(continued from front flap)
Wisconsin. He examines them at several
stages in the evolution they have undergone
since the advent of revolutionary technologies
in building construction, energy supply,
transportation and communication
that gave the metropolis its peculiar and
still changing structure.

Porter offers some startling and extraordinarily challenging ideas about what can be
done so that cities can compete with suburbs
as places to live. He tells in a practical way
how they can be helped to regain their
financial independence. If this sane voice in a
chaotic wilderness is heeded, THE
RECOVERY OF AMERICAN CITIES—
imaginative, lucid, tightly-reasoned—could
profoundly influence both urban theory
and public policy.

D1029269

THE
RECOVERY
OF
AMERICAN
CITIES

Paul R. Porter

ANNEXE DE LA BIBLIOTHÈQUE
u Ottawa
LIBRARY ANNEX

Université d'Ottawa
BIBLIOTHÈQUES
Ottawa
LIBRARY ANNEX
LIBRARIES
University of Ottawa

Universitas
BIBLIOTHECA
Ottaviensis

THE TWO CONTINENTS PUBLISHING GROUP, LTD.
A SUN RIVER PRESS BOOK

Library of Congress Cataloging in Publication Data

Porter, Paul Robert, 1908-
 The recovery of American cities.

 "A Sun River Press book."
 Includes index.
 1. Cities and towns—United States.   I.   Title.
HT123.P64   301.36'3'0973   75-39090
ISBN 0-8467-0152-9

Copyright © 1976 by Sun River Press
All rights reserved. No part of this publication may be reproduced, stored in a
retrieval system, or transmitted in any form or by any means, electronic,
mechanical, photocopying, recording, or otherwise, without prior written
permission of the copyright owner.

Production by Planned Production

Text design by Joyce C. Weston
Commercial artwork by Nelson Reyes

Printed in USA

Two Continents Publishing Group, Ltd.
30 East 42 Street
New York City 10017

and

Sun River Press

Acknowledgment

When some of the ideas presented in this book were being developed, Ben Fischer, President of Action Housing, Inc., of Pittsburgh, and the late Clarence Senior, a wise student of migrations, were patient and helpfully severe critics. My wife, Hilda, was constant in her support. To them and to many others who gave information and advice, I am gratefully indebted.

Contents

Tables

Maps and Charts

THE
RECOVERY
OF
AMERICAN
CITIES

1. REASONS FOR HOPE

From Rural to Urban

The transition of American society from mainly rural to mainly urban has been a rough passage. The change began before we were a nation and gradually gained momentum as the growth of trade and manufacturing drew farm youth and immigrants to new kinds of jobs in cities. The historian, Samuel Eliot Morison, reminds us that "measured by numbers, the urban movement was stronger than the westward migration; and its effect on the American character has been equally important."

Very often the reality of urban life did not match the promise, at least quickly, and periodically a frustration gave rise to stormy times—stormy enough that in the past decade the faith which has infused our history as a nation has seemed to sputter and fade. The troubles which follow a major influx of new arrivals, however, are not new, especially when there are ethnic differences between the established and the new residents. Morison writes of Baltimore's "sinister reputation for mobbing as early as 1812." A riot in 1843 directed against Irish who had settled in the Kensington district of Philadelphia resulted in casualties of 30 killed and 150 wounded and the destruction of many houses by fire. During a period of three decades beginning in the thirties there were repeated riots in New York City. The worst, aggravated by resistance to Civil War draft calls, occurred in 1863. The *Encyclopedia Britannica* reports it as follows:

> For five days in July, 1863, many thousands of rioters, mostly impoverished Irish immigrants . . . swept the city, looting, burning and killing. Negroes were hanged from streetlights and trees.

1

Warships trained guns on the city as they (the rioters) clashed repeatedly with the police, national guardsmen and the army. At least 2,000 were killed and 8,000 wounded, and all business halted in the face of the armed conflict.

The grim riots which shook Los Angeles, Detroit, Baltimore and other cities in the late sixties of our century were, thus, not without precedent and anyone would be rash to predict that the last has been seen. Nor is dissatisfaction with urban life confined to residents of what we now call the inner city. The discontent is general and is directed also to what we now call the metropolis (since the word "city" is no longer an inclusive term for an urban settlement).

The pervasive discontent finds voice in some of the most melodramatic language of our time. People do not move to suburbs. They "flee." Suburbs always "sprawl," except when they are "a white noose around black cities." Cities are "sick" and "dying." They even have a "death wish," however that is determined. People do not use automobiles out of need. They have a "love affair with the automobile," and the disdain with which the words are pronounced makes it clear that the affair is not a respectable one. Such are the harsh clichés about our urban society which are regularly encountered in the daily press and in scholarly reviews.

The language is too purple. It does not accurately describe the reality. The dark view which has lately gripped many critics of American life must be ascribed in part to fashion, that ever inconstant measure of what is acceptable in dress and thought. Tocqueville might have been writing of contemporary America when he wrote thus of the English in 1833:

> In past times what most distinguished the English people from any other was its satisfaction with itself; then everything about its laws and customs were good in its eyes. . . . Today everything has changed. In the England of our times a spirit of discontent with the present and hatred of the past shows itself everywhere. The human spirit has fallen into the opposite extreme. It only looks for what is wrong around it, and is much more bent on correcting what is wrong than in preserving what is good.

Contrary to the dark view, this book presents a belief that in another two decades or so the worst of our troubles arising from the rural to urban transition can be behind us. It is not foolish to envisage the recovery of cities, although it must be acknowledged that at this time the words make a strange combination. *The recovery of cities.* In our accustomed awareness the words clash, like "the goodness of evil" or "the exuberance of senility."

The gloomy view of city prospects, seemingly confirmed by the financial crisis of New York City, ensures that any argument that a turn in the tide of events now actually favors the recovery of cities will be met with profound skepticism. I will make that argument.

When I speak of recovery, I mean two things being regained which cities have conspicuously lost: an ability to compete with the more attractive suburbs as a place of residence, and financial independence. "The city"—so it is widely said—"must in one way or another obtain access to the tax base of its suburbs, because cities are no longer a viable political unit." Statements of this kind usually mean some variant of one of these alternatives: Either a city must be enabled to absorb its suburbs, or it must be permanently subsidized by the federal government which has access to the tax base of suburbs.

The possibility that cities can absorb their suburbs at this late date must be dismissed as unreal. Virtually all large cities now have fewer residents than their suburbs, and the rate of their population loss has shown a startling acceleration since the 1970 census was taken; even such formerly fast-growth cities as Dallas and Los Angeles have begun to lose population. The political power of cities shrinks accordingly.

The alternative possibility of a permanent subsidy has more substance. All large cities are already subsidized, and in the absence of their recovery such dependence will continue, but for both cities and the rest of the nation it is a dreary omen of enfeeblement and strife.

Cities can neither absorb their suburbs nor safely rely upon their generosity, but there is a third alternative. With temporary assistance from the rest of the nation, cities can come to compete with their suburbs as a place of residence and by doing so can also regain their financial independence.

My conviction that cities can recover—completely within two decades or so—grows out of a first-hand study of ten cities and their metropolitan areas, placed in historical perspective. The ten are New York City, Baltimore, Detroit, St. Paul, Minneapolis, St. Louis, Dallas, Fort Worth, Los Angeles, and, as a small industrial city, Kenosha, Wisconsin. Merely to list them suggests the broad diversity that governed their selection. They vary widely in region, size, age, history, economic base, topography, governance, civic effort, relationship to their metropolis, population density, and racial and ethnic composition. I have lived in two and known all during more than forty years as an occasional visitor.

The Artichoke Pattern

The inquiry into the ten cities centered on their inner cities.

Partly this was because inner cities contain the greatest contrasts: flourishing central business districts surrounded by slums, failing industrial districts and surplus railway yards. But another reason was that inner cities are sensitive barometers of change. The conventional study of an inner city is a still photo, reasonably accurate unto its day but soon dated. Some faces reappear in one photo after another. But in the span of a decade there are also many changes. Many families who once lived in an inner city are now in better homes in the outer city, and the grown children of some have bought houses in suburbs. Blacks, too.

The pass-through process does not reach all inner city residents, but any true account of inner cities must register its prevalence and its strength. Geographically, a metropolis grows like the trunk of a tree, in increments at the perimeter, but in the urbanization of people the growth of a metropolis is akin to that of an artichoke in which new stock forms at the center as older stock pushes outward. Consistently, this has been the pattern in our cities, although it is not the case in some Latin American and European cities where new arrivals congregate in shantytowns in the outskirts.

The artichoke pattern has been a fateful one for American cities. Because inner city housing is the oldest and usually the cheapest, inner cities are inevitably the first urban location of most new arrivals from the countryside. Never in our history was the formation of a new urban stock greater in volume than in the two decades following World War II. Ben J. Wattenberg and Richard Scammon, in *This U. S. A.*, describe the exodus from farms to cities in this period as "one of the greatest single migrations in the history of the world; greater than the American immigration during the peak 1894-1914 years."

It was made possible, at least in the form that it took, by a second migration which was as great in volume although much shorter in distance. This was the movement from cities to suburbs which vacated city housing for new arrivals. Oddly, the second migration would probably have drawn much less attention than it did if many cities, especially those most often in the news, had not ceased to grow by annexation. Had more city boundaries also moved outward, the outward movement of older urban stock would have been more readily recognized as simply a continuance of a process as old as American cities themselves.

What might have happened if powerful social forces behind each migration had not coincided in these particular decades is a matter about which we can only speculate, but in the fact that they did coincide is to be found the principal cause of the crisis of cities. Behind the movement from farm to city was a powerful renewal, after the Depression and a major war, of the mechanization of agriculture. It is a trend as old as

McCormick's reaper, invented in the forties of the past century, but it rose to peak strength after World War II as tractor power rapidly replaced horse power. In the same period there occurred the strongest and the longest sustained rise in affluence among people who already lived in cities. In part, this may be attributed to rising productivity and a better management of the national economy, but a major factor was the upsurge in trade union organization in the thirties. In time it brought workers an income level that enabled many to move to suburbs along with a larger number of professional and clerical workers. (The AFL-CIO estimates that more than half of its members live in suburbs.)

The scornful critics who comprehend the second migration only as unseemly "flight" to "sprawling" suburbs have missed something very reassuring in American life. For millions reared in crowded cities the ownership of an individual house surrounded by a patch of green has meant attainment of a significant part of *their* American Dream. A middle-class black who moved to a Baltimore suburb put it simply: "I wanted a home I could walk around." Such longing for more living space is widely shared; urban land per capita has approximately doubled since World War II. It is an old longing. New York City's first subway, linking Manhattan Island with then undeveloped areas of Queens and the Bronx, was opened in 1904. In almost every census count since 1910 the population of Manhattan Island has declined.

Thus, two migrations linked in tandem—from farm to inner city and from inner city to outer city and suburbs—and both flowing in the largest volume ever until recently, have flooded cities with poor ex-farmhands looking for unskilled city jobs and have drawn from cities many of their higher-income residents. In the cities the need for social services zoomed upward and the tax base shrank, until cities became heavily dependent upon subsidies from the rest of the nation.

And then an event occurred which is so profound in importance that it gives solid hope that the recovery of cities may be realistically contemplated. The migration from farm to city sharply slackened.

Meanwhile, the pass-through process continues and a near-severing of the link between the tandem migrations has caused the population count of inner cities to plummet. Detroit and St. Louis lost more than a third of their inner city population between 1960 and 1970. Even in Dallas, a city of major overall growth, there was a 5% loss and the rate of decline is increasing.

A judgment may now be ventured with reasonable confidence that the long transition from a mainly rural to a mainly urban society is drawing to an end. This does not mean that there will not be further migration from rural areas to cities. But a resumption of a large scale migration for a sustained period of time is no longer possible because the reservoir of potential urban residents who remain on farms or in small towns is now too low to sustain another big migration.

At first glance, the fact that one out of four Americans is still classified as nonurban, or rural, seems to contradict this statement. But the farm population in 1974, as estimated by the Census Bureau, was down to 4.4%. Even if once more it could be halved, which seems unlikely, and all who left farming moved to cities the number would be too small to have a major effect. The proportion of today's rural population, if not stable, approaches stability. Besides a corps of very productive farmers, an urban society needs the support of miners, loggers and fishermen. Many who have a nonurban residence hold an urban job, especially in construction and factory work in outer suburbs. Many render services to urban travellers along the intercity highways or in vacation resorts, and all need the support of retail clerks, teachers, doctors and local government officials in the nonurban areas where they live. It should be recognized that many people who are classified as nonurban are performing urban-type jobs in locations outside the city where the rest of society that is technically urban needs them to be performed.

In the shadow of a 100-story skyscraper, those which reach to 20 or 30 stories may seem hardly worth noting, and in comparison with an event so profoundly important as an approaching end to the transition of American society from mainly rural to mainly urban, other circumstances favorable to the recovery of cities may appear dwarfed. But only in the comparison. In themselves they have a large significance, and an understanding of them is basic to shaping the policies of recovery.

The first of these additional causes for hope is the falling birth rate. Even if it falls no further, it has already eased the burden of fast-expanding schools, will soon reduce the largest of the welfare programs, and in another decade and a half it will have ended the abnormal condition of a lopsided proportion of beginners trying to enter the ranks of the employed. Once a better balance between beginners and experienced workers returns, the attainment of full employment will be made less difficult, and that situation, too, will be favorable to the recovery of cities.

The story of housing in recent years provides a fascinating example of how mood and fact may move in opposite directions. Overcrowding in city housing was a heritage of large-scale immigration, and much of the housing which was built was built in the half century between the Civil War and World War I, when immigration was highest, was of wretched quality when new. By today's standards it is easy to scorn such housing, but it was built for people who arrived in cities terribly poor. Not until about 1950 did we begin to turn the tide against seemingly permanent overcrowding. Since then the volume of new construction has been spectacular. In 1970 one out of three homes had been built in the preceding two decades—a rate of growth well above that of population. The magnitude of the achievement is not fully appreciated until we remember that in the same time several million rural homes were abandoned. A huge amount of unfit housing remains, but we now know from recent experience that the goal of a decent home for every American family is within our reach in another two decades or so. Count the achievement in housing as another cause for hope.

The evolution of the structure of metropolises toward a large decentralization of employment, as well as of residence and trade, carries a less evident omen for the cities at their center. In the absence of a well-conceived recovery effort, the condition of cities could be worsened. But decentralization is not necessarily harmful to cities. Indeed, a general reduction in the distance between homes and jobs would free capital for the redevelopment of blighted areas that is now wastefully claimed by excessive transportation. If we act wisely, the recovery of cities can be assisted by the powerful and irreversible trend toward decentralization.

Relocations of Urban Workplaces

Before we explore the implications of the tapering off of large scale migration to cities we should note also some other major developments which must change our accustomed ways of thinking about cities. One of these is the decline of large cities as manufacturing centers. Contrary to a popular view, this is not the result of a decline of manufacturing employment per capita. Now, as a half century ago, a quarter of the labor force is engaged in manufacturing. In this time the labor force remained at close to 40% of the population except for a bulge during World War II; the great expansion of the white-collar trades, which was especially large in government and services, was balanced by the big decline of employment in agriculture and, to a lesser extent, in mining. In our fluid society many children of factory workers became professionals and executives and many children of farmers became factory workers, but the ratio of factory workers to total population remains fairly constant.

Then why have most large cities declined as manufacturing centers? It is because industrial districts in the inner cities are the most obsolete and the least suited for efficient production, and factories have moved out. Factories have also moved from outer cities and inner suburbs. Increasingly, they have gone out to industrial parks in the metropolitan outskirts, where ample land is available at moderate cost and where access to major highways is easy. Enough plants leave the metropolis altogether for small cities and rural small towns to result in the net decline of most large metropolises, as well as cities, as manufacturing centers.

Baltimore and Minneapolis have established municipal offices and budgets to try to halt the departure of factories and to attract new ones. Possibly the rate of departures can be slowed, but these cities have had meager success in attracting new industry. By contrast Columbia, Maryland, the new city in the Baltimore metropolitan area, has been attracting manufacturing plants with relative ease. The decline of large cities as manufacturing centers is a universal phenomenon determined by pressures of a competitive economy and appears certain to continue.

A major consequence of this trend, of course, is that many inner city residents find it increasingly difficult to obtain steady work. Public education helps some inner city youth to qualify for the white-collar jobs which have proliferated in the central business district, but many others with less education find that living in the inner city keeps them from achieving self-reliance. For them, the pass-through process is not working.

In contrast to the consistent outflow of blue-collar jobs from cities, trends in the location of white-collar jobs are mixed, but the strongest trend has been a vertical concentration in central business districts. Another example from New York City provides a telling statistic. During the sixties, jobs in the city's garment industry declined by 45,000 (a fifth of the total), while in the same period jobs in Wall Street brokerage houses increased by the same number. In all of the large cities—even in Detroit, the laggard—towering new glass-sheathed job stacks have risen to provide more office space in revitalized central business districts. And as is well known, a high proportion of such jobs—in many cities, a majority—are filled by suburban commuters, who cross spreading moats of decay to reach their island workplace. The combination of the outward move by higher-income office workers to distant homes and the concentration of their jobs in the central city has greatly lengthened the average journey to work—which is what the transportation crisis is mostly about.

There is, however, a rising countertrend to concentration at the center. Most noticeably in the sixties, secondary office work centers multiplied, sometimes in the outer city but more commonly in suburbs. Bloomington, almost unknown outside of Minnesota, competes strongly with Minneapolis and St. Paul as a location for office work, and is on the point of passing Duluth as the state's third largest city. Many large corporations have chosen suburban Clayton in preference to downtown St. Louis; Columbia and Towson compete with Baltimore; Arlington is a minor rival to Dallas and Fort Worth. On a lesser scale some large corporations have moved their headquarters to campus-like settings outside cities. In this manner Southern California Edison has quit Los Angeles; General Mills, Minneapolis; 3M, St. Paul; IBM and two dozen others, New York.

The most rapid growth of secondary centers in the sixties occurred in metropolitan Los Angeles. In 1960 five-sixths of the total high-rise office space was in downtown Los Angeles and most of the rest was strung out along the five-mile Wilshire Corridor. In the next decade downtown office space grew by one half. By most standards, this was a spectacular revival of downtown. Nonetheless, at the same time, nine other centers —six of them new—combined to bring their total high-rise office space above that of downtown Los Angeles.

The strong surge in the growth of outlying office work centers in the past decade and a half should not be a surprise. It follows the strong growth of suburban shopping centers that began in the fifties and the construction of highways which wholly or partially encircle cities and their inner suburbs. It is a part of a basic change in the structure of the metropolis itself.

We have noted a major movement of manufacturing from cities to outlying sectors—an accelerating trend for two decades—and an outward movement also of department stores and specialty shops, which, until the early fifties, were found only in the traditional downtown locations. These reduced inner city employment; the growth of outlying office work centers has not. The phenomenal increase in white-collar employment has occurred both downtown and in secondary centers.

There are reasons to believe, however, that while central business districts will remain strong, the future growth may be mostly in the new centers. The high cost of downtown real estate is one reason. An even more compelling reason may be that more employers are coming to recognize that the journey to work has become too long, too vexatious, and too costly. Once a conviction takes hold that strategically located secondary centers may have a competitive advantage over downtown, a shift of new investment capital to the new centers could occur quickly.

The Technologies that Shaped the Metropolis

To better appreciate the significance of the changes in metropolitan structure which have become pronounced in the past two decades or so, it is helpful to look back not quite a century to the emergence of the technologies which gave rise to the metropolis and imparted to it its peculiar structure. The year 1880 is a good place to start because it was a census year. It was also approximately the beginning of a fabulous quarter century of new inventions and their commercial development in energy, construction, transportation, and communication. They comprise the technological base of the metropolis and although they have since undergone many improvements they have been neither superseded nor basically changed.

In 1880 St. Louis, greatest of the river boat cities and with a population of 351,000, had just yielded its rank as the third most populous city in the nation to Chicago, the first city to owe its eminence mainly to railroads. For a time its universities and seminaries enabled St. Louis to continue as the cultural capital of the Middle West but this, too, was lost to Chicago. By 1876 it had reached the geographical boundaries that contain it today, and was the fourth largest city as late as 1910 (surpassed soon thereafter by Detroit). But St. Louis was not able to annex, and in time it took on more of the characteristics of an inner city than any other in the nation, except perhaps Newark.

Baltimore, prospering as a seaport and as the terminal of a great railroad, was sixth in population. Detroit, benefiting from the excellence of Michigan hardwoods, had become the capital of the carriage industry and had acquired a number of machine shops for the repair of lake boats. In 1880, therefore, when the city's population had barely passed 100,000, Detroit already harbored the two skills which would make it the automobile capital of the world.

Minneapolis was then the leading center for lumber manufacture; logs were floated from the North by river, and St. Anthony's Falls provided the power to drive sawmills. Soon the city would lose this industry altogether, but it was beginning to mill wheat and had a population of 47,000. Eight miles downriver, St. Paul was flourishing as a railroad center and state capitol and was not far behind in population. The population of Los Angeles had almost doubled in a decade—to 11,000. Dallas and Fort Worth, which had been trading villages (the latter a military post as well) since about 1850, were recorded in the census count for the first time in 1880.

Kenosha, originally Southport, had its beginning in a union of Great Lakes traffic and rich farmland. It was a warehouse and shipping port for Southern Wisconsin wheat until the Dakotas were opened to better yields, and it manufactured boxes for cheese sent to the East by water until the railroads came. By 1880 the first industries had failed and had been succeeded by leather tanning, machine shops, and a wagon industry. From the earliest days, the city's settlers insisted upon good public schools—Kenosha had the first high school in the state in 1849—and with only occasional faltering in more than a century and a quarter, school boards have passed on the heritage from one generation to the next. (In the second year after publication of Darwin's *Descent of Man*, interested residents were introduced to the theory of evolution through a series of lectures at the Unitarian Church.)

The population of New York City, still confined to Manhattan Island except for a small annexation in Bronx County, had surged to nearly 1.2 million; if Brooklyn, Williamsburg, and other cities which were absorbed in 1898 had been included, the total would have been nearly two million. The population density of the island had reached 51,000 per square mile. In the next three decades it would rise to 103,000, but already by 1880 it was three times the highest density ever reached in any other American city. The exceptional density is one of the reasons why conclusions appropriate to New York often do not fit the situation of other cities.

New York, however, had a low profile. The tallest building was Trinity Church; for more than six centuries cathedral towers and church spires had stood above all other man-made structures except the pyramids of Egypt. Higher than all but church spires were masts of sailing vessels in New York harbor. It is fitting, therefore, that the Statue of Liberty looks across the bay to the skyscrapers now massed on the tip of Manhattan Island. It is their forebear. When the statue was completed in 1886, its construction showed that walls need be no more than a cloak around a steel frame. The designer was Gustave Eiffel, who a few years later designed the famous tower that bears his name, and his purpose with both was to demonstrate the construction potential created by the new technology of wrought iron and steelmaking. Although steel bridges were coming into use—Eads had bridged the Mississippi at St. Louis in 1873, and the Brooklyn Bridge was but three years from completion—the height of large buildings was still limited, as from time immemorial, by the strength of load-bearing walls.

A steam-powered passenger elevator had been introduced in a New York department store in 1857, and some other buildings installed hydraulic lifts, but it was the electric elevator, invented in 1889, along with steel-frame construction which constituted the building technology of the new skyscraper age. Barely a decade after its invention new buildings had reached 30 stories. The Empire State Building topped off at 104 stories in 1931. Lately, it has been slightly surpassed in height by the twin Trade Center buildings in New York and the Sears building in Chicago, an achievement in one-upmanship probably more satisfying to vanity than practicality.

A century ago the horsecar was the prevailing mode of public transportation in cities. Two well-known French paintings, Renoir's *Pont Neuf* and Pissarro's *Boulevard des Italiens,* have preserved for us a record of what some cars were like. In Paris they had, besides the enclosed coach, an open upper deck reached by a spiral staircase in the rear. By 1880 most horsecars were drawn on rails. Manufacture of the cars by John Stephenson had become one of New York City's largest industries, and Stephenson supplied not only the American market but exported cars to Europe, China and India.

The use of horses for public transportation was near its end, however. Since 1871 New York had had elevated trains drawn by steam locomotives. The Centennial Exposition in Philadelphia featured a steam-powered monorail car, but there were no buyers. Meanwhile, a variety of inventions using electricity appeared. In 1876 the telephone was introduced, and the incandescent lamp two years later. In 1879 the Bell Company began serving a few hundred New York subscribers from a central exchange. The first central power generating plant was completed in London in January, 1882, and the second in New York in the following September. The first electric streetcar in the United States ran in Richmond, Virginia, in 1888, shortly after it had been introduced in Germany and ever since, electric motive power has supported one of the two main forms of urban transportation. The first electric elevated trains ran in Chicago in 1895 and the first American subway train was operated in Boston in 1898.

The internal combustion engine gave rise to the other form of metropolitan transportation, and even it needed electricity for ignition. The first practical automobile, the Benz, was built in Germany in 1885, followed by the Daimler a year later. The Duryea was the first manufactured in the United States, in 1893. The first Ford was sold ten years later. The quickness with which the automobile filled a transportation need may be seen in a minor historical footnote: Between 1904 and 1908, 241 United States automobile manufacturers entered the market. By borrowing the principle of the assembly line from the Chicago meat-packing industry, Ford was able to surpass all others by producing cheaply. In 1925 the list price of the Model T was $290.

The automobile could be driven wherever a road or street existed, and it did not take long to lay a pavement. The flexibility of the automobile's variable path gave it a huge advantage over fixed path transportation restricted by a central power source, and the low cost of the automobile made it possible for most families to own one.

It has often been said, wrongly, that the automobile created the suburb. The commuting suburb had come into being at least a half century ahead of it. According to the *Columbia Historical Portrait of New York*, the city of Williamsburg, across the East River from Manhattan Island, was described in an 1853 guidebook as "almost exclusively a city of residences" occupied by citizens "of the sterling middle class" who worked in New York and commuted there by ferry.

Other suburban towns were developed along railroads, such as the Philadelphia Main Line suburbs and those of the Chicago North Shore. What the automobile did to suburbs was to bring them within the price range of millions who could not afford to live in the expensive ones. It made suburban living democratic. It did so by making possible the development of the large expanses of land lying between the rail lines radiating from the hub. By bringing this land within the urban pattern, the automobile both moderated the cost of urban land and allowed urban dwellers to own more land per capita.

For an effect so big, the technologies which made possible the transformation of cities into metropolises were remarkably few: steel-frame construction, the electric elevator, electric-powered trams and trains, the automobile and surely also the telephone, although conceivably the telegraph might have sufficed. As in most successful technologies, invention was followed by a spurt of technical and commercial development and then a long period of gradual technical improvement and broadening commercial acceptance. Before the end of the first decade of our century, the basic patterns had been established.

Some new technology, still unknown, may come to have a profound and revolutionary effect on urban settlements, but the prudent assumption at this time must be that most of the impact of existing technologies on cities and suburbs, like migration from the countryside, has already been felt—except in one important respect. The exception is that the net effect of relevant technologies, so far as it can be foreseen, will be favorable to the decentralization of metropolitan employment, rather than further centralization at the hub.

Most manufacturing technologies require an increasing amount of space per worker; for this reason, among others, manufacturing will continue to move outward. Computer technology is favorable to decentralization of some kinds of office work; with computers it is possible to retrieve information instantly at terminals widely separated from the place it is stored, and processing and other space-consuming operations can be divorced from expensive downtown real estate. Building technology is neutral; steel-frame construction and electric elevators are as serviceable in secondary centers as they are downtown. The automobile is a decentralizing force; it has been so in regard to residence from its introduction, and in regard to shopping and manufacturing for more than two decades. Now it is multiplying the locations suitable for office buildings in the suburbs.

Alone among the technologies that significantly influence the structure of metropolises, fast rail transit is not adaptable to the decentralization of employment. Because of its expensive construction, it is only practical for carrying a large volume of passengers in corridors that converge upon the

metropolitan hub; it cannot, like automobiles and buses, serve the web
pattern of traffic that links homes and workplaces in outlying areas. If
more subways and commuter railroads were built to carry white-collar
workers to the hub, they *might* deter the decentralization of nonlocal
office work, although this assumption is increasingly open to doubt. In
any event, the staggering construction costs of fast rail transit are forcing
a shift in transportation planning—most significantly in the U. S.
Department of Transportation, which provides most of the financing—to
less expensive and more flexible modes of mass transit. The evidence,
which we will examine in later chapters, all points toward a strong growth
of suburban office work centers, competing with downtown, in all except
the smallest metropolises.

The Policies of Recovery

Recovery will be a major departure from existing urban policies,
and our starting point in conceiving new policies is the changed
relationship between the tandem migrations. Growth of the metropolis
through newcomers has been slowed and will not be resumed on a large
scale; the dwindling urban-start migration will hereafter have greatly
reduced needs for housing. Meanwhile, as the children and
grandchildren of earlier arrivals improve their education, skills, and
income, they continue the historic move-up migration to better housing
in more desirable neighborhoods—often beyond the city. Thus the inner
city, the most vulnerable part of the metropolis, loses population;
housing which only the poor will occupy is abandoned; and large
residential districts, along with failing industrial districts, slip into ever
deeper decay.
   What a superb opportunity for cities!
   This land of dwindling use lies close to the greatest concentration of
jobs to be found anywhere in the metropolis. Most of the jobs also pay
well—enough so that the men and women who fill them can afford to live
in suburbs, as many do. To redevelop this land is, of course, an old
dream, and during four decades of a federal housing policy fragmentary
urban renewal has taken place. But as long as low-income housing was in
acute short supply, and as long as there was a strong stream of migration
from the countryside, renewal policy (with some exceptions) has been to
preserve this land for low-income residents.
   The policy, like most buildings on the land, is obsolete. The proper
goal should be to transform the decaying districts into new
neighborhoods attractive enough *to compete with suburbs* as a place of
residence for people who work in the central business district.
   Standing alone, however, a policy of making inner cities competitive

with the strongest suburbs is neither adequate nor just. It must be accompanied by a complementary policy, a policy that enables those whose residence in the inner city prevents their being self-reliant to relocate outside cities for convenient access to jobs which they can fill.

The inner city residents who are most subject to unemployment are the youth, and this will continue to be the case for about a decade and a half. There are simply more beginners in the labor force, because of the earlier high birth rate, than private employers can use. As an interim measure, the youth who are surplus to normal employment should be recruited for transitional employment in useful public service (and thereby directed away from apprenticeship in crime). They should have access to vocational training for future jobs in the private economy, and be prepared for relocation in communities where they may enjoy the dignity of self-reliance, and the public may be relieved from the obligation to support them on welfare. These youth should represent a large fraction of inner city residents who would eventually leave the city and resettle.

Together, the complementary resettlement policies would substantially reduce the huge mismatches between residence and workplace which developed when the tandem migrations were at peak strength. Together, they would also progressively bring to an end the need of cities for subsidies. Abnormal costs for social services would decline as many inner city residents moved to locations where there were good chances of steady work (assuming an expansive national economy). City tax revenues would rise as slums were converted into neighborhoods competing with suburbs. In time, a city's needs could again be met from funds of local origin (although this would require some changes in federal taxation, to be noted shortly). An important by-product of the two policies would be a shortening of the average journey to work, which would reduce the per capita demand for transportation.

Two other recovery policies are needed. First, the federal government should assume a merely neutral stance with respect to decentralization of metropolises, a position that would end a tilt toward increased downtown congestion.

Many cities, with federal support, are engaged in promoting a major expansion of the central business district. If successful, this will require a major increase in subsidized transportation. The effort is understandable but unfortunate. The cities have attempted to compensate for an outward flow of major taxpayers by building up the tax base at the center, thereby tying their future to a permanent condition of costly congestion. It is an error which is likely, in time, to be self-defeating, since the congestion will make competitive office centers in suburbs more attractive, and some cities, at least, will be left with an enduring large volume of vacant commercial space. This may be the condition of New York City now. If inner cities were made into attractive places to live, the taxes their residents would pay would be a more practical source of revenue.

Lacking a recovery concept, many cities are caught up in plans which will make congestion worse. There is the proposed Central City in Los Angeles, Baltimore's MetroCenter (symbolic of the greater congestion that would result, the words are crowded together), and Metro '85 in Minneapolis. Central City would nearly double downtown employment by 1990. As the plan has been conceived, Vermont school teachers, Nevada sheepherders and divers other nonbeneficiary taxpayers are expected to support such folly. There would be the use of federal funds to clear sites for commercial buildings. Then the federal government would contract for office space—one third of the proposed new office space has been earmarked for government use, including state and local. Finally, the federal government would provide a huge subsidy for the construction and operation of a subway, deemed an essential support for the plan.

If local electorates wish to subsidize ventures like Central City and MetroCenter, and let themselves in for a seemingly endless need for more subsidies, they should, of course, be privileged to do so. But they alone should bear the cost. Federal funds should not be used to tilt commercial development toward a particular location, whether downtown or suburban. Subject to reasonable local zoning, the location of office space can best be determined by a free market.

In fairness to their sponsors, it should be said that the plans are consistent with what the federal government encourages local governments to propose in their bids for federal assistance. The federal government frequently even pays much of the cost of preparing such plans.

The fourth recovery policy is that federal aid to local governments (or most of it) should be conditional upon their effective action to overcome the need for aid as early as possible. A quarter of a century ago the United States Government successfully employed this principle in Marshall Plan assistance to nations of Western Europe. The same principle is appropriate to the recovery of cities.

Each city in need of aid would be expected to develop and pursue a comprehensive recovery program. Basically, the program would consist of the complementary resettlements outlined in the first two policies: making the inner city a desirable place to live; enabling poor inner city residents to move where the jobs are. Although it would be a federal objective to withdraw from local affairs as rapidly as possible, the federal government, in the interests of the nation as a whole, would need to ensure that subsidies were not used improvidently.

The policy will require a fresh way of looking at federal grants to localities. Only in part are they a true subsidy, that is, an unearned, nonrepayable transfer of resources from the rest of the nation. In large part they are a return of funds of local origin, that is, federal taxes paid by local residents. At the present time there is no way of knowing what part of the total federal payments to a locality consists of subsidies and what part is a return of local-origin funds. In the accounting, all are "grants."

We can make a practical distinction between subsidies and nonsubsidies—that is, the local-origin funds—if we think of the latter as revenues from an *implicit local income tax* which has been included for convenience and by custom in the federal individual income tax. In truth, that is exactly what the local-origin funds are. When the Congress establishes the rates for the federal income tax, it sets them high enough to permit federal agencies to return a part of the revenues to the same communities from which they are collected. In providing for this revenue round trip, the Congress has implicitly recognized a need for a local income tax (however it may be collected and put into the hands of local governments) to supplement conventional local taxes such as those on property and retail sales.

Now let us carry this line of reasoning one step further. Visualize a specific and uniform percentage of the federal individual income tax being earmarked for an *automatic* return to the community from which the tax was collected. Visualize the percentage being high enough that the great majority of local governments—those that do not need a subsidy—will be able to meet their needs without any other payment from the federal government. What I have just described is what would happen if the *implicit* local income tax, which is real but unrecognized, were converted into a *universal* local income tax, with recognized legal status.

The local-origin revenues that economically depressed communities—all large cities, many small ones, and some suburbs—would thus receive would not match the total of what they customarily receive as federal grants. Their subsidy would need to be continued while they recover. However, for the first time we would be able to isolate the subsidy from local-origin funds, and thus be in a position to concentrate an effort on making subsidies unnecessary.

By making the return of the local-origin funds automatic, we could by a single act dispense with the clumsy and erratic system of revenue sharing, categorical grants, and block grants as the method of returning funds to communities which do not need outside help. How clumsy the present system is was described by Senator Edmund S. Muskie to the National League of Cities in December, 1975. He related that 186 different federal programs for community development were spread over 21 federal agencies. Said Muskie: "We got into this quite innocently as we tried to respond to problems on a piecemeal basis, but the result is an administrative monster."

The Universal Local Income Tax, incidentally, should not be confused with revenue sharing, which is an improvisation unrelated to a principle, and perpetuates the fiction that the federal government is "sharing" revenues which more rightfully may be regarded as local.

Two important qualifications need to be made concerning an automatic return of proceeds from the Universal Local Income Tax. In many communities there is not just one local government but several. Because the overlapping governmental functions of cities, counties, and special districts vary widely from one state to another, each state government should determine how revenues from the Universal Local Income Tax would be apportioned among local governments that overlap. Also, no local government should receive a sum from this tax that would be greater than a specified ratio to conventional tax revenues. Without such a limit, some wealthy suburbs could receive back more than they spend on government.

When New York City officials point out that federal taxes collected in the city are much larger than the federal grants that the city receives, the figures they commonly cite include corporate income taxes. Taxes paid by corporations do not belong in the proposal made here. The earnings on which they are paid are derived from operations that in many cases are conducted on a regional or national scale, and to include these taxes would give an unfair advantage to New York City (which is the collection point for nearly a fifth of all corporate income taxes), to an industry capital such as Detroit, and to regional business capitals such as Atlanta, Dallas, and Minneapolis. Nonetheless, New York City's spokesmen have a valid point. The city still has many high-income residents, and if the Universal Local Income Tax were established, the city would certainly be much less dependent upon the federal government than it is today. New York City would still need a transitional subsidy in order to recover, but it would be proportionately less than in many other cities.

Unhappily, the understanding that we need has been muddied by the city's financial crisis. The drama of the crisis has temporarily eclipsed two other facts of greater long-term importance: All large cities now need and receive federal subsidies (taking into account welfare payments to city residents), and any local government that receives a federal grant for a specified purpose—whether the grant is a subsidy or only a return of local-origin funds—thereby submits a part of its budget to federal control.

Unlike the city's recovery, which is necessarily a long-term process, a balanced budget can be achieved in two or three years by austerity, a revision of pensions, and a refinancing, deferral or write-down of debt payments. When a city government defaults or is in serious danger of doing so, some outside control over its financial operations is a likely prospect. It may be harsh and humiliating, whether exercised by a referee in bankruptcy, some committee of federal officials protecting a guarantee of city bonds, or simply a finance control board set up by a state government. But when the emergency is over, the basic weakness of the city will remain. Austerity, no matter how severe, cannot cure it. Only recovery can.

The amount of debt per capita is obviously not the only guide to a city's ability to repay what it owes, and it is not necessarily reflected in ratings given to municipal bonds at their time of issue. Nonetheless, it can tell us quite a bit about the chances of other cities to avoid the kind of financial crisis which befell New York City. The Census Bureau issues reports on the amount of debt owed by local governments; the most recent year for which both reports of debt and of population estimates are available is 1973, but it is recent enough. In that year New York City's per capita debt was about $1,540 (in 1975, when the total debt was larger and the population smaller, the per capita sum was about $1,700). Fifty-four other cities have a population of 250,000 or more, and in 1973 this was the ratio of their per capita debt to that of New York City: about three-fifths, Atlanta and Washington, D.C.; one-third to one-half, Los Angeles, Philadelphia, Baltimore, and 18 other cities; one-quarter to one-third, Chicago, Detroit, Newark, and 10 other cities; less than one-quarter, St. Louis, Minneapolis, Pittsburgh, and 15 other cities.

"Sufficient to the General Happiness"

The policies of recovery stand apart from contemporary liberal and conservative doctrines but are in the tradition of an American policy which is older than the nation and has been one of its most successful. When the young George Washington worked as surveyor for Culpeper County, Virginia, he was helping to carry out a policy of government assistance to people who wished to resettle so that they might improve their opportunities. The policy was a part of the rich heritage of Colonial Virginia to the nation, and Washington continued it as President in his support for the settlement of Kentucky and the Northwest Territory. Jefferson and Lincoln made two big additions to it, the former by the Louisiana Purchase and the latter by his support for the Homestead Act of 1862. Indirectly, federal grants of free land to railroads also served a resettlement purpose.

In a time when so much of government is grimly technocratic, it restores perspective to recall that the nation's founders were not abashed to speak of happiness as a proper aim of government. Jefferson's "life, liberty and the pursuit of happiness" was the most memorable statement. To Hamilton "the national happiness" was dependent upon a strong national government. The words of Edmund Randolph, however, may better than the others set forth concisely a proper role of the federal government. Its role, he argued at the Constitutional Convention, should be *"sufficient* to the general happiness."

Those few words sum up the balanced standard of ambitious commitment and sense of proportion which must govern the policies of recovery. In supporting a quest for the general happiness, the federal government should not do too little, as in times past it has. For the two decades or so during which most cities will need a *diminishing* subsidy, we must look to the federal government to provide it. But neither, by a standard of sufficiency, should it essay too much, as today it does. Although the guardianship for those local governments which require a subsidy cannot be wholly ended until the subsidy is no longer needed, the detailed intervention that now prevails should be eliminated.

For the many local governments that do not need outside resources, but only their automatically remitted share of the federally collected local income tax, the guardianship could be quickly ended altogether.

2. THE TANDEM MIGRATIONS: ONE STILL SURGING, ONE NEARLY SPENT

Three Historical Phases of Their Relationship

In the great age of geographic discovery, after it had been accepted that the North American continent was a barrier to a westward route from Europe to Asia, many explorers and their royal or mercantile sponsors nonetheless dreamed that a practical northern route by sea might still be found. The hope was known as the Northwest Passage and it was pursued until almost the end of the eighteenth century.

Another Northwest Passage tempts many scholars of urban affairs. Surely, it is held, there must be universal laws which govern the growth and decay of cities and which, when discovered, can be expressed in a mathematical model wherewith the pattern of the future may be predicted. Thus armed with knowledge of what an unplanned future holds, we can then use the model as a "planning tool" to change the future. Just as the invention of the compass, the astrolabe and the sextant made the explorations possible, so it is thought that the remarkable computer will unlock the magic knowledge still withheld from us.

It is an appealing thought, buttressed by the fact that we know too little about how human settlements grow and change. It would be unwise to dismiss the possibility that someday a plausible model of "the natural life cycle" of cities may be constructed (even to a span of 250 years, as one mathematician has attempted without troubling to study the history of cities). After all, a landless route around North America was eventually discovered, and Amundsen, working his way through ice floes, made the transit by stages in three summers. (By one of history's neater ironies, his journey coincided with the start of work on the Panama Canal.) But by then hope that a commercially valuable passage through the Arctic could be found had long since been abandoned for more practical routes. And so with the recovery of cities: It is a need too urgent to await the discovery of the Northwest Passage sought by builders of urban models.

One of the frustrating problems in constructing a model of cities is that there is no standard city. Every one differs from every other. A city (or what experts now call a central city) is a political jurisdiction which is only a part of the larger settlement that we call a metropolis. It may be no more than a quarter of the whole, as in the case of St. Louis, it may be as much as two-thirds, as in the case of Kenosha, and occasionally even more. But it is also impossible to pin down what the whole is; we must rely on arbitrary definitions. The Census Bureau has two for all settlements above 50,000 in population. One is the Urbanized Area and the other is the Standard Metropolitan Statistical Area (SMSA). The latter consists of whole counties and usually contains some rural population. Most economic data that we will use for analysis are available only in reports based on the SMSA; consequently, it is our most frequent measure of the metropolis. But in a chapter on transportation our unit of measure will be the Urbanized Area because that is the measure prescribed in the legislation which governs the U. S. Department of Transportation. Also, in the case of Los Angeles and New York City (following a common practice) we define their metropolitan areas more broadly than does the Census Bureau.

The explorations made in this and following chapters, whereby we seek the understanding on which practical policies of recovery may be based, do not disclose any "laws" of urban development nor do they confirm the existence of a "life cycle" for settlements. (The presumed parallel between settlements and biological organisms is tenuous and reflects more of mysticism than of demonstrable fact.) But, distinctly different in nature from patterns which may be described as natural laws of development, we can identify various historical trends which interact upon each other, and by understanding them better we can arrive at policies more fitting than those we have.

The tandem migrations of urban-start and move-up have been until recently the most decisive forces in the evolution of the settlements we know today. It was because of the urban-start migration that the settlements grew much more rapidly than was possible through natural increase of population. And it was the move-up migration which justified the other; it continually nourished the hopes which brought people to cities.

They are not the only significant migrations, however. There is another consisting of people already urbanized and whose change of location is not induced—significantly, at least—by a change in social status. It is the migration which has enabled metropolitan areas such as those of Dallas, Los Angeles, Phoenix, Denver, and Atlanta to grow much more rapidly than those of Detroit, St. Louis, New York, Boston, and Buffalo. Mainly, this transfer migration is induced by shifts in employment opportunities; without it all metropolises would grow at about the same rate. Much of it is from suburb to suburb with only minor effect on cities.

During a long era in which the tandem migrations moved approximately in unison even the worst city housing was in demand. The era spanned roughly a half century, from the outbreak of World War I until the mid-sixties, when a gap began to show between the migrations. Throughout most of this era much of the worst housing was also overcrowded, sometimes dreadfully so. But, as we have seen, the housing shortage was being reduced even before the stream of new arrivals slowed.

The overcrowding was the heritage of a still earlier era when the relationship between the move-up migration and the migration of new arrivals was the reverse of what it is today. Then there had been more new arrivals than people moving up. When our cities were much younger, the housing vacated by people moving to something better was far from enough to provide shelter for the big stream of foreign immigrants. The solution was to create instant slums. Block after block of city land was filled with cheap rental housing for people who were terribly poor: the six-story walk-up tenements for Jewish garment workers on New York's lower East Side, Baltimore's cramped brick rowhouses for Italian and Polish immigrants who loaded ship cargo, and the tiny, look-alike wood frame houses for Scandinavian lumber workers in the upper Powderhorn district of Minneapolis. Many of these dismal structures still remain.

Both migrations have always responded to the business cycle. The Panic of 1893—in today's parlance an acute recession or a three-year mini-depression—caused a slump in immigration, but with economic recovery the flow of immigrants rose to its highest level. More than a million entered the United States in 1910, and nearly all settled in cities. The outbreak of war in Europe stopped immigration and the pre-1914 level was never reached again. The Johnson Act of 1921 restricted

immigration by the application of national quotas, and more severe
restrictions came three years later. Since then the stronger current of
new arrivals has come from American rural areas. Now it has spent its
force.

When Confidence Prevailed

We glimpsed briefly our ten cities as they were in 1880 on the eve
of the new technologies that shaped the metropolis. We will understand
better what the frayed link between the tandem migrations portends if
once more we take a backward look. The view which serves us best is to be
found on the eve of the automobile-based suburb.

The year is 1920. In that year, for the first time, music was transmitted
by radio in Pittsburgh and London, and the broadcast industry was born.
No city yet had a commercial airport; scheduled passenger flights were
still seven years away. Nearly everybody who went from one city to
another traveled by train. One could take a night boat from New York to
Boston or Norfolk. A motorist setting out from the now established
automobile capital of the world was soon bouncing on dirt roads.

In 1920 the young avant-garde architects, Ludwig Mies van der Rohe
(once plain Ludwig Mies), in Berlin, and Charles-Edouard Jeanneret
(later Le Corbusier), in Paris, having learned Eiffel's lesson that walls of
steel-frame buildings need be only drapes, were independently
preparing designs and articles which, when published the following year,
would make them rival leaders of a new vogue in architecture variously
known as the "functional" or "international" school. The new
architecture would prevail and after mid-century most new commercial
and government buildings would be clothed in austere slabness. Arguing
for only "skin and bones," Mies van der Rohe prophetically called his
design "The Glass Skyscraper."

All cities were growing then, and all of any importance were growing at
a rate faster than the nation as a whole. We were well on our way to
becoming an urban society. When the 1920 census data became known it
was found that for the first time a slight majority of the American people
now lived in urban areas, i.e., in cities and towns of at least 2,500 persons.
The rural population was increasing but it had grown by a mere 3% in ten
years, compared to a 29% urban gain. The family farm was still supreme
as a production unit, and horse power was the main source of energy for
agriculture. The tractor was yet a novelty, but farmers who were
prosperous owned automobiles that could be used in good weather.

Of our ten cities, only New York, St. Louis, and Baltimore had been of
major rank in 1880. In the next forty years the population of New York

Table 1

POPULATION OF TEN CITIES, 1790-1973 (in thousands)

Year	New York City	Baltimore	Detroit	St. Louis	Los Angeles	Kenosha	Minneapolis	St. Paul	Dallas	Fort Worth
1790	49	14								
1800	79	27								
1810	120	47								
1820	152	63	1							
1830	242	81	2	5						
1840	391	102	9	16						
1850	696	169	21	78	2	3				
1860	1,175	212	46	161	4	4	3	10		
1870	1,478	267	80	311	6	4	13	20		
1880	1,912	332	116	351	11	5	47	41	10	7
1890	2,507	434	206	452	50	7	165	133	38	23
1900	3,437	509	286	575	102	12	203	163	43	27
1910	4,767	558	466	689	319	21	301	215	92	73
1920	5,620	734	994	773	577	40	381	235	159	106
1930	6,930	805	1,569	822	1,238	50	464	272	260	163
1940	7,455	859	1,623	816	1,504	49	492	288	295	178
1950	7,892	950	1,850	857	1,970	54	522	311	434	279
1960	7,782	939	1,670	750	2,479	68	483	313	680	356
1970	7,896	906	1,511	622	2,816	79	434	310	844	393
1973	7,647	878	1,387	558	2,747	79	382	287	816	360

Source: U.S. Bureau of the Census decennial census figures since inception (1790), plus Census Bureau estimate for 1973.

almost trebled and in St. Louis and Baltimore it more than doubled. The population of St. Paul was multiplied by 6; Minneapolis and Kenosha, 8; Detroit, 9; Fort Worth, 15; Dallas, 16; Los Angeles, 52.

Anyone familiar with American cities would have named St. Louis and Baltimore high on the list of pleasant cities in which to live (unless one happened to be black). They were urbane in a way that would never be matched by the newer cities. They had, for example, come to maturity at a time when the city park movement—the movement that began with the design of New York City's Central Park by Frederick Law Olmsted—was at its peak strength in exerting a humanizing influence on city structure. (During the business panic of 1857 the city of New York had hired hundreds of the city's unemployed to hasten completion of the park.) St. Louis had been host to the 1904 World's Fair, and afterwards the fair grounds became the nucleus of Forest Park. This park and Baltimore's Druid Hill Park remain among the nation's best.

By 1920 Detroit's carriage industry and machine shops had become the larger part of the new automobile industry. In 1900 there were 8,000 automobiles in all of the United States. There were 458,000 in 1910. In the next decade the number raced to over 8,000,000, and Detroit became the nation's fourth most populous city. The rise of Detroit profoundly changed every other city in the United States. Even by 1920 the effect was big within cities, though not yet outside them. Arterial streets were being widened and renamed "avenues" or "boulevards." For the past five or six years developers of new residential areas in cities had been betting that their customers, even if they did not yet own an automobile, would want a house suited to the new age. The larger new houses had an inside garage. Modest bungalows had a driveway and a shed. For this reason building lots were larger and population density was less than in older neighborhoods. If you wish to be an urban archeologist and identify the beginnings of the automobile age, look for the neighborhoods where the original street curb no longer runs in an unbroken line but is molded to fit individual driveways. However, in cities where rowhouses were common, as in Baltimore, look instead for alley entrances to rear-yard garages.

Ironically, there was an exception to the new trend and it was in Detroit, of all places. In the early years of the automobile industry, not many people (Henry Ford excepted) expected automobile workers to be able to buy the product they were making. Detroit's real estate developers obviously did not. From about 1905 to about 1920 they built acres upon acres of houses of the kind that factory workers were then expected to be content with. Lots were too small to hold both a house and a car. That misjudgment was a principal reason why in later years, after the industry's workers had formed a union and won high wages, the city lost population heavily to more spacious suburbs.

The Twin Cities had grown from small cities to large ones. Minneapolis now clearly outranked its downriver rival as a regional business capital. The city's last lumbermill had closed, a consequence of ruthless overcutting of timber in Northern Minnesota and competition from the Pacific Northwest. But the flour milling industry, supplied by the booming wheat production of the Great Plains states, had expanded hugely. It served a national market and provided a stable economic base.

Dallas and Fort Worth were no longer frontier towns. The former had prospered as a center of the cotton trade and was already the business capital of a region destined for strong growth. The surge in automobile production had spurred a search for more oil; although the big East Texas discovery had not been made, there had been lesser ones; Dallas was manufacturing oil field rigs, financing wildcatters, and growing fast.

Dallas began its growth where a rocky bottom afforded the safest crossing of the Trinity River, and it is a jest in Dallas that the end of one day's journey by wagon train determined the location of Fort Worth. In truth, there was a stronger reason. When the fording of rivers was still a dangerous part of travel, the pause in the trail that became Fort Worth was the best place to cross the Trinity's Clear Fork. Moreover, adjacent high land was suited for a military outpost to protect westward-bound settlers. When the first railroad in the region reached Fort Worth and ended there, the city's first large growth was founded on the ruin of the famed Chisholm Trail, whose mythology lives on as a staple of TV entertainment. No longer was it necessary to drive cattle to Kansas; they could be loaded into cattle cars at Fort Worth for shipment to Chicago. And then as a regional market developed, Chicago packing houses established branches at Fort Worth.

As late as 1920 meat packing was one of the few industries in which companies had established branch plants to produce for regional markets. The practice, already a boon to Fort Worth, would be widely adopted during the next half century by major corporations in most industries, and it would be an important element in a large shift of population from the Northeast and the Middle West to the Southwest and Pacific Coast—especially to Texas and California. The burgeoning automobile industry would adopt the branch plant innovation in the twenties, and in time Los Angeles would assemble more automobiles in a year than Detroit.

Sandwiched between Chicago and Milwaukee, Kenosha was destined to remain a small city, but it had a foothold in the automobile industry (which it still has as the main manufacturing location of American

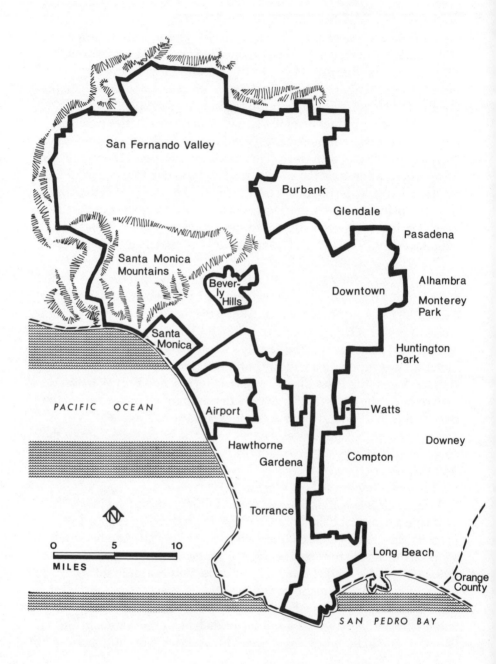

Figure 1. *The Peculiar Boundaries of the City of Los Angeles*

Motors). By 1920, outnumbering the descendants of the Anglo-Saxon settlers and of the early German immigrants, were many who had been born in Italy, Poland, and the Baltic states, living in their separate neighborhoods. The school administration, with the aid of volunteers, had established a day care center at which women working in the then active tannery might leave their small children.

Los Angeles was especially different from every other city. A town forty years earlier, it now had a population of more than a half million and was growing faster than any city except Detroit. Los Angeles had a broad range of natural assets for growth. Oil in the ground was one. Over 2,000 wells were being pumped in the city's Signal Hill district. A benign climate was another—in the long run, the greatest. By now Los Angeles and nearby towns were a mecca for a very special migration, new in history: a migration of the elderly who wished to spend their remaining years in a pleasant place blessed by a mild climate. Climate and ample space for production lots had been decisive in drawing the still young movie industry from New York.

Los Angeles, the terminus of two major railroads, was on its way to becoming one of the world's great seaports. The harbor towns of San Pedro and Wilmington, unable to compete with Long Beach, had persuaded Los Angeles to annex them and to provide the money for port development. They were fifteen miles from the city line and the laws of California did not permit a city to establish a colony, in the manner of the city-states of Ancient Greece, which was not connected to it by land. To annex the harbor towns it was necessary for the city to annex also a half-mile-wide connecting strip—a negotiating feat which required some imaginative deals in the state legislature. The spindly-legged annexation has given the city the shape of some rare bird perched on San Pedro Bay.

Cities Lose Control of Their Destiny

By 1920 the word *suburb* was entering the common speech but the suburbs which then existed owed little to the automobile. Speak of suburbs, and people thought of New York's Mamaroneck and Rye, Philadelphia's Ardmore and Bryn Mawr, or Chicago's Winnetka and Lake Forest—towns in a line astride a railroad, like pieces of shishkebab on a skewer. While the automobile was still a rich man's plaything, railroads were running commuter trains for well-to-do people who worked in the central business district and were acquiring spacious homes on the outskirts of little towns along the railroad. The first such homes had been summer homes. Then real estate developers and railroads found a mutual interest in promoting year-round homes in rail-based suburbs. Since a right-of-way and tracks were in being, a large part of the necessary railway capital had already been provided.

Although in 1880 John Stephenson manufactured horsecars, he did not ordinarily use them; his fashionable home long stood next to his works near New York's Madison Square. At that time many thousands of others also did not need transportation to work. In the needle trades and in cigar-making whole families worked for miserable piecework pay in their homes. But in forty years profound changes had taken place. The island was now too crowded for heavy manufacturing like Stephenson's. State legislation had banned the home sweatshops, and the per capita demand for transportation had risen sharply among both the poor and the well-to-do. While new arrivals had doubled the island's population, descendants of earlier settlers pushed almost to the outer limits of Brooklyn, Queens, and the Bronx. Commuter trains brought quick-stepping throngs from Long Island, New Jersey, and Westchester County. The city now had a second subway, and in the twenties contracts would be let for a third. Running for mayor in 1929, Norman Thomas would exclaim, "We can never catch up with ourselves as long as there is no limit to the congestion of workers in skyscrapers of ever greater rise. . . . We run our race against subway congestion on a treadmill."

Meanwhile a dispersed residential pattern was emerging in the broad basin of the little Los Angeles River. One of the flourishing myths of our time is that the automobile was the cause of the spread-out nature of Los Angeles and what is now its metropolitan area. It happened another way. Before automobiles came into general use, the pattern had been firmly set by the Pacific Electric Railway. Chartered in 1901, it soon became the largest electric interurban system in the United States. It, too, provided commuting services on lines which radiated from the hub, but it also did two things that were different. It built new tracks to serve communities not yet in being and it developed a network of connecting lines. Before the automobile became competitive, more than 300 residential districts in four counties were being served by 2,700 daily trolley runs on the elaborate network. Downtown Los Angeles and the harbor area and downtown and Pasadena were linked by express trains running on reserved tracks. Beaches and a mountain peak were no more than an hour away for residents of Los Angeles and the suburbs which the trolleys were creating.

Transportation was an incidental purpose. As told by Spencer Crump in *Ride the Big Red Cars: How Trolleys Helped Build Southern California,* the railway lost money on its operations in all but a few years. Its main purpose was to promote the sale of land owned by the railway's owners. Henry E. Huntington, nephew of the builder of the Southern Pacific and himself the builder of the Pacific Electric, described his objectives in a published interview in 1904: "It would never do for an electric line to wait until the demand for it came. It must anticipate the growth of communities and be there when the home builders arrive or they are very likely not to arrive at all, but go to some section already provided with the arteries of traffic." Huntington saw to it that the arteries of traffic favored the great acreages owned by himself and his associates. After their speculative holdings had been sold to developers, their interest in the railway waned. Routes were progressively abandoned as riders turned to automobiles. But the big red cars in their heyday brought to the residents of Los Angeles and its trolley-based suburbs a spaciousness that was ahead of the times.

Automobile-based suburbs really began to grow when people could live outside the city without getting stuck in the mud. Harry Truman, an elected official of Jackson County, Missouri, started unknowingly toward the White House by paving county roads. Similar paving, although not resulting in a related political eminence, occurred in the twenties on the edge of all the nation's cities. Until water and sewer lines were laid, the pioneer residents of the automobile-based suburb could make do with a well and a septic tank, but hardtop roads were indispensable.

In those days residents of new settlements along the city's edge tried to persuade cities to annex their land, and almost as frequently city residents refused their requests rather than accept the cost of providing municipal services.

Many years earlier the citizens of St. Louis had deliberately ruled out further annexations by seeking and obtaining the status of a county. Later Baltimore did the same, and by 1920 Baltimore and St. Paul, like St. Louis, had reached the boundaries that they have today. In the twenties Minneapolis made a minor annexation and none thereafter, Detroit a major one and none thereafter. In that decade Los Angeles expanded almost to its present area. Cities would have more freedom of action today if they had pushed their boundaries further before suburbs became uppity, but few people could then perceive that their city would become a minor component of a metropolis. *Metropolis?* What is the fellow talking about?

Later, when feasible at all, annexation became a process of untidy compromises. Detroit had been obliged to accept Hamtramck and Highland Park as independent municipalities, although surrounding them. Los Angeles, Dallas and Fort Worth made similar concessions to local autonomy. A dozen independent municipalities are scattered inside Fort Worth like South Seas islands. But because Dallas, Fort Worth, and Kenosha continued to annex into the sixties, they are, among the ten, the most suburban in characteristics. Most of the later growth of Los Angeles occurred in the big San Fernando Valley, which had been providently annexed in 1915. Its major development became practical when freeways pierced the intervening Santa Monica Mountains. It is essentially suburban.

The element of chance in annexations should remind us that a boundary between the outer city and inner suburbs is artificial and arbitrary, defining a political jurisdiction and not a difference in kind. Whatever description may be given to this type of residential district, St. Louis has less of it than other cities. We cannot talk about cities without generalizing, but if we are to avoid glibness we must constantly remember that they are not cut from a single cloth.

Stranger even than the thought that more people would live in suburbs than in cities, would have been a suggestion in 1920 that cities would become *victims* of prosperity. It was nonetheless predictable that both bizarre eventualities would occur if certain things happened.

If a city's boundaries became fixed, if the population of the city and its immediate vicinity continued to grow, if enough housing was not available in the city, and if good transportation could be provided, then inevitably the expanding population would overflow into new residential districts outside the city, and in time the new districts would hold more than the old.

If, also, the newer homes outside the city were more attractive than the older ones in it, and if rising incomes, along with easier terms of home financing, made it practical for many city residents to choose the more attractive homes, then, as certain as the sunrise, cities would be hurt by prosperity.

Given the premises, the logic was unassailable. It was just that the premises were too hypothetical to be taken seriously. But all these things did come to pass.

The Great Resettlements

If distant historians should be baffled when they try to reconcile the language of our time with reality, their bewilderment may be forgiven. Reading the written word, they might understandably conclude that no one ever settled in a suburb except in *flight* from the city. But when they come to the pictorial evidence, how attractive today's suburbs will appear in comparison with other refugee camps! No tents in dusty fields. No communal mess halls. Even the barracks were of a one-family size, had a split-level design and were set amid shade trees and azaleas on broad lawns.

Most resettlements of people respond both to a pull and a push: opportunities which appear to beckon and dissatisfactions to get away from, hopes and fears. Whether the pull or the push may be stronger varies from place to place, from time to time, and in accordance with the situation of those who move or stay put: their age, responsibilities, financial condition, work training, the knack of making good or poor guesses. Consequently, there is usually scope for disagreement among thoughtful people concerning the motivations which are dominant in a large resettlement of people. But there are useful clues: If most of those who relocate obtain better housing, or better jobs, or better chances for their children, it is fair to say that in their resettlement the pull factor was dominant.

Flight, as a characterization of the massive movement from cities to suburbs, is an overwrought metaphor. Repeated so often that it becomes the conventional wisdom, a dogma, it dulls the mind to an understanding of what really happened. What did happen was something more prosaic: Cities increasingly lost their ability to compete with suburbs as a place of residence. They were outclassed in pulling power. This, and not its few black citizens, caused Minneapolis to lose 27% of its population between 1950 and 1973.

Newness is always an attraction. It was especially so in a time of revolutionary change in mechanical household equipment. When furnaces were converted from coal to oil or gas or electricity, when air conditioning was being introduced, when the icebox gave way to the electric refrigerator and the washing machine to the automatic washer, houses designed to incorporate the new equipment had—in a word which in this period was newly added to popular speech—the *built-in* advantages. Then there was the matter of space. The verdict has not been unanimous. Many people like to live in a high-rise apartment, even if located in a suburb. But a greater number choose a detached home with an individual lawn or a suburban townhouse in a green setting.

During the twenties the urban-start and the move-up migrations flowed at about the same rate, and in that decade more of the move-up occurred within cities than outside them. An exception was St. Louis, which had the smallest reserve of vacant land. The city population rose by 49,000 while the suburbs, with a gain of 111,000, more than doubled. Population increase in the city of Los Angeles was 661,000 and in the remainder of the county it was 611,000.

Probably the best definition of the metropolis of Los Angeles has been given by the Security Pacific Bank; it calls the metropolitan area the Sixty Mile Circle, and defines it as the land area within a 60-mile radius drawn from downtown. The circle contains 97% of the population of the counties of Los Angeles, Orange, San Bernadino, Riverside, and Ventura.

When demographers first introduced the concept of a metropolis, the thought of 10 million people residing in the Sixty Mile Circle must have seemed as far-fetched as a separation of India from the British Empire. If the speculation was entertained, the Depression put the prospect into cold storage—or seemed to.

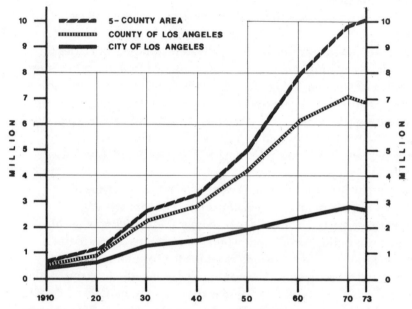

Figure 2.   *Population Growth in Los Angeles and Its Metropolitan Area, 1910-1973*

Its chilling effect on suburban growth may be seen in the record of total new housing starts. Nationwide, it had been nearly a million in 1927. They were a tenth of that figure in 1932, and recovery was slow. There was also negligible migration to commuter suburbs during the war years.

When the end of the war released pent-up wants, many people rushed to obtain new housing. During the war there had been full employment and a build-up of savings; now the savings were available to support a long accumulated demand for goods. When spent, they sustained a continuing high level of employment, which generated rising incomes, which spurred home-buying in suburbs. The longest period of prosperity in American history was beginning, and in the next quarter of a century it would erode the financial standing of almost every American city.

To say that cities have been the victims of prosperity seems to fly in the face of common sense—to draw a theme from the theater of the absurd—and especially so in the mid-seventies when cities have been caught in the squeeze of a severe recession. It is to say, in effect, that cities in their present condition face a no-win situation: Whether the national economy flourishes or falters they will be hurt. Prosperity, by enabling so many former residents of cities to leave them (like a wasting illness that leaves a person vulnerable to pneumonia), has weakened cities more than periodic recessions.

Not merely the fact of rising incomes sent city dwellers to the suburbs; there was also the effect of a momentous revolution in home financing which had begun on a muted scale in 1935 with the creation of the Federal Housing Administration. The FHA was a new government agency empowered to insure home mortgages. (Similar powers were later given to the Veterans Administration.) By greatly reducing lenders' risks, the insurance fostered low down payments and a longer mortgage life.

Before the FHA set a new standard, mortgage bankers typically required a 35% down payment and repayment within seven to ten years. At the end was a menacing balloon payment. If that could not be met, all that the homeowner had invested might be lost. In the early Depression years it happened often.

Conceivably, competition among lenders in the conventional mortgage market might have led to the relatively easy financing terms (apart from current interest rates) that we now take for granted. Consumer credit blossomed in the postwar years; if easy financing could be arranged for refrigerators, perhaps it would have been done also for homes. Possibly. But it seems equally possible that it was the other way around: The pace the government set for home financing may have been the stimulus for easier credit in other areas.

What might have been the consequences for our time without rising incomes and liberal credit terms for home ownership? The tandem migrations would have been severely slowed—not halted altogether, but slowed the way traffic is reduced to a crawl many miles behind the congesting bottleneck. Easy home financing opened the valve for the great stream of city dwellers, excited by the prospect of a home in attractive suburbs and sharing enough in the rising affluence to afford the monthly payments. Without this flow of people, the other stream behind it would have been dammed. How else would the newcomers from the countryside have been housed in cities except in the housing being vacated as people moved outward? Hypothetically, new houses could have been built for them. But the hypothesis is pretty well demolished by the facts. Since there is not much by-passed land in cities on which to build, it would have been necessary to demolish existing housing in order to build for more people. But where? In the inner city where the existing housing was least valuable? But there the density was already the greatest. In the outer city then, in order to spread density more evenly? That would have meant destruction of newer and better housing while retaining the worst.

In a small degree some rebuilding to higher density on slum sites did occur with generous federal funding. The big Pruitt-Igoe complex in St. Louis was such a case, although when it was authorized it was intended for people who then lived in the city, not for newcomers. To have added a huge migration from rural areas to a city's existing population would have required so much rebuilding to higher density that the possibility must be dismissed as one which was never real.

Again hypothetically, the people who were made surplus on farms might have settled in shantytowns at the edge of cities, as in Paris and Bogota. They might have, that is, if residents of suburbs had abandoned zoning practices.

It must be supposed that the mechanization of agriculture, being an independent force, would have occurred anyway, with a consequent large reduction in agricultural employment. If the farm-to-city immigrants could not have occupied housing being vacated in cities, from which they could look for work, their only plausible alternative would have been to remain in the rural housing they had, bad as it was. But their distress could not have been ignored. There would still have been a large welfare program, with more dispensed in rural counties and less in cities. The "rural problem" would have overshadowed the "urban problem."

By stretching our imagination we can visualize a hypothetical postwar history in which the big city-to-suburb and farm-to-city migrations did not take place. In this fancy, it is easy to list urban misfortunes which, if they existed at all, would have been small in relation to those we have known. But the misfortunes which would have taken their place are harder to imagine. Given the magnitude of rural poverty, even before so many farm workers were displaced, it is evident that the problems would have been big ones. Despite the wrenching effect on cities, it is difficult to believe that our society would today be better off if the great resettlements of the past three decades had not occurred.

The Emptying Inner Cities

The inner city is the place where the tandem migrations touch. Most poor arrivals must make their start there because it is where housing is cheapest. At the same time, some inner city residents—sometimes whole families, sometimes just children who have matured—move up to better housing, usually in parts of the outer city from which others are moving to suburbs.

When the urban-start migration falls off and the move-up continues strongly, a drop in inner city population must be expected. It happened in eight cities where inner city population changes between 1960 and 1970 were computed, ranging from a modest 5% in Dallas to a stunning 35% in Detroit and St. Louis.

The inner city, it should be said, is not easily defined. In popular usage the term connotes both a geographic area and a social condition, and while the city's poorest are largely concentrated in the oldest area, the overlap is anything but tidy. In only two of the ten cities—Detroit and Dallas—have city governments defined their inner city for statistical analysis. In the other cities, except New York and Kenosha, I identified census tracts which were similar in location and social characteristics to those in the Detroit and Dallas models and then computed population changes in them. The results are shown in an accompanying chart. Kenosha was omitted because population was not recorded there by tracts until 1970, and New York because of the city's peculiar geography and the sheer size of the task. However, a partial inspection shows heavy population losses in some of New York's older low-income districts such as Central Harlem and the South Bronx.

Inner city population losses were heaviest in those cities where there were population losses as a whole—in outer cities and inner suburbs as well. Cities which gained in population, and therefore had a tighter housing market had smaller inner city losses. As one might expect, move-ups were easiest where the housing market was slack. Minneapolis is one such city; there all but one of ten officially defined districts lost population. The Twin Cities Citizens League, a civic organization distinguished by the high quality of its studies, found in 1973 that approximately one half of all owner-occupied homes (a half of all homes in Minneapolis and found mainly in outer districts) were occupied by one or two persons. When such houses come on the market, as they may be expected to do with increasing frequency because of the advanced age of many of the owners, they will draw residents from the inner city.

The only Minneapolis district to gain population during the sixties has a story worth telling. It is officially known as Calhoun-Isles, but to national television audiences it might fittingly be called the Mary Tyler Moore district. It consists of stately old houses like the one glimpsed occasionally in the popular program as the main character's residence. The houses were built about 1915. At first the developers proposed to drain the area's several lakes in order to have more land on which to build. Enough citizens rallied to oppose it that the city council turned down the request. In the end both nature-lovers and developers were happy, because when the new houses were built along the shores of the lakes the district quickly became the most fashionable in the city. It remained so until after

World War II. Then during the fifties, as maturing children moved away, the population of Calhoun-Isles fell by 8%. Recovery began when many of the spacious and well-preserved old homes were divided into apartments for young professionals like those portrayed in the TV show. In 1970 more than a third of the residents were single adults, mostly young.

The Slippery Slope of Population Losses

A point of view frequently heard pins hopes for cities on anticipated troubles for people who live or want to live in suburbs. Rising gasoline prices, it is said, will force a return to the city. Or suburban no-growth advocates will block further sewer hookups and thereby force up the price of suburban real estate and save the city. The flaw in an approach that stakes a city's future on reluctant residents is that it will work only in the short term.

There is more reason to believe that in time the falloff in new arrivals will keep some—not all—people from moving out. In the face of a slackened demand for city housing, some city homeowners who had planned to move to the suburbs will change their minds because they cannot sell their city home at the price they had counted on. Thus far, however, the reverse has been true, with dismaying results for many city administrations. As a guide to the allocation of revenue sharing funds based in part on population, the Census Bureau now makes sophisticated periodic estimates of population. The most recent published estimate is for 1973; the astonishing results are shown in an accompanying table. Dallas, Fort Worth, and Los Angeles are now losing population; the rate of loss has increased in St. Louis, Minneapolis and Detroit.

The prudent assessment is that from whatever city that hath lost—heavily, anyway—still more shall be taken. The reason is to be found in certain demographic peculiarities. Trying to show how demographic trends affect a city is like trying to get a true picture from the distorted images in a wall of funhouse mirrors. No single statistical mirror will tell us what we need to know. We must look at several, and because sooner or later all trends are curves, every one of the mirrors has a warp. Look from one place, and we get one distortion. Change the perspective, and we get another. The best we can do is to construct a composite mental image which will be truer than any we see.

Let me draw the image first; then I shall show how I arrived at it:

There is a real prospect—not certain, but probable—that in the next decade or two some cities will begin to have fewer births than deaths. In other words, a loss from *natural decrease* will be added to the loss from net migration now going on. Natural decrease has marked the later stages

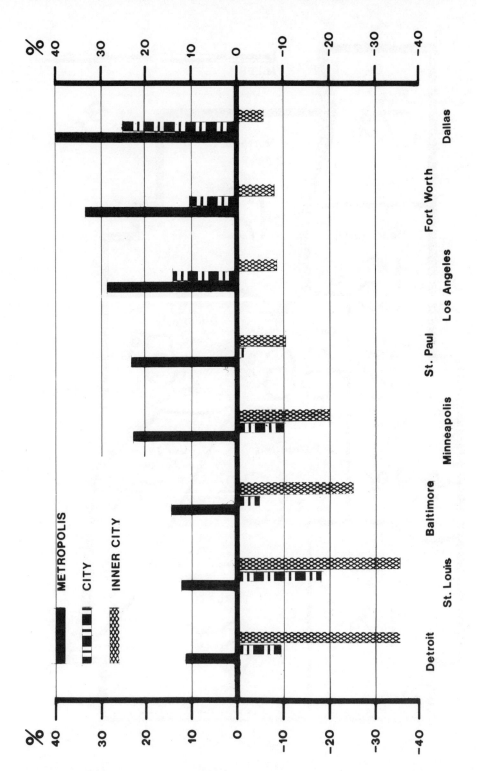

Figure 3. *Population Changes in Eight Cities, Their Metropolises and Their Inner Cities, 1960-1970*

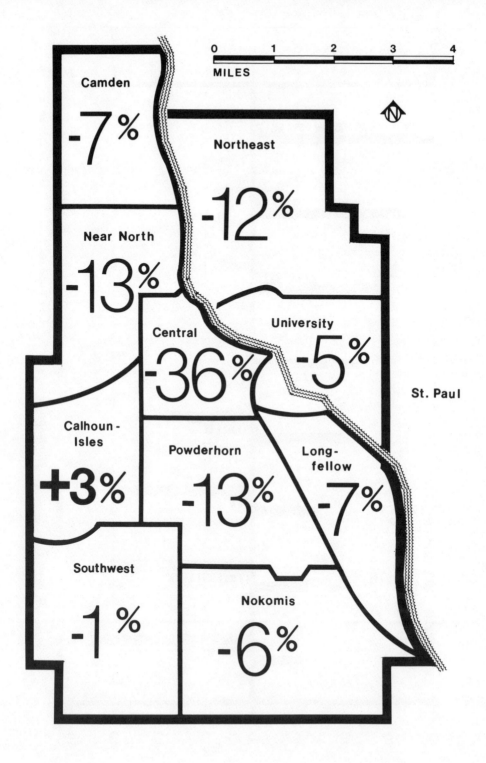

Figure 4. *Population Changes in Minneapolis, by Districts, 1960-1970*

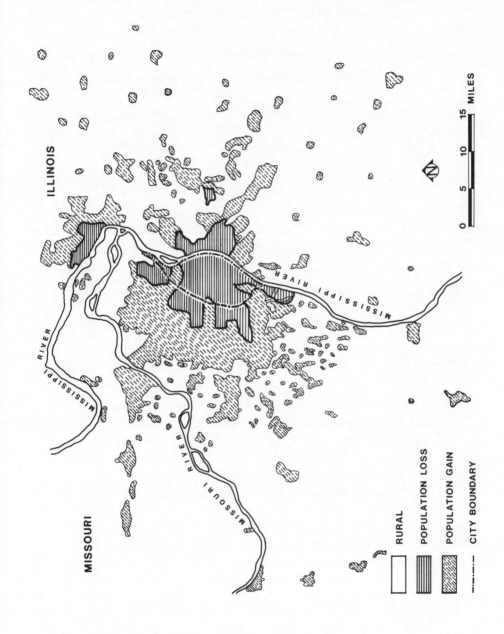

Figure 5. *St. Louis and Its Urbanized Area, Showing Districts of Population Gain or Loss, 1960-1970*

POPULATION CHANGES IN TEN CITIES
1960-70 AND 1970-73

	Percentage Changes		Numerical Changes	
	1960-70 %	1970-73 %	1960-70 (000)	1970-73 (000)
Dallas	+24.2	− 3.4	+165	− 29
Kenosha	+16.1	+ 0.6	+ 11	+ 0.5
Los Angeles	+13.6	− 2.5	+337	− 69
Fort Worth	+10.4	− 8.6	+ 37	− 34
New York City	+ 1.5	− 3.1	+114	−249
St. Paul	− 1.1	− 7.3	− 3	− 23
Baltimore	− 3.6	− 3.1	− 33	− 28
Detroit	− 9.5	− 8.3	−159	−125
Minneapolis	−10.0	−12.0	− 48	− 52
St. Louis	−17.0	−10.3	−128	− 64

Source: Census of Population, 1960 and 1970, and U.S. Bureau of the Census estimate for 1973

Note: In the 1960-70 period annexations accounted for 7% of the population increase in Dallas, 30% in Fort Worth and 73% in Kenosha.

Table 2

of the decline of old mining towns and rural villages, but it has never yet happened in a large American city. St. Louis, hedged into the boundaries it had in 1876, is the most vulnerable. Minneapolis and Detroit appear to be not much less so. The prospect is remote in semisuburban Dallas, even if the United States birth rate falls still more.

During the sixties the rate of natural increase in St. Louis, 7.3%, was less than half the rate in Dallas, a suburbanlike 16.2%. St. Louis had an abnormally low rate because so many families in the childbearing years had already moved to suburbs. Since this continues, and since the national birth rate has continued to go down, the rate of natural increase in St. Louis will almost certainly be lower in the seventies. In the eighties it may go below zero.

When we look at St. Louis' loss from net migration we see a staggering rate of 24.4% for ten years. We know that normally the city-to-suburb movement is strongest among people in their childbearing years.

The population loss in the critical age group which could help to repopulate cities may be seen in a comparison of population profiles according to age—a profile drawn, say, in 1960 and again ten years later. Our population has not increased in neat, uniform steps. Rather, we have had a highly volatile birth rate during the past half century. It began to decline in the twenties and fell sharply during the Depression. After World War II came the baby boom, cresting in 1957. The birth rate then declined, slowly at first and then precipitously. It is now the lowest we have ever known.

A comparison of population age profiles shows, among other things, a record of people growing older, and as people grow older the down-up-down birth rate is seen as a rolling wave: trough, crest, trough. Because fewer people were born in the thirties than in the twenties, the number of Americans who in 1970 were between thirty and forty years old was smaller than the number in this age group ten years earlier. Even in Dallas there was a dip in this age group. In a city such as St. Louis, where the rolling wave coincided with a heavy loss from net migration, the drop was severe. Indeed, the loss in this and still younger age groups was so severe that there are now fewer people under age forty than at any time since 1890. The city is not the most promising place in which to practice gynecology.

One of the reasons why the national birth rate declined after 1957 was that the low birth rate in the thirties and the war years resulted in fewer potential parents. Demographers call the relationship an echo effect. The more recent fall will have its echo, and the echo will resound as in a cavern in those cities which have been partly emptied by earlier migrations to suburbs.

A Historic Function Grown Obsolete

We have arrived at a situation like nothing we have known before. Until recently the inner city played a key function in the evolution of metropolitan settlements: It was the starting place in urban living for the terribly poor. The function was a grim one in an ugly setting. For at least the last half of the nineteenth century and most of this one, inner city housing, poor at best, was overcrowded. Nonetheless, a start was made which enabled most who arrived in inner cities, or their children, to leave them.

Traditional functions of the inner city as a business center and as a cultural center remain strong, but the function of offering an urban start to new arrivals is nearly played out. The big surge caused by the rapid mechanization of agriculture cannot be repeated. Restraints on foreign immigration are not likely to be relaxed in any major way. New curbs on illegal immigration are probable.

The consequences will be much more severe in some cities than in others—St. Louis, for example, at one extreme and Dallas at the other—but all will be affected. If cities on a steep downhill slope of population loss are to attract new residents for whatever population level that may seem fitting, they must in the future draw them mainly from suburbs.

Where else?

COMPONENTS OF POPULATION CHANGE IN TEN CITIES
1960-1970

	Total Change %	Natural Increase %	Net Migration %
St. Louis	−17.1	+ 7.3	−24.4
Detroit	− 9.5	+ 7.8	−17.3
Minneapolis-St. Paul[a]	− 6.6	+ 9.2	−15.8
Baltimore	− 3.6	+ 9.0	−12.6
New York City	+ 1.1	+ 7.8	− 6.7
Fort Worth[b]	+10.4	+12.7	− 2.3
Los Angeles[c]	+12.4	+10.3	+ 2.1
Kenosha[b]	+16.1	+15.8	+ 0.3
Dallas[b]	+24.2	+16.2	+ 8.0
FOR COMPARISON			
Suburbs of			
St. Louis	+28.5	+13.8	+14.7
Dallas	+61.8	+18.9	+42.9
United States	+13.4	+12.3	+ 1.1

Source: U.S. Bureau of the Census

[a] Data for the two cities are combined in the census report on this subject. They are not available separately.

[b] Annexations accounted for 7% of the population increase in Dallas, 30% in Fort Worth and 73% in Kenosha.

[c] Includes data for Long Beach.

Note: The published census report on components of population change is based on preliminary data in the case of New York City which differs from the final data used in Table 2.

Table 3

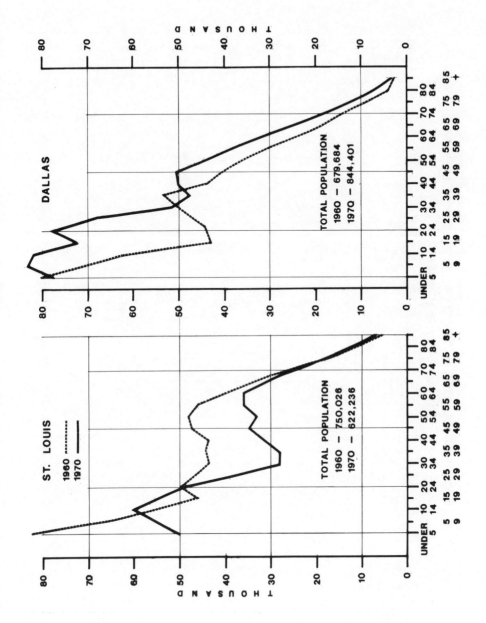

Figure 6.   *Population Profiles of St. Louis and Dallas, by 5-Year Age Groups, 1960 and 1970*

PERCENTAGE CHANGE IN POPULATION IN TEN CITIES BY 5-YEAR AGE GROUPS, 1960-70

(Persons Under 40 in 1970)

	Born in the Sixties		Born in the Fifties		Born in the Forties		Born in the Thirties	
	Under 5 %	5-9 %	10-14 %	15-19 %	20-24 %	25-29 %	30-34 %	35-39 %
St. Louis	-39	-17	+ 7	- 1	- 1	-21	-36	-37
Minneapolis	-29	-16	+ 8	+ 9	+29	+12	-20	-37
Detroit	-23	-17	+ 1	+22	+38	+ 8	-32	-42
Baltimore	-26	- 3	+11	+24	+30	+ 4	-25	-34
St. Paul	-24	- 7	+ 7	+25	+39	+20	-16	-29
Fort Worth	-13	0	+19	+46	+82	+15	-16	-22
New York City	-10	+ 6	+ 9	+24	+35	+16	-12	-19
Kenosha	-10	+22	+31	+57	+47	+36	- 2	-27
Los Angeles	- 9	+ 9	+26	+56	+67	+33	- 1	-15
Dallas	- 3	+16	+36	+66	+77	+46	+ 2	-10
FOR COMPARISON								
Suburbs of								
St. Louis	-11	+20	+54	+85	+74	+39	+ 5	+ 2
Dallas	+27	+66	+84	+92	+96	+90	+67	+52
United States	-16	+ 7	+25	+44	+51	+24	- 4	-11

Source: Based on data from U.S. Bureau of the Census

Table 4

3. THE EVOLVING METROPOLIS

New Competition for the Hub

To judge from surface appearances, the central business district of most large cities has never been healthier. At the center of anemia it pulses with vitality. Higher income residents, retail trade and manufacturing drain away to suburbs, but sleek new job stacks rise to dizzying greater heights to contain the daily flood of white-collar workers who pour in from the metropolitan outer reaches. Ringed by decay, the clustered skyscrapers wear the look of modernity, wealth, power, and assured permanence.

Nowhere has the increase in new office buildings been more spectacular than in the dual central business districts of deeply troubled New York City: Wall Street and Midtown. At the end of World War II office space on Manhattan Island (mostly concentrated in the two districts) amounted to 86 million square feet. By 1964 another 64 million had been added. Then, in a surge of new construction surely never equaled before, 80 million more square feet were added in the next decade. The gain since 1964 is enough to provide office space for 450,000 workers at an average of 180 square feet each—the norm in the new World Trade Center, which alone has the capacity to accomodate 50,000 workers.

The new skyward thrust expresses the confidence of investors in the continuing supremacy of the metropolitan hub that is hard to square with the evolving nature of metropolises. Office space in New York City has been recklessly overbuilt; estimates of vacant space range from 13 to 18% of the total. Such improvident investment was spurred, in part, by federal legislation that made commercial real estate a tax haven for big investors. The real problem of central business districts, however, is more fundamental than a prospect of some defaults on high-figure mortgages. In all of the large cities that were studied, central business districts are encountering competition, in a degree hitherto unknown, from fast growing secondary office work centers. Mostly they are in suburbs, but in spread-out Los Angeles and Dallas such centers also flourish in their outer cities.

The total investment in central business districts—in buildings and the maze of underground installations—is so huge, so impractical to reproduce in less than several generations, that a city's central business district may be expected to continue as the *principal* job center of corporate administration, finance and related professions. But it would not be surprising if most new growth occurred in the emerging secondary centers.

This conclusion rests in part on the record of growth in secondary centers during the past decade or so. But since the visible evidence is fairly recent it is desirable to appraise it in light of what we can discover about the nature of changes in the structure of metropolises as they continue to evolve.

The Theories of Burgess and Hoyt

When I studied urban sociology at the University of Kansas nearly a half century ago, the first explicit theory of the growth and structure of urban settlements was just beginning to ripple through the profession. The author of the theory was Prof. Ernest W. Burgess of the University of Chicago, and while the structure of the city he described—too simply—could be observed by anyone, he found a meaning in it which no one previously had developed systematically.

Burgess first presented his theory in 1924 in *Publications of the American Sociological Society,* but the best known version appeared the following year in a book, *The City,* which he co-edited with Robert E. Park. The gracefully written essay (it was at a time when sociologists still esteemed the English language) was aptly titled "The Growth of the City," and in it he identified the outward migration of distinct cultural groups through concentric zones in a movement extending over several generations and corresponding roughly to their rise in income and education. In an analogy in an earlier chapter I compared the tandem migrations of urban-start and move-up to the growth of an artichoke in which the older stock pushes outward as new stock forms at the center. The characterizations are mine but they are consistent with his theory of urban growth.

Drawing his observations mainly from Chicago, Burgess noted "the tendencies of any town or city to expand radially from its central business district," and added:

Encircling the downtown area there is normally an area in transition, which is being invaded by business and light manufacture. A third area is inhabited by the workers in industries who have escaped from the area of deterioration but who desire to live within easy access of their work. Beyond this zone is the "residential area" of high-class apartment buildings or exclusive "residential" districts of single family dwellings. Still farther, out beyond the city limits, is the commuters' zone—suburban areas, or satellite cities—within a thirty- to sixty-minute ride of the central business district.

Burgess's account of the move-up migration by Jews in Chicago then is suggestive of the black move-up in Baltimore that will be discussed in a later chapter. After noting the first residential zone beyond the central business district—the zone of deterioration—he wrote:

The next zone is also inhabited predominantly by factory and shop workers, but skilled and thrifty. There is an area of second immigrant settlement, generally of the second generation. It is the region of escape from the slum, the *Deutschland* of the aspiring Ghetto family. For *Deutschland* (literally "Germany") is the name given, half in envy, half in derision, to that region beyond the Ghetto where successful neighbors appear to be imitating German Jewish standards of living. But the inhabitants of this area in turn look to the "Promised Land" beyond, to its residential hotels, its apartment-house region, its "satellite loops" and its "bright light" areas. [Chicago's downtown is locally known as The Loop.]

And on to Suburbia.

Burgess was principally interested in the process of growth, as is evident when his ideas are examined firsthand, but the part of his theory that drew most attention was his description of the city's structure as a series of concentric zones. He qualified the description with the remark that "complications are introduced by the lake front, the Chicago River, railroad lines, historical factors in the location of industry, the relative degree of the resistance of communities to invasion, etc." Nonetheless, his description of a city's structure was too sparse, and critics seized upon this weakness while undervaluing his description of the dynamic process of growth.

Homer Hoyt, an economist, offered an alternative interpretation of the structure of cities, which he described as a sector theory. He based his theory on a study of the pattern of residential rents which he conducted in 142 cities for the Federal Housing Administration in the late thirties. The areas of high rents, he found, did not lie wholly in an outer zone or form a complete ring around a city but, instead, were sectors on high ground or along a lake front or a park or along the lines of fastest transportation to the city's hub. Hoyt's study, published in 1939, did not disprove an outward movement of residents as their incomes rose, but he showed the series of concentric zones to be highly irregular in shape. Although he and many of his followers have regarded his ideas as an alternative to the Burgess theory, they are more properly an amendment to it.

A third presumed theory of urban structure should be noted because its name—the multiple-nucluei theory—suggests that it anticipated the emergence of the secondary office work centers that became common during the sixties. However, this is to read more into the theory than is to be found in the original essay in which it was advanced. The secondary centers noted by the authors, two geographers, C. D. Harris and E. L. Ullman, were mainly ports, industrial districts and sales locations for products such as automobiles that require a large amount of display space. R. J. Johnston, a New Zealand geographer who has written an admirable summary (*Urban Residential Patterns*) of the many criticisms and elaborations of the Burgess and Hoyt ideas, ranks the Harris-Ullman theory well below the contributions of Burgess and Hoyt in importance. His judgment appears to be sound.

Burgess and Hoyt gave stimulus to many others. Johnston cites the works of approximately 100 sociologists, economists, and geographers who have criticized their ideas or sought to adapt them to particular models of urban growth. No one, however, has offered a comprehensive theory which replaces the basic ideas put forward by Burgess a half century ago. No one has proposed a revision more important than Hoyt's.

Nonetheless, since their time there have been major changes in things which they took for granted. Suburbs, not cities, now hold a majority of the population in most metropolises. Industry is not moving into the "zone of deterioration." It is moving out. The urban-start migration which continually repopulated inner cities has sharply dwindled. And although Burgess and Hoyt both took note of the emergence of secondary business districts or "satellite loops" (*central* implies others), neither suggested that they might seriously compete with the central business districts or acquire the nonconventional forms that they are taking today. In order to appraise the present relevance of their ideas to the recovery of cities we need to take account of changes since their time.

Jobs in Cities: More White-Collar, Fewer Blue-Collar

One of the popular myths muddying our understanding of the settlements in which most of us live is that we are becoming less of an industrial society than we were. Even persons trained in precision often make the mistake. Thus we find an official White House science adviser in the Nixon administration writing of "our chosen development of a 'post-industrial' society oriented toward communication, information, education and services, instead of manufacturing." *Instead?* If he had said *instead of agriculture and mining,* he would have been correct with respect to jobs, although not output. But not *manufacturing.* The ratio of manufacturing jobs to total population in 1970 was almost the same as it was a half century earlier, and during the sixties it increased slightly.

The big changes that continue to occur in both the nature of jobs and their location are important to our inquiry because of their profound effect on the evolution of urban settlements. The most revealing way to look at the changes in jobs is in relation to population growth. A 10,000-person microcosm is a suitable size for an accurate measure of the changes.

To begin with, in a 10,000-person model of the whole United States in 1970, 3,900 were engaged in some civilian job compared to 3,680 a decade earlier. This was not a long-term change, but only a reflection of an improvement in the state of the economy. Beneath it, however, were others of a long-term character. Jobs which are mostly white-collar in nature rose during the sixties from 2,016 to 2,360 per 10,000 persons—a whopping 17% gain. The ratio of blue-collar jobs rose only 1%. The difference in these rates of gain is apparently what the White House science adviser had in mind.

There was a further change in the basic shift from rural to urban jobs. In a 10,000-person microcosm in 1970 there were only 170 working in agriculture, compared to 303 in 1960 and 985 in 1920.

Within these changes in kinds of jobs were also large changes in where they were performed. Although New York City is not wholly typical, it does illustrate general trends in most jobs. Between 1960 and 1970, when the city's population rose by 1.5%, the number of manufacturing jobs fell from 947,000 to 773,000—down 18% in a time of rising prosperity. More than a third of the manufacturing job loss was in the clothing industry, but

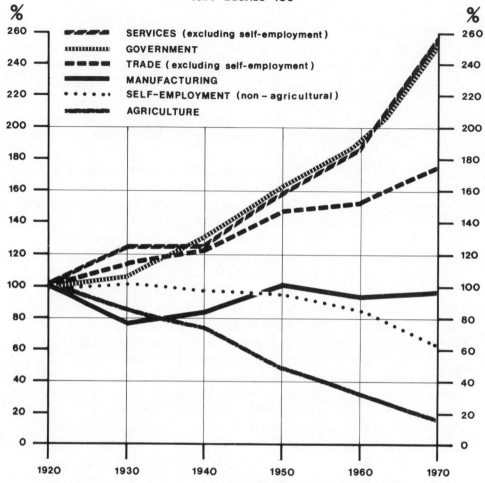

Figure 7. *U. S. Employment Per Capita, by Major Categories, 1920-1970*

Table 5

EMPLOYEES PER 10,000 PERSONS IN THE UNITED STATES, 1920-1970
(Civilian Wage and Salary Employees Except Where Otherwise Stated)

	1920	1930	1940	1950	1960	1970
Mostly urban						
1 Manufacturing	1,005	776	831	1,007	937	952
2 Transportation and public utilities	377	299	230	267	223	221
3 Contract construction	80	111	98	154	161	166
4 Mostly blue collar	1,462	1,186	1,159	1,428	1,321	1,339
5 Trade	421	471	511	620	635	734
6 Government	246	256	318	398	466	617
7 Services	223	274	279	356	414	571
8 Finance, insurance, real estate	111	120	114	127	149	181
9 Self employed (non-agriculture)	411	415	408	398	352	257
10 Mostly white collar	1,412	1,536	1,630	1,899	2,016	2,360
11 Total mostly urban (lines 4 and 10)	2,874	2,722	2,789	3,327	3,337	3,699
Mostly non-urban						
12 Agriculture (including self employed)	985	839	722	473	303	170
13 Mining	117	82	70	60	40	31
14 Total mostly non-urban	1,102	921	792	533	343	201
15 Total civilian employees (11 and 14)	3,976	3,643	3,581	3,860	3,680	3,900
Unemployed and military						
16 Unemployed	201	352	614	217	215	201
17 Civilian labor force (15 and 16)	4,177	3,995	4,195	4,077	3,895	4,101
18 Military	36	21	41	109	140	108
19 Total labor force (17 and 18)	4,213	4,016	4,236	4,186	4,035	4,209

Source: Based on data from the U.S. Census Bureau and the Bureau of Labor Statistics

losses occurred in all but five of 66 industries which were reported. The exceptions: book and magazine publishing, jewelry, soap, and plastic products. Construction jobs declined 13% despite the spurt in new office buildings.

These losses were more than offset. The city's net gain in jobs was 225,000, or 6%. The largest source of new jobs, by a wide margin, was the city government. The Bureau of Labor Statistics shows an increase of about 145,000 city jobs, or more than a 50% growth. Most of the growth appears to have been in programs which had federal support. Jobs in banking rose by 52% and in the brokerage business by 91%; together these main branches of the financial world created 90,000 new jobs in the city. Many of them were presumably filled by commuters. On the other hand, the losses in manufacturing caused an increase in the city's welfare burden.

Another way of measuring the decline of most cities as manufacturing centers is by the number of factories. The U. S. Census of Manufactures provides an actual count every four or five years. Small factories can be relocated easier than large ones, and for this reason a loss in the number of factories is usually proportionately greater than the actual loss of jobs. Nonetheless, it is an important indication of a trend. An accompanying table shows changes during a 14-year period. (Part of the gain by Dallas and Fort Worth resulted from annexations.)

NUMBER OF MANUFACTURING PLANTS, NINE CITIES
1958-1972

	1958	1972	Change %
New York City	35,544	24,312	−32
Los Angeles	9,149	7,598	−17
Detroit	3,363	2,398	−29
St. Louis	2,135	1,461	−32
Minneapolis-St. Paul	1,947	1,504	−23
Baltimore	1,623	1,239	−24
Dallas	1,406	1,809	+29
Fort Worth	615	771	+25
United States total	299,017	320,710	+ 7

Table 6

The outward relocation of factories began well before 1958 (Hoyt mentioned it in his 1939 study), but the annual rate grows larger. It should not be supposed that all factories will quit cities; many must be adjacent to a lake or a river or a major rail terminal. But before a leveling off occurs, further losses seem certain. A major reason was given by a special Industry Advisory Committee to the Minneapolis City Planning Commission in 1960. "Minneapolis, on the whole, operates in an obsolescent industrial plant," it said. The committee recommended an attempt to redevelop obsolete industrial districts but was skeptical that it would have much effect.

The city government established an industrial development commission, as the committee recommended, and it can point to successes in persuading several companies to remain in the city. But relocations continued at a heavy rate. In 1970 the commission polled the managements of 135 factories and warehouses which had relocated in suburbs. Space for growth was the most important reason to relocate. The 135 firms that were polled had an average of 700 square feet of land per worker in the city but an average of 4,700 in the suburbs. Floor space in the new buildings averaged 584 per worker against 366 when in the city. For the additional space the firms which relocated paid property taxes that averaged twenty-two cents per hour per worker in suburbs compared to seven cents per hour per worker in the city. Total employment rose by 27% after moving.

**REASONS CITED BY 135 INDUSTRIAL COMPANIES
FOR LEAVING MINNEAPOLIS**

Reason	Firms Citing This Reason %
Room for expansion	76
Low cost of land and new construction	67
Travelling convenience of employes	56
Civic-industrial climate	45
Availability of labor	28
Favorable tax structure	16
Low cost of truck transportation	16

Table 7

Large manufacturers often relocate in stages by transferring some production to branch plants. The experience of a Detroit automotive parts plant is illustrative. A quarter of a century ago all of its operations were in the city. When growth in production reached the capacity of the city factory, it built branches in several Michigan small towns. In the early fifties most of its workers walked to work or arrived by bus. About twenty parking spaces on company property met the needs of executives.

As workers' income rose in response to a strong automotive market and collective bargaining, more and more of them could move to suburbs and did, thereafter making the journey to work by automobile. When on-street parking became inadequate, the company bought tracts of nearby houses and razed them for a parking lot.

At the same time the neighborhood deteriorated. To hold critically important research and development engineers, the company provided them with new offices in a suburb. Then all administrative offices followed to another suburb. More production was shifted to branch plants outside the metropolis. There has been no dramatic closing, just cumulative cutbacks in jobs performed in the city. It is considered to be only a matter of time until the old factory which once employed 3,000 workers will be shut down.

At an increasing rate many factories are now relocated outside of metropolitan areas altogether, a move made easier by the new interstate highways. A comparison between twelve metropolises which have a population of two million or more and the rest of the nation provides a startling contrast. Bear in mind that 31% of all Americans lived in these twelve metropolitan areas in 1970. Consider then how new manufacturing jobs were distributed. In the nation they grew by 2,553,000 between 1960 and 1970 but by only 214,000 in the twelve biggest metropolises. In relation to population, manufacturing jobs in these twelve fell by 8.7%, rose by a modest 1.6% in the twenty-eight next largest (over 750,000 in population) and by a strong 9.2% in the rest of the nation.

In the data I have reported (and much more that could have been) there is an important point, I think, which is missed by persons who protest against the spread-out nature of suburbs. If the outer suburbs could not provide the land manufacturers consider they need for efficient production, many more factories would relocate outside the metropolitan areas altogether.

A clue lies in the willingness of those Minneapolis manufacturers to pay three times the property taxes per hour of work that they paid in the city. They could do so profitably because of production economies that could be realized with the ample additional space their move provided.

A Tolerant View of Suburban Sprawl

Urban traditionalists feel about suburbs the way that devotees of the iambic pentameter felt about free verse a couple of generations ago. The form itself offends them. Their most damning indictment, repeated insistently, is that suburbs sprawl.

Sprawl is a loaded word. Like evil, it calls for an automatically negative response. In Shakespeare's time it meant to jerk convulsively, as in agony, and in *Titus Andronicus,* the cruelest of Shakespeare's plays (if he truly wrote it, which many of his admirers doubt), the vengeful Lucius orders:

First hang the child, that he may see it sprawl;
A sight to vex the father's soul withal.

In its modern meaning of being spread out it has long been used to describe the ragged edge of urban settlements. "Overgrown cities sprawl over the neighboring green fields," wrote the American historian, James Harvey Robinson, in *The Mind in the Making* in 1921. *Cities* then. It has been a description of suburbs almost since the latter appeared in common speech.

Suburban sprawl is the more easily disdained if the definition of it is elastic. The difficulty in defining precisely what it is that vexes the soul is illustrated by a recent joint undertaking of HUD, the Council of Environmental Quality, and the Environmental Protection Agency. The three federal agencies contracted with a consulting company for a study of *The Costs of Sprawl.* No one can fault the study for inadequate research. The bibliography surely set an all-time high in exhaustiveness: A total of 253 pages were devoted to listing books, articles, and other study reports used as source material. But nowhere was there a definition of the subject that the report deplored.

One can only deduce from the text what it is that the report and those behind it consider sprawl to be, and that deduction can not be made with confidence. With varying emphasis at different times, the authors seem to view sprawl as some combination of low population density, the presence of by-passed areas among patches of developed land, a grid pattern of streets, an imbalance between population and shopping facilities, and something less than total community planning.

It is instructive to test this somewhat variable concept of sprawl against the reality of new cities, which are often cited as the right alternative to sprawl. Even wholly planned new cities, such as Columbia, Maryland, and Reston, Virginia, must begin with a low population density, and a major purpose of their planning is to make certain that their ultimate density will be well below that of old cities.

The wisest attitude toward population density is the one our ancestors painfully learned to accept with respect to religious doctrine: Let a great variety prevail. The right level of density is a question which theologians of urban planning love to debate, but as long as choices are available the issue is more likely to be settled by the moving van than by the arguments. In his book, *The Last Landscape,* William H. Whyte devotes a chapter to "The Case for Crowding." Crowding is good, he says, because it is more efficient. Efficient for what purpose? The satisfaction of residents? He does not say. As one contemplates the thousands of books that have been written about the urban condition, one is led to speculate about the efficient use of paper and writing talent. A reader struggling to winnow the really significant books from all the chaff has reason to wish for less sprawl in the intellectual landscape. Happily, however, for Mr. Whyte and most of the rest of us, the efficient use of books—if that is the way to view it—is left to book buyers to decide. In much the same manner, the efficient use of residential land will most wisely be left to the marketplace decisions of home buyers and renters. Who else has a more legitimate interest?

Because the presence of by-passed land amid new residential districts is easily observed, it, probably more than any other factor, gives plausibility to the sprawl indictment. Critics ask: Why should not the by-passed land be developed before land that is further removed from the center? Usually, the land is by-passed for one of three reasons. It may have less commercial value than land farther away; it may, for example, lie in a flood plain. Or its owner may hope to obtain a better price by waiting. Or the reason may be noneconomic: An owner-occupant may simply wish to continue living on the land. Is it really important enough to a public purpose that these reasons should be overridden? Obviously not many local electorates have thought so, despite the vexation of critics who are not very pleased with suburbs in any event.

The hostility of some critics to what Victor Gruen has scornfully described as "spread, sprawl and scatteration" is both doctrinaire and lacking in historical perspective. Many residents of Reston are ready to rally against contemplated tax rates on farm land that would threaten the survival of a popular peach orchard lying between their homes and the metropolitan center. Surely the two environmental protection agencies who contributed to the report do not hold that such rural vestiges as a peach orchard or, for that matter, a dairy farm, reduce the quality of an urban environment.

A bit of historical perspective will help to distinguish "suburban sprawl" from truly serious problems. The spread-out, ragged edge of human settlements is normally only a transient stage in the development of an area. It has been the norm of development of cities as well as of suburbs. One reason why St. Paul and Baltimore had only minor population losses in the sixties is that within the boundaries of each city there had been by-passed land on which homes were built in that decade.

A graphic historical record of *city sprawl* may be found in maps published by the St. Louis City Plan Commission. The commission's publications have the admirable quality of being written to aid citizens in understanding the city's problems, and in a book which presents the commission's development program there is a fascinating set of maps which show areas of new development at various times from 1840 onward. Up until 1920 all of the maps show an outward moving *sprawl zone* very much like the ragged edge of the metropolitan area shown in Figure 5. There was a notable outward thrust following the introduction of horse-drawn trams which served new areas of development. Today the St. Louis sprawl zone is about twenty miles further from the city center than it was 135 years ago, but its character is the same.

The old sprawl zones have long since been "citified" with intensive development: many fine homes, many that were of wretched quality when built, some of the nation's finest parks, campuses, industrial districts, and commercial centers. Any hindsight critic can find many faults with the development pattern, but at the time the development took place it was as good as any in the nation.

Lest these comments be misunderstood, let it be said that they are not a rejection of planning, beauty, or the better use of land. Our own satisfaction and the heritage we leave can be substantially improved by a more consistent reliance on these admirable virtues, even if we are often unsure of the standards by which they are to be judged. But if we are to focus our energies on the most important urban task—the recovery of cities—we must constantly bear in mind an overwhelming fact which urban traditionalists are loath to accept: Cities and suburbs compete with each other as places of residence, and it is a competition which suburbs, imperfect as they are, are winning hands down. As long as suburbs become more attractive and cities do not, the competitive position of cities will grow weaker.

It would help clear our minds of some harmful nonsense if we were to recognize that many suburbs, especially the newer ones, represent a major advance in the quality of urban residence. In his witty and common sense book, *Urban Choices: the City and Its Critics,* Roger Starr gives an entertaining account of how judgments may change with the passage of time. In the latter part of the eighteenth century the ancient city of Bath was substantially rebuilt to be a fashionable resort. The result horrified Tobias Smollett, novelist, editor, surgeon, and a gentleman who found few things pleasing. He described the new buildings, Mr. Starr recalls, as

> contrived without judgement, executed without solidarity, and stuck together with so little regard to plan and propriety . . . as if some Gothic devil had stuffed them altogether in a bag, and left them to stand higgledy piggledy, just as chance directed.

Yet in our time, Lewis Mumford, an urban critic no less difficult to please, has written

Even now, after a century and a half of change, the heart of Bath has qualities of design that even the best examples in Paris, Nancy, London or Edinburgh do not surpass. . . . Nothing in the rest of the Eighteenth Century city reaches this level of planning.

We may be confident that the suburban spaciousness so roundly deplored by today's heirs of Mr. Smollett will win praise from future heirs of Mr. Mumford.

The Principle of Critical Mass in the Evolution of Suburbs

An important competitive advantage that most suburbs have is that, on balance, they evolve toward giving ever more satisfaction to the needs of their residents. A particular neighborhood—or subdivision, if you prefer—may have the same physical characteristics that it had when newly opened ten or fifteen years ago (except that the trees now give more shade), but not too many miles away a magnificent new enclosed shopping mall offers all the goods that once were available only at the distant downtown. As is said in the computer and weapons industries, it is a second generation product, as different from the early suburban shopping center as the modern automobile is from the Model T.

The early shopping center itself was a new urban form. Instead of the immemorial practice of shops lining two sides of a commercial street, the new center typically occupied a whole block, on three sides of which specialty stores faced inward around a parking apron, with the fourth side open to the arterial road it adjoined. National chains were quick to see the opportunities of locating stores convenient to the new suburban class—predominantly young families with incomes above the city average. Except for Sears Roebuck, the national chains were more specialized in their merchandise than were the downtown department stores, but together a group of specialty shops could provide an equivalent range.

The new shopping centers cut deeply enough into the sales of the downtown department stores that the latter had no choice but to go suburban, too. The early type of shopping center, however, could not provide the space they needed. Some imaginative architects and developers created a new form: great enclosed malls embracing rival department stores at opposite ends of one or more axes and linked by broad corridors which recreate the pattern of ancient bazaars. On all sides of the mall, like a great moat, is the parking apron. Never again will downtown have the preeminent shopping location that it once had.

Downtown associations, of course, fought back—more imaginatively in Minneapolis than anywhere else. Several blocks of plain Nicollet Avenue were converted into graceful Nicollet Mall. Straight curbs gave way to a wavy pattern which reclaimed some street space for sheltered bus stops and a bit of landscaping, while diverting some auto traffic to other streets. More important, a network of covered walkways was constructed which bridged streets and cut through office buildings at a second floor level. They are especially welcome during the city's frigid winters.

And population continued to drain from the city—a 10% loss in the sixties, 12% between 1970 and 1973—as if the downtown improvement had never been made.

James W. Rouse is justly respected as the creator of Columbia, Maryland, but it is less well known that the Rouse company is also a major builder of shopping malls. Valuable as Columbia is as an example, the malls may have larger direct consequences on the future course of urban development because they go a long way toward reducing the differences between planned new cities and the suburbs of not long ago.

"Towns, suburbs and even little cities are totally different organisms from great cities," wrote Jane Jacobs in *The Death and Life of Great American Cities.* It is a sweeping overstatement (not her only one); the differences are far from total. But put more moderately, she has a useful point. While there is virtually no difference between outer cities and inner suburbs (except as political jurisdictions), there is a huge difference between inner cities and outer suburbs. In one sense that difference is reduced as suburbs gain much of what was traditionally available only downtown: a full range of shops, good restaurants, and even theaters and concert halls. In another sense the difference is made greater because by these gains suburbs grow more independent of the hub.

In the evolutionary stage that we are now witnessing some of the most important functions of the city are being reproduced in suburbs. The structure that serves the functions, however, is not duplicated. The suburban structure is looser and more diffuse, as permitted by the mobility of automobile transportation.

Before suburbs could reproduce the nonresidential functions of cities there had to be a large enough concentration of residents in an area—a critical mass, so to speak—to induce merchants and investors to take a gamble. We do not know the size of the critical mass, and it probably cannot be closely measured because it must be accompanied by other factors—for example, adequate transportation routes to strategic locations. However, when the critical mass is reached under favorable circumstances, it can trigger, as we now know, a chain of swift developments.

Can we infer from this line of reasoning that some critical mass of suburban residents—no doubt a different one—will also trigger a major transfer of employment from the central business district to dispersed employment centers in suburbs (and, in some cases, outer cities)?

Up to a point, the answer is already yes. A high enough concentration of residents to require an infrastructure of highways, water supply, and waste disposal has been sufficient to attract a substantial volume of light manufacturing to outer suburbs. As we noted earlier, there has also been a rapid growth of white-collar centers in suburbs and in some outer cities.

Secondary office work centers have multiplied most strongly and most swiftly in the Los Angeles metropolis. Until 1956 the height of buildings in Los Angeles (the city hall excepted) was limited to 140 feet because of a fear of earthquake damage. Once the limitation was lifted, high-rise construction spurted entirely out of proportion to the growth of the area. (The total still just about equals the vacant high-rise space in New York City.) Downtown Los Angeles is acquiring an impressive skyline of buildings in the 40- to 60-story range, but other metropolitan area centers together outrank it in total high-rise space.

The question is no longer whether suburbs can compete with the metropolitan hub as centers for office work traditionally performed downtown, but, instead, how serious that competition may become. The judgment at this time must rest on an estimate of the future.

In Quest of Understanding

As one searches among American professional studies for enlightenment on the evolutionary prospects of metropolises, one is impressed by the great number of studies that have been made, mostly in universities, and generally also by their technical competence, their specialization, and the absence of a unifying theme.

The rigor of analysis that is basic to technical competence is notably evident in the works of Brian J. L. Berry, geographer, Richard F. Muth and Wilbur R. Thompson, economists, and Leo F. Schnore, sociologist (to be unfairly selective), but none of these widely respected scholars has ventured far from the bounds of his profession, although Berry appears to do better than most.

One finds that a general practice among economists, sociologists and geographers who specialize in urban studies is to attempt to crystallize their findings in the form of a generalized model which can be used to

**VOLUME OF OCCUPIED HIGH-RISE* OFFICE SPACE IN LOS ANGELES
CENTRAL BUSINESS DISTRICT AND COMPETITIVE CENTERS
1960 AND 1970**

	Million Square Feet	
	1960	1970
Central business district	11.4	16.5
Other centers	2.4	18.5
Distribution of other centers		
Within Los Angeles city boundaries		
Wilshire Corridor	1.7	6.5
Century City	0	2.4
International Airport	0	2.0
Hollywood	0.3	1.7
San Fernando Valley	0	1.4
Beverly Hills (separately incorporated)	0.4	1.3
Westwood	0	1.0
Outside city's boundaries		
Orange County	0	1.6
Pasadena	0	0.6

Source: Los Angeles Committee for Central City Planning, Inc.

*High-rise in this instance means eight stories or more.

Table 8

predict events in cities they have not studied. Economists, especially, are
addicted to models that can be formulated as a mathematical equation.
(Historians, including Marxists, view predictive models of human
behavior somewhat as they view astrology.)

While models have a usefulness as stepping stones to larger
understandings, they have inherent weaknesses when used for
prediction. A model, even a complex one, is always much simpler than
the facts. Consider, for example, this statement by Professor William
Alonso in his paper, "A Theory of the Urban Land Market."

The model presented in this paper corresponds to the simplest
case: a single-center city, on a featureless plain, with transportation
in all directions. However, the reasoning can be extended to cities
with several centers.

At best, only a few prairie towns might fit this description, and it is to be doubted that any of them have equal transportation in all directions. Real cities have not only the natural features of geography such as hills, flood plains, and waterfronts but also innumerable man-made features which affect the value of land. Along with all of these, rent of urban land may be affected by unusual behavior patterns.

In fairness to Professor Alonso, he made it clear that his model was "purely theoretical" and he only hoped that it might "provide a logical structure for econometric models which may be useful for prediction." It seems unlikely, however, that we are close to devising a model that could predict the bizarre rent pattern in the rapidly emptying inner city of St. Louis. How could we codify the St. Louis landlords who, concluding that their properties are not worth the continued payment of taxes, are waiting for an eventual city takeover and meanwhile charge rents low enough to draw tenants from subsidized public housing (which is also free of a tax burden)?

Many models have another weakness: an implicit assumption that what has been true in the past will continue to be no less true in the future. The chart used earlier in this chapter shows what mathematicians call an exponential curve for the growth of service and government jobs. Clearly they cannot continue to grow at this rate or they would displace all other kinds of work. Model builders also usually suggest that their models will be helpful in formulating public policy but, paradoxically, the models are so mechanistic in predicting human behavior as to leave little room for the influence of wisdom or folly.

Strangely, there seems to have been little effort by American scholars to develop a unified theory from the many specialized studies, despite tribute paid to "interdisciplinary studies" and "comprehensive planning" as desirable objectives. The principal attempts at some kind of synthesis appear to have come from the New Zealand geographer, R. J. Johnston, and Murray Stewart, a Britisher, who have also drawn upon British and Commonwealth studies.

A high proportion of the American studies are detailed demonstrations of ideas developed by Burgess a half century ago: for example, the migrations of Dutch in Kalamazoo, of Russians in Minneapolis, or Italians in New Haven. They are interesting but are elaborations of a kind which in architecture is known as rococo.

In refreshing contrast to the scrollwork craftsmanship of so many American scholars, the late Greek architect and planner, Constantinos A. Doxiadis, boldly sought to plumb the secrets of all settlements. He emphasized the interdependence of all fields of urban study before the word *interdisciplinary* became fashionable, and to provide an inclusive term coined the word *ekistics* from the ancient Greek word for household (from which also comes the word *economics).* In 1968 Doxiadis wrote in his book *Ekistics:*

> We need a total Ekistic theory into which all phenomena can merge and by which all phenomena can be explained. . . . For the time being I think I can present a basic Ekistic theory which can gradually grow into a total one. . . . Only if we look at the whole picture of this Earth with all its settlements, can we recognize the substance of this nature and evolution, and define their conditions. When we achieve this, we will be able to recognize the abnormal cases, the deviations, the diseases and conceive their therapy.

His approach was to define all settlements as some combination of five elements: nature, man, society, shells (buildings), and networks. His "basic" theory is derived from 54 "laws" he formulated which govern the possible combinations. (Example—"Law 50: the right form for a human settlement is that which best expresses all the static positions and dynamic movements of Man, animals and machines within its space.")

Doxiadis was invited by the Detroit Edison Company to apply his theory to a major study of Detroit and its environs, which the power company funded at a cost of several million dollars. Wayne State University collaborated. The study extended over five years, and the results were published in 1970 in three thick volumes. The selected criteria for a recommended program to the year 2000 led to a hypothetical 49 million alternatives which were reduced by computer screening to seven. The one finally proposed would establish a twin city for Detroit at St. Clair, forty miles to the northeast, plus nine smaller new cities, all to be linked by an ultrafast transportation network based on a still hypothetical new transportation technology. If the recovery of Detroit was among the 49 million alternatives, the computer was not programmed to disclose it.

The only other major study of a metropolitan region that I am aware of is one of the New York City region that was conducted a decade before the Detroit study. It, too, required five years to complete, drew assistance from six universities and funding from four foundations. The study director was the versatile Harvard economist, Raymond Vernon, who earlier had been a State Department official and who since has conducted a monumental study of multinational corporations.

The study, which was made on behalf of the Regional Plan Association, Inc., a private body, was reported in nine volumes, beginning with *Anatomy of a Metropolis* and concluding with *Metropolis 1985.* It is a descriptive study which readily makes evident the region's peculiar geography and its unique place in the national economy. One of the study's many great merits is that it did not attempt to project a universal model from a New York condition or to illustrate general "laws" of urban development. Nonetheless, as a by-product of an inquiry into the nature of the nation's largest urban region, the study is of unrivaled importance in demonstrating the complex interplay of history, geography and economic and social forces in the evolution of a metropolis. In *Metropolis 1985* and in a later, slender volume, *The Myth and Reality of Our Urban Problems,* Vernon portrayed the then evident consequences of the outward movement of residences, trade and jobs, while avoiding dogmatism, clichés and overblown interpretation. In my view, he underestimated the forces which have led to the strong growth of secondary business centers, but this development came after the study.

Vernon's career detour into urban affairs was for a brief five years, but I would place him after only Burgess and Hoyt as an illuminator of the growth and structure of the metropolis.

The Rationale for Recovery

Somewhere between the miscellaneous specialized findings common to the universities and the overreach of Doxiadis, who, like Icarus, flew too close to the sun with wings too fragile, there is a place for an orderly interpretation of a broad field of knowledge, a theory, which will help to provide a clear understanding of the continuing evolution of the metropolis.

This book is directed to a more modest task: an understanding of what is needed for the recovery of cities which have been weakened by the evolution. The following comments, which in part are a restatement of earlier conclusions by Burgess, Hoyt, and Vernon and in part go beyond them, are not offered as an adequate theory, but it is believed that they provide the rationale for recovery.

1. The tandem migrations of urban-start and move-up described in Chapter 2 established a pattern of urban growth in excess of natural population increase, an attraction of the least skilled to the cheaper housing common to the older central area, and an outward movement of residents to newer and more spacious housing as their skills, income, and status rose. The pattern is subject to many irregularities arising from particular geographic, historical, economic and social circumstances which make every metropolis partly unique, but its basic character is unmistakable and universal, and leaves cities disproportionately burdened with the poverty associated with the urban-start migration.

2. Each day every metropolis is a little different from what it was the

day before. It does not merely grow bigger (as virtually all large ones still do). Minute changes from a hundred causes have a gradually accumulating net effect of reducing the dependence of residents on the hub, and of enabling them to fulfill needs and satisfactions from homes, shops, and jobs newly located in outer areas. The metropolis grows more decentralized.

A web pattern of travel to new and expanding trade and job centers is overlaid on the traditional radial pattern. The new centers do not duplicate the old hub, made compact by fixed-path transportation, but assume looser, still evolving forms specifically responsive to the nature of the automobile.

3. In the foreseeable future, the decentralization of metropolitan functions and structure may be expected to continue and in some respects to accelerate. Two powerful forces, in particular, favor such prospect. The net effect of the technologies in construction, transportation, and communication which made large settlements practical also support their decentralization; the automobile especially has powerfully promoted it by opening new land to development and thereby reducing the per capita cost of land. Rising incomes (partly made possible by urban patterns of work) allow people to move to homes of greater convenience and spaciousness, principally available in outer areas, and the outward movement of residence exerts a gravitational pull on retail trade and employment. Against the forces of present technologies and a more broadly shared prosperity, efforts to arrest decentralization have the effect of a drizzle on a duck's back.

4. The location of white-collar work that serves nonlocal markets has seemed to resist metropolitan decentralization and even to run counter to it. This, however, should be regarded as a short-term phenomenon caused by five factors: a spectacular per capita increase in white-collar work in general; the opening of new freeways to the hub (which cannot increase indefinitely); momentum (which in physics is governed by the same law as inertia); vigorous civic-business efforts to expand the property tax base of the central business district, including subsidized downtown renewal; and improvident investment in new office buildings as a federal tax shelter, especially in New York. In the long run, these exceptional stimulants are likely to be offset by increasing costs of commuter transportation and the lower rents and easy parking available at suburban locations. The central business district may be expected to remain preeminent because of the huge investment it represents, but most future growth in office work will probably occur in outlying areas.

5. Further decentralization of the metropolis need not be harmful to the recovery of cities. Even if the central business district should grow no further, it will remain the major employment center for middle- and

high-income employees, whose convenience would be served by nearby
residence in inner city areas ripe for reconstruction. A chance to convert
decayed and obsolete districts into new neighborhoods which will
compete with suburbs as places of residence is powerfully increased by
the dwindling of the urban-start migration.

6. Well-conceived policies can significantly alter the evolution of a
metropolis. However, because cities have been gravely weakened, their
recovery is beyond their present resources. They will need external aid
for a generation or so in progressively diminishing sums. For reasons
largely beyond the control of city electorates, cities have been obliged to
bear a disproportionate share of the economic and social costs of the
tandem migrations which have converted American society from one that
was mainly rural into one that is mainly urban. As a simple matter of
equity the rest of the nation thus has an obligation to help cities to regain
competitiveness as a place of residence and an ability to meet their needs
from revenues of local origin. But this is the only obligation to them
which the rest of the nation has: to help them to recover. There is no
obligation to subsidize them a single year beyond the time required to
become independent of outside help. The cities, too, have an obligation:
to make the most of the recovery opportunity when offered to them.

4. SHORTER JOURNEYS TO WORK

The Novel Idea of Reducing a Need

A part of the solution to the vexatious problem of transportation in urban areas is simply less travel. The average distance between home and job has become too long, and of all the alternatives that can be imagined for making the journey faster, more comfortable, less expensive, less demanding in its claim on new capital, less wasteful of imported energy, less damaging to the environment, and less divisive as a political issue, none goes to the heart of the matter so surely as shortening the journey.

The idea, it must be conceded, goes counter to a way of thinking that is deeply imbedded in custom. Throughout the whole era of post-horse transportation the only public policy in response to the unremitting growth in per capita demand for transportation has been: increase the supply. The one-way nature of the demand-supply relationship becomes more apparent when we reflect on the transportation issues that stir public debate. All of them pertain to aspects of supply: the mode, what routes should be established or enlarged, the timing, cost, and financing.

The major prevailing issue, as generally perceived, is a question of mode; in oversimplified form, mass transit versus the automobile. No more than two decades ago the prevailing wisdom called for more freeways to the metropolitan hub. The new wisdom, no less certain of its rightness, calls for more mass transit to the hub—transit from deep in the suburbs, that are now extended farther than ever. Both the old and the new wisdom accept the indicated level of demand without question. They differ only in how to supply it. To hold a third position—that demand itself is excessive, and on a per capita basis it can and should be reduced—is to court the risk of seeming daft.

Whether the third position is sensible or fanciful is a matter of perspective. In the context of the recovery of cities, it becomes practical to shorten drastically many journeys to work.

From Glamor to Realism

Although the recovery of cities would substantially reduce the amount of new investment in urban mass transportation that is now thought necessary, this potential major relief from an onerous tax burden has no place at this time in the urban policies of the federal government. It could hardly be otherwise, because the executive and legislative branches both lack a concept of recovery. It is encouraging, therefore, to find a trend in the thinking of the Department of Transportation which, while not related to a recovery idea, is sympathetic to bringing homes and jobs closer together.

The conventional mission of transportation planners has been to project a demand for transportation under indicated conditions and show how to meet it, as far as practical, to the satisfaction of users. It was not considered to be within their province to ask if the journeys are really necessary. The fact that it is now being suggested that a reduction in per capita demand would be sensible is a measure of an interesting evolution of official thinking since the first legislation providing federal grants for urban mass transportation was enacted in 1964.

In the beginning high hopes were placed in the magic of more money and bold new technology. The outer space program was then becoming a mammoth effort, and it had an influence on the way we thought about earthly travel. "If we can put men on the moon, we can . . ." was a frequent introduction to science-fiction versions of the daily trip from suburbs to the metropolitan hub. The planning of BART, as the San Francisco Bay Area Rapid Transit system is known, as a conventional subway and surface railway had begun as early as 1951, and in most respects that was what was built. But the glamor theme was running strongly when construction finally got under way, and much was made of the addition of computer control of train starts, stops and speeds, door openings, and announcements of destinations. The computerized operations were enough to cause former President Nixon to prophesy, after a demonstration ride, that the San Francisco Bay Area would become "as widely renowned in the future for the space-age efficiency of BART as it has been in the past for the romance of the cable car."

It was a rash prophecy. The early operating record was a series of bungles. Taped voices put passengers on the wrong trains; trains made unscheduled stops in mid-tunnel and arrived at wrong destinations; doors flew open while trains were hurtling at eighty miles an hour. No doubt the troubles can be overcome in time, but until then a new BART management has made at least a tactical retreat from the Space Age.

Before the BART experience dampened a faith in gadgetry, proposed dual-mode systems enjoyed a vogue among some planners who made glib assumptions about capital costs and energy consumption. In 1967, when HUD still had responsibility for federal assistance to mass transit, the agency published a booklet under the authoritative title, *Tomorrow's Transportation,* which described uncritically a proposed new system wherein self-propelled vehicles, similar to a small automobile, or maybe a golf cart, would be driven from suburban homes to a suburban transfer station from which they would be whisked on a guideway to a downtown terminal and driven from there to parking garages. Doxiadis, believing dual-mode transportation to be closer to technical feasibility than was the case, relied heavily on it in his recommended program for the Detroit urban area. New technology of a kind which might make a major difference in urban transportation has not materialized, and both technical and economic obstacles remain formidable. By 1974, Claude S. Brinegar, then Secretary of Transportation, was ready to settle for a "lovable bus," if anyone knew how to invent one.

Even in the absence of a major new technology, the revival of interest in mass transit gave a strong stimulus to the idea that metropolitan areas which did not have a subway should build one—an idea initially encouraged by the new Department of Transportation. A subway (which might become an elevated or a surface railway in lightly populated districts) was seen as an answer to a host of problems. It could provide so fast a service from suburbs to the metropolitan hub that commuters would prefer it to automobiles, and congestion in the central city would be greatly reduced. Money scheduled for more freeway construction could be used to help build the subway. Since most routes would be underground, the number of homes and commercial firms displaced would be small in comparison with freeway construction. The convenience and (ignoring the experience of New York) the presumed comfort of riding a subway train to work would induce more commercial growth in the central business district, thereby enlarging the city's tax base. Some enthusiasts argued, contrary to the experience of cities which have long had subways, that the construction of a subway would arrest a city's loss of population and bring a higher residential density.

In 1970 an amendment to the Urban Mass Transportation Act
authorized long-term financing of mass transit, with a strong emphasis on
rail rapid transit. Baltimore and Atlanta moved quickly to obtain
commitments of federal aid for initial segments of new subways. Los
Angeles, Detroit, Buffalo, and numerous other cities, in concert with
their suburbs, speeded up their planning. Joint rail systems were
proposed for Minneapolis-St. Paul and Dallas-Fort Worth.

The stage of second thoughts about widespread adoption of subways
began when the Department of Transportation started adding up the
costs. During the Brinegar regime the Department began to caution local
governments that it would not support new subways if buses could meet
the need. In a speech which signaled the turn, Brinegar said:

> Many relatively lightly populated areas are seriously considering
> installing fixed guideway transit systems, not primarily as solutions
> to today's transit problems, but more as a deliberate means to shape
> future economic growth and to increase central city urban density.
> These may be desirable local objectives, bringing new jobs,
> increased land values, and higher tax bases, but I think it is
> important to recognize that they are *not* direct, near-term
> transportation objectives. . .
>
> I am concerned that too many big fixed-rail projects are being
> proposed based largely on these latter objectives. . . . The billions
> of dollars that such systems cost are simply too high; the national
> benefits, in a public transit sense, are simply too low.

His successor, William T. Coleman, Jr., reaffirmed this line of
thinking in a policy guideline issued in late 1975. Federal assistance for
the construction of a subway or other rail rapid transit facility is still
possible, but in the future an applicant will be obliged to demonstrate
that its needs cannot be met by better traffic management and a less
costly investment. The new policy will apply to all mass transportation
investments in which the federal contribution would be $100 million or
more. The sum is low enough to submit any new subway to the test of a
comparison with alternatives.

Under the new policy, the Department's Urban Mass Transportation
Administration will give assistance in an amount no greater than the
standard federal share of the alternative which it considers to be most
effective in relation to cost. If Los Angeles (as an illustration only, without
prejudging the eventual decision) should hold that it needs a subway, and
UMTA concludes that mass transit needs in the area could be met
adequately by buses using reserved freeway lanes, UMTA would limit
federal assistance to a share of the bus alternative. If the Southern

California Rapid Transit District (the agency for Los Angeles and its suburbs) still wanted a subway, it would have to pay all of the additional cost. The difference, as we shall shortly see, is huge.

The new policy incorporates a second important restriction also, in support of the stated aim of ensuring that federal funds will be "utilized in the most prudent and productive manner." The federal commitment will be made in increments which serve needs of five to ten years. Further commitments will depend upon periodic reviews of long-range plans. The purpose is to "preserve maximum flexibility to respond to changing urban conditions, technological change, and shifting land use and travel patterns."

Such is official policy at this stage of its evolution. A hint that more than this is needed has come from C. Kenneth Orski, Associate Administrator for Policy and Program Development of the Urban Mass Transportation Administration. In a recent speech he said:

> Even established urban areas are in a constant state of change and a start can be made to redirect the process of their growth and development in ways that will decrease the need for transportation. This can be done by providing housing and a good environment close to places of employment so as to reduce the necessity for long commuting trips, and by clustering activities to create self-contained neighborhoods in which distances between homes, schools, shops, playgrounds and community facilities are small enough to be covered on foot or bicycle.

His remarks go beyond anything that the Department of Transportation can accomplish directly, but they are a refreshing contribution to public discussion. More than in any other federal agency which has a large influence on urban affairs, the ideas encountered in the Department of Transportation are adaptable to the recovery of cities.

The Potential Impact of a Change in the Law

The Brinegar-Coleman policy, as it seems fair to call it, is officially described as a rule of cost-effectiveness. In more ordinary language it means federal aid for whatever is adequate at the least cost, but no more than that. Since some modes of transportation are much more costly than others, defenders of the policy will have little difficulty in occupying the high ground in a controversy over its application.

The policy also has far-reaching implications, some of which are not readily apparent. In time, as the policy is applied in a sufficient number of cases, latent issues which are inherent in the basic legislation will be brought to the surface, and some are consequential enough that they will surely cause a further evolution of policy. Two such issues—the shortening of journeys to work and equity of benefit—are particularly germane to the theme of this book.

The logic of the Brinegar-Coleman policy of cost-effectiveness, when related to a 1974 amendment to the Urban Mass Transportation Act of 1964, must sooner or later lead to the question: Why should not approval of a transportation plan be based on proposed changes in land uses, to shorten journeys to work?

One of the stated purposes of the Act is "to encourage the planning and establishment of areawide urban mass transportation systems needed for economical and desirable urban development." The original Act then specified that the equipment and facilities for which federal aid might be given would be those "needed for an efficient and coordinated transportation system." It would take tortuous reasoning to find that shorter journeys to work are implied by the language of the original Act.

The 1974 amendment, however, redefined the equipment and facilities eligible for federal aid as those "needed for any efficient and coordinated mass transportation system which is *compatible with socially, economically, and environmentally sound patterns of land use.*" (Emphasis added)

The amendment has made the issue of shorter journeys to work germane whenever a local transportation agency applies to the federal government for financial help in purchasing equipment and facilities. To comply with the amendment, the Urban Mass Transportation Administration must now know in each instance the pattern of land use in the area served by the transportation system for which federal aid is sought, and it must have criteria for determining what is "socially, economically and environmentally sound" in land use patterns.

Consider the pattern of land use in inner cities. In the central business district there is the greatest concentration of jobs, predominantly white-collar, to be found anywhere in the metropolitan area. On the borders of the great job stacks are large patches of land which each year is more poorly used: failing industrial and warehouse districts, excess railway trackage, and dismal stretches of obsolete housing no longer in demand by new arrivals and progressively abandoned when the occupants can afford something better.

What use of such land would be more economically sound than its conversion into new neighborhoods which could compete with suburbs, especially for people who work nearby, and by being competitive would reduce a need for transportation? Would not the new use be socially desirable? And what travel can do less damage to the environment than travel which does not occur?

The creation of *travel-reducing* patterns of land use is basic to the recovery of cities. The Urban Mass Transportation Administration has not been given a mandate to promote the recovery of cities. But it *has* been directed to ensure that transportation systems which it may support with capital assistance must be compatible with sound patterns of land use. By a reasonable interpretation of the new legislation, land-use patterns which would reduce a need for transportation have obvious merit and fit the prescribed standard of soundness completely. It would be appropriate, therefore, for the Urban Mass Transportation Administration to require that applicants for aid submit information on what their communities are doing, or propose to do, to create travel-reducing patterns of land use.

The millions of Americans whose taxes support federal aid for mass transit but themselves do not benefit from it have a legitimate reason to expect the responsible federal agency to spend no more of their money than is necessary. The issue may be put this way: The evolution of federal transportation policy has made shorter journeys to work in the urban areas of New York and California a proper concern of people who live in Wyoming and Vermont.

Indeed, two out of five Americans live in communities which are not eligible for federal financing of mass transit. The aid is restricted to urbanized areas that have a population of 50,000 or more. When a total of 203 million Americans were counted in 1970, about 85 million lived outside such areas. There are no urbanized areas at all (as officially defined) in Wyoming and Vermont, and only one each in eight other states.

Moreover, within eligible urbanized areas there are great numbers of people who cannot use mass transit in their daily travels to work if the transit system is efficient—which the law says it must be in order to qualify for federal aid. Here we must distinguish between two distinct patterns of traffic—the conventional radial pattern and the newer web pattern superimposed upon it. All mass transit systems are primarily radial in their structure and resemble wheel spokes converging upon a hub. For travelers who work at the hub and live within a corridor served by a radial route, mass transit can be an efficient subsitute for automobile travel.

The travel needs of people who work at a distance from the hub are quite different. As trade and employment become more decentralized, web patterns of traffic become common. The paths from homes to jobs that collectively make a web, however, are individually so different in the

location of their terminals that it is difficult to group enough journeys
together to make mass transit efficient. Rail transit requiring a major
investment in fixed guideways is quite impractical. Buses offer greater
promise, but even under assumptions most favorable to mass transit the
automobile will remain the only practical means of travel for a majority of
travelers in urbanized areas.

Mass transit no longer serves the travel needs of most blue-collar
workers (except in New York City), and it is not realistic to suppose that it
can be made to do so in the future. Factories in need of more floor space
will continue to move from cities to the metropolitan outskirts or beyond.
Most retail clerks are now employed in suburban locations. Mass transit
following radial routes cannot do much to help them or the growing
number of white-collar workers employed in the new outlying office
centers. As we saw in our examination of "The Evolving Metropolis,"
there is an inexorable trend toward decentralization which makes it
certain that in every large urbanized area there will be many workers who
cannot benefit from mass transit.

Understandably, officials of the Urban Mass Transit Administration
feel that equity of benefit is a matter which should be threshed out at a
local level. The governing legislation twice provides that parties with "a
significant economic, social or environmental interest" in a federally
aided transportation project must be given an opportunity to be heard at
public hearings. If equity of benefit is not made an issue in local hearings,
federal officials cannot be faulted for not raising the issue themselves.

However, as the relative cost of automobile transportation continues to
increase, which we must assume to be the long-term outlook, it may be
expected that people who depend upon the automobile for traveling to
work will grow increasingly unsympathetic toward the use of their taxes
to support money-losing mass transit systems. Elected officials of
blue-collar suburbs and perhaps trade unions that have been passive or
friendly to the idea of mass transit in the abstract, will add their voices to
others against subsidized transportation for affluent commuters. Equity
of benefit from big federal grants for mass transit is not yet a divisive
issue, but that doesn't mean that it will remain so. The two large groups of
non-beneficiaries—the two out of five Americans who live outside
eligible communities and the many within such communities for whom
mass transit is not practical—may be expected to find that they have a
common interest. And while UMTA officials may justifiably hold that
equity of benefit within eligible communities is a local concern, they are
obliged to take account of the issue as it affects the tax burden of
outsiders. The Brinegar-Coleman policy—as far as it goes—is a
recognition of that obligation. But it does not go far enough, and in time
the issue of equity will surely carry the evolution of national

transportation policy beyond acrimonious conflicts over modes of travel
to the more fundamental issue of reducing an inflated per capita demand.

A Jolt from a Survey of Local Plans

In 1974 the Department of Transportation submitted a startling
(but little noted) report to the Congress. Even when allowance is made
for a large margin of error in estimates of transportation needs set forth in
the report, it is evident that the transportation plans of many local
governments are on a collision course with reality. The revisions which
must be made point relentlessly toward (1) less expensive systems, and (2)
actions which will reduce per capita demand. The Department drew the
first conclusion and not yet the second, but we may make our own
judgment on what the figures mean.

For all their faults, the estimates are the best available at this time. This
is their history: In 1972 the Department on its own initiative prevailed
upon the governors of all states to assemble estimates from local officials
of their transportation needs to the year 1990. With this information as a
start, a second survey was then conducted. Governors and local officials
were asked to review their earlier estimates (resulting in a modest
reduction) and to describe concretely the anticipated increase of mass
transit of any kind between 1972 and 1990 (for which generous federal aid
was assumed). A summary of the estimates was published as a report to
the Congress, titled "A Study of Urban Mass Transportation Needs and
Financing."

The biggest jolt in the estimates is that despite anticipated major new
investments in mass transit and more than twice the number of passenger
trips by mass transit—from 6.4 billion to 13.8 billion in 1990—the mass
transit share of total urban travel was expected to increase very little. In
all urbanized areas, the national average percentage of mass transit would
rise from a mere 5.5% of total transportation in 1972 to a still mere 6% in
1990. The average share in the nine largest urbanized areas would remain
constant at 11%, although some figures were up and others down. In the
urbanized area of New York City the mass transit share of all passenger
trips was expected to fall from 24.6% to 17.4%, although the largest
investment per capita was planned in this region. Statistically, more
cause for optimism was found in the Los Angeles area. There, with
support from an assumed new subway, the mass transit share was
predicted to grow by one half—*from 2.5% to 3.7%.*

Several things need to be said about the estimates. The first is that their
reliability is open to serious question. If passenger trips by mass transit
double while their share of the total remains unchanged,

then—mathematically, at least—the number of passenger trips by automobile must also double. This projection is hard to reconcile with common sense. Note that if total trips doubled and the number of urban travelers were to increase by one third (the Department, with the aid of the Census Bureau, projected a 31% gain in population in the same urbanized areas between 1972 and 1990), passenger trips per capita, not just passenger miles, would rise by 50%—an improbable prospect.

The report to the Congress states that the estimates are not regarded as accurate, but describes them as "an indicator of national trends and preferences which are subject to further refinement in light of more cost-effective alternatives, and negotiation at the time of grant application." It is in that perspective that they are judged here.

We can judge them better by bringing them into a single focus, which is done in an accompanying table. The projected investment for each mode of mass transit is recorded three ways: in millions of dollars, as a percentage of all mass transit, and, crudely, on a per capita basis for each of four categories of urbanized areas. The crudeness of the per capita projections is inherent in the fact that population will be greater in 1990 than in 1970 (the year used here) and will grow more rapidly in some urbanized areas than in others. It will almost certainly grow more slowly in the nine largest areas, which the study reported separately, than in the others as a group. (The nine largest are the regions which center upon New York City, Los Angeles, Chicago, Philadelphia, Detroit, San Francisco, Boston, Washington, D.C., and Cleveland.) If so, the per capita differential between the nine largest and the others will be greater than indicated in the table.

The figures shown in the table correspond to the value which the dollar had in 1973. In these inflationary times, a fairly stable measure of the cost of mass transit is the housing it could buy, since the dollar cost of each may be expected to change at a similar rate. The $58 billion projected for mass transit would pay the construction cost of 2.3 million houses at an average of $25,000 per house, excluding the cost of land. It is instructive to reflect on what might happen if the anticipated investment in mass transit were cut in half and the saving devoted to the construction of new housing.

Could the projected investment be cut by one-half? In fact, merely by a shift from planned investment in rail transit to buses it could be cut a great deal more than half. The most significant line of figures in the table is the one which shows investment in rail rapid transit as a percentage of all. For practical purposes, *rail rapid transit* means subways with elevated or surface tracks in outlying areas. Two-thirds of the total mass transit investment is projected for this mode. Even as an average in urbanized areas other than the nine largest it is expected to be a half of their total.

The estimates project the construction of 1,582 miles of additional rail rapid transit. The total estimated investment for this mode, $38.6 billion, includes the new construction and operating equipment to go with it,

PROJECTED CAPITAL INVESTMENT IN MASS TRANSPORTATION IN URBANIZED AREAS, 1972-1990, SHOWN IN 1973 DOLLARS
(Population of Urbanized Areas: 50,000 or More)

	All Urbanized Areas	*9 Largest Urbanized Areas*	*All Other Urbanized Areas*	*New York Urbanized Area only*
Capital investment ($ million)				
Rail rapid transit	38,600	27,700	10,900	12,600
Commuter rail	5,300	5,200	100	2,800
Bus	8,000	3,000	5,000	800
Other	6,300	500	5,800	0
Total	58,200	36,400	21,800	16,200
Mode as % of total				
Rail rapid transit	66.3	76.1	50.0	77.8
Commuter rail	9.1	14.3	0.5	17.3
Bus	13.8	8.2	22.9	4.9
Other	10.8	1.4	26.6	0
Capital investment as dollars per capita in urbanized areas (1970 population)				
Rail rapid transit	326	560	158	778
Commuter rail	45	105	1	173
Bus	68	60	73	49
Other	53	10	84	0
Total	492	735	316	1,000
1970 population as % of total	100	42	58	14
Investment as % of total	100	63	37	28

Source: Based on data in A Study of Urban Mass Transportation and Financing, *a report to the Congress by the U.S. Department of Transportation.*

Table 9

plus some new operating equipment on existing lines. Because the new equipment for old lines is included in the total figure, it is not practical to make a reliable estimate of the cost of the new construction and matching equipment on a per mile basis. But if hypothetically we suppose that all new equipment were for the new lines, the cost per mile would be $24.4 million. This sum, which is the maximum that can be calculated from the total cost, is absurdly too optimistic. The projected cost of the proposed Los Angeles 116-mile subway-elevated is $57 million per mile in 1973 dollars. The original estimate for the 98-mile subway-elevated in Washington, D. C. was $25.5 million (or 1,020 houses) per mile. Inflation and cost overruns have raised the latest official estimate to $46 million per mile. Instead of about 1.5 million houses as the price of 1,582 miles of new subways, the true price would be nearly twice as many houses.

Besides the proposed investment in rail rapid transit, the report to the Congress shows a proposed investment of $5.3 billion in 21 new miles of commuter railway systems (conventional railroads), including 732 new railroad cars for both the old and new trackage.

What transportation capacity could be bought with the projected investment in rail transit? Capacity is commonly measured in *seat miles* —that is, the number of seats in a vehicle multiplied by miles traveled by the vehicle in a given time. Working from the collected estimates, the Department calculated the capital cost of rail transit to be 86 cents per seat mile and of buses, including a large sum for planned busways, to be 17 cents per seat mile.

It can be argued that although the capital cost of rail transit is five times higher per seat mile, the operating cost is lower. As calculated by the Department, operating costs per *passenger mile* are expected to be 10 cents for rail transit and 14 cents for buses (in 1973 dollars). Taking the estimates at face value and ignoring interest costs, the difference in the amount of capital which rail transit would require could be recovered from savings in operating costs in 82 years. Perhaps the Methuselah Club will think the waiting worth while.

For people who live near a subway station and work near another, rail transportation offers the fastest service. However, fast service by bus is possible when buses use freeway lanes reserved for them or travel on special busways. Of the $8 billion projected for investment in bus transportation, $3.1 billion is intended for the construction of 1,400 miles of busways or exclusive bus lanes—a mileage almost as large as is planned for rail rapid transit. Exact comparisons are not practical, but it is clear that a dollar spent on buses will buy much more transportation than one spent on subways.

It is not difficult to understand why the two Secretaries of

Transportation who have had access to these figures have insisted upon a policy of cost-effectiveness which seems likely to scuttle most new subways which are being planned.

The Scapegoat Automobile

The second conclusion to be drawn from the figures we have reviewed—that a reduction in per capita demand should be an integral part of a national transportation policy—overshadows in long-term importance the conclusion that the Department of Transportation has accepted and is responding to through the Brinegar-Coleman policy.

Even when the projections to 1990 are discounted for error, they are still a jolt. Some of the figures, moreover, are about as accurate as can be expected. This is generally true of those which pertain to the present, such as patronage of the various modes of transportation and the costs of each. The weaknesses derive from faulty assumptions about the future.

Working from reliable data about the present use of mass transit, it is a simple mathematical exercise to calculate how much it must increase under believable future conditions in order that automobile travel be held to its present level. If we assume a 31% increase in transportation users from 1972 to 1990 (corresponding to a projected increase of population in urbanized areas as a whole) and assume also no change in passenger trips per capita, the mass transit share would need to rise from a national average of 5.5% in 1972 to 28% in 1990 for there to be no increase in automobile passenger trips. To reduce automobile trips by a quarter, the mass transit share would need to rise to 46%. It would need to be substantially higher than that in the largest metropolises.

Whether or not the mass transit share can be increased enough to reduce dependence upon automobiles as population increases, or even to hold automobile traffic at present levels, it should certainly be possible to do better than raise the national average from 5.5% to 6%. Economic aspects of urban travel are now more favorable for mass transit—buses, anyway—than when the estimates were prepared. Since then there has been a sharp and probably permanent increase in gasoline prices (in relation to other living costs). Also since then the Congress has voted to supplement capital aid for mass transit with operating subsidies. Still more things may be done to make driving to work, or some of it, more expensive. The idea of stiff taxes on parking in congested zones appears to grow in favor, both as a revenue measure and as a restraint on automobile use. Thus, it is reasonable to believe that by a combination of generous subsidies to mass transit and sharply higher costs for automobile use, the mass transit share could be increased significantly beyond the trivial growth indicated in the 1974 report to the Congress.

The combination is nonetheless a fragile support for a long-term policy. The more effective it may become, the more will it also be politically divisive, with potentially ugly overtones. Fuel costs can be cut by recourse to less powerful engines. Air pollution can be reduced by better emission controls. In time both will probably be done, with the result that much of the present opposition to automobiles might be deflated—without, however, reducing traffic congestion. A high tax on downtown parking could reduce the congestion without necessarily causing a significant shift to mass transit. Instead, a tax high enough to be a major deterrent would probably accelerate the growth of competitive office centers in outer cities and suburbs.

Finally, it is necessary to look well beyond the near-term year 1990. With each year's passing it will become more urgent that a transportation solution be found that is better than a mere change of mode. Population will continue to increase. So will the size of urban areas—probably at a rate faster than population growth, as has been the case throughout this century. The theory that greater reliance upon mass transit would turn the latter trend around and lead to a higher population density was pinned to an expected increase in rapid rail transit. The theory was probably wrong, anyway. As long as people want more space and can afford it, any mode of fast transportation—freeways or subways—that reaches deep into suburbs will reduce population density in areas where people feel crowded. The population of Manhattan Island began to fall within a few years after the first subway was opened. But whether the theory was right or wrong, the policy of cost-effectiveness undercuts the expectation that subways will be widely adopted. It is difficult to believe that more buses will reverse the decline of population in cities.

We cannot solve our transportation problems by treating the automobile as a devil. To blame the automobile has at least the negative merit of being a more civilized way to vent emotions than to blame a religious or ethnic minority, which unhappily has been a frequent human response to baffling frustrations. But scapegoats of any kind are no help to understanding.

Devil theories flourish when we are unable to find persuasive rational explanations of problems that trouble us deeply. In considering urban transportation—as also in the case of housing and welfare dependency—we find ourselves handicapped by a poverty of conceptual thinking in the government and in the universities concerning the nature of the evolution taking place in metropolitan settlements. We can observe, in the wake of dispersed residence, a recent rapid growth of outlying office centers which compete with the hub. The mobility that the automobile affords is clearly a factor in such a trend. Urban traditionalists, deploring the trend, seize upon the circumstance that the automobile is an instrument of the change and hold it more responsible than it actually is.

As we saw in the preceding chapter, the powerful decentralizing trend in the evolution of large settlements—one which continues even after the urban-start migration has tapered off—is not caused simply by a particular mode of transportation, influential though it may be. It is the result of rising incomes and the net effect of all technologies that have a significant bearing upon metropolitan structure. Instead of being resisted, the decentralization should be welcomed.

Inasmuch as journeys to work can be shortened either by bringing homes closer to jobs or by locating jobs near the homes of the people who fill them, the emergence of suburban centers for non-local white-collar work is a fortunate event that can significantly reduce transportation needs. If the volume of commuting should also be reduced by making inner cities competitive with suburbs, we will be able to view the problem of urban transportation in a more relaxed and confident perspective. It is not the number of automobiles in use that makes the automobile the problem it is today. It is, rather, the length of the daily journey, the amount of fuel consumed and of waste products thrown into the air, and excessive concentration in zones subject to congestion. Shorten enough journeys and the other effects become tolerable.

Interestingly, the actions that will shorten journeys are also favorable to a switch from automobile travel to mass transit. Many people who will not use buses, even express buses, for travel from suburbs to the hub would find buses preferable for short distances. The automobile may be expected to remain the predominant mode between suburban homes and suburban offices, but there is probably a potential market for transportation by jitneys and little buses—*paratransit* is the contemporary generic word—which could travel variable routes like some airport limousines and the experimental Dial-a-Bus.

Hazards in the Present Method of Financing

A logic of events, we have found, is broadening urban transportation policy to include intervention by the federal government in the affairs of local governments to foster reduction in the per capita demand for transportation. While the reduction is desirable for several good reasons, the prospective intervention is worrisome. Any intervention of such far-reaching scope entails the danger of inadvertently damaging local communities. We should ask ourselves if there is not a better way to the desired end. In fact, the hazard exists already in the delicate task that the Urban Mass Transportation Administration must perform in deciding that federal aid may be given for very expensive rail transit in one urban area but not in another.

Until now the agency has been engaged mostly in rescue operations to prevent local mass transit systems from deteriorating further or collapsing altogether. Kenosha was without public transportation for seven months in 1971 after its private bus company quit. UMTA money helped the city to establish a publicly owned system which now carries 3,500 passengers daily during the school year and 1,500 in the summer. (Population of the city and adjacent urbanized area was 84,000 in 1970.) Most of the agency's grants have been for the purpose of saving failing systems and modernizing them with new equipment. Assistance has been given to extend or upgrade rail rapid transit in New York City, Chicago, Philadelphia, and Boston, as well as the commitments to Baltimore and Atlanta. But for the most part, the really difficult decisions—whether or not to support a subway for Los Angeles or the proposed joint rail system for Dallas and Fort Worth—have not yet been made.

An authorization by the Congress in 1974 of more than $10 billion for use over a six-year period is large enough to bring closer the hard decisions about capital investment. Of this sum, $6 billion may be used for capital assistance at the discretion of the Secretary of Transportation. Another $4 billion is to be distributed in accordance with a formula and may be used by the recipients for either investment or operating expenses. Federal aid may be used to pay up to 80% of capital costs and up to 50% of operating costs, provided that such uses conform to specified standards.

The formula establishes the amount of aid for each urbanized area with a population of 200,000 or more in accordance with the density of population in the area. In the case of areas with fewer than 200,000 people (but more than 50,000), an aggregate sum computed the same way is given to the governor of the state for distribution. The results vary widely and somewhat strangely, illustrating the inherent difficulty in applying any formula to diverse conditions. Generally, the formula favors the larger cities and their suburbs. In addition, then, to the fact that two out of five Americans live in communities that are not eligible for mass transit aid and that many who live in aided communities will not benefit either, the issue of equity is further aggravated by large differences among communities in the amounts given them on a per capita basis. The New York City area, as a whole, will receive 30% more under the formula than it would if the amount per capita were the same among recipients; Dallas will receive 27% less.

An accompanying table shows the effect of the formula in the nation's
25 largest urbanized areas. If the money which may optionally be used as
an operating subsidy were to be distributed solely on the basis of
population, each area would receive $33.56 for each resident it had at the
time of the 1970 census. The figure for each urbanized area in the table is
the amount that is more or less than the $33.56 average, and represents
the effect of the density factor.

Even if the amount of federal aid determined by formula truly
corresponds to needs of each of the aided communities, which is
doubtful, the allocation is so crude and unconvincing as to add needlessly
to political tensions that already exist. Nonetheless, the amounts of
money which must be spent on investment in public transportation vary

**PER CAPITA ADVANTAGE OR DISADVANTAGE IN 25 LARGEST
URBANIZED AREAS RESULTING FROM ALLOCATION OF MASS
TRANSIT AID IN ACCORDANCE WITH THE POPULATION DENSITY
OF EACH AREA**

Urbanized Area	*Amount above the per capita average* $	Urbanized Area	*Amount below the per capita average* $
New York City	10.06	Dallas	−9.13
Philadelphia	4.61	Kansas City	−8.11
Los Angeles	4.47	Minneapolis-St. Paul	−7.58
Chicago	4.24	Atlanta	−6.22
Baltimore	3.60	Milwaukee	−6.03
Buffalo	3.53	Seattle-Everett	−4.99
Washington, D.C.	3.26	Cleveland	−4.85
Miami	2.02	Pittsburgh	−4.59
Detroit	1.36	Houston	−4.51
San Francisco–Oakland	0.68	San Diego	−4.38
		Cincinnati	−3.70
		Denver	−2.63
		San Jose	−2.13
		Boston	−0.93
		St. Louis	−0.54

*Source: Based on data published by the Urban Mass Transportation Administration and by
the Census Bureau.*

Table 10

widely on a per capita basis from one community to another. The circumstance is recognized in federal law, both by the formula and the broad discretion entrusted to the Secretary of Transportation. The basic political issue is not that needs differ, but whether the controlling decision should rest with the federal government—as is inevitably the case when it pays 80%—or with the affected communities. Allowing the latter to make the big decisions affecting them would obviously require a different method of financing.

The nature of the difference in needs may be seen in a brief comparison between New York City and Los Angeles and their respective suburbs. The nation's two largest urbanized areas stand at opposite poles in transportation modes, and will surely continue to do so as far into the future as we can imagine it. No American city will surpass New York in dependence upon subways. Few great cities, if any, will continue to rely upon automobiles more than Los Angeles. The reasons have little to do with the wisdom or folly of their present residents. They are rooted deep in history, and in the different space requirements of work performed in each city.

When it became possible to generate electricity at a central power station, both the surface trolley and the subway were born. By the time vehicles could be powered by wire or rail, Manhattan Island was already nearing its peak in population density. Because of the density, the city moved almost directly from the horse trolley to underground trains. (Preparation for the first subway helped in 1898 to produce the union of the five counties that have comprised the city ever since.)

The city's largest industry, then as now, was the garment industry. Initially, most of the work had been performed by miserably paid recent immigrants in the crowded tenements where they lived. For this reason a high population density could be achieved with minimal transportation needs. State legislation forced a shift of work from home to factory, but the nature of the work was such that jobs could be stacked in layers in multistory loft buildings. Most other industries that were practical in a densely populated city were those that had small space needs per worker. The combination of an already existing high population density and the ease of job-stacking created a situation more favorable to subways than has been found in any other city.

The city's subways, in conjunction with the new building technology (steel-frame buildings with electric elevators), fostered a high concentration of both office and factory employment on the island. At the same time the subways initiated a major shift of population to Brooklyn, the Bronx, and Queens, which was later extended to suburbs by commuter railroads and the automobile.

The transportation destiny of Los Angeles was radically different.

When New York was building its first subway, Los Angeles had one-thirtieth of New York's population. It responded as quickly as New York to the new technology of electric-powered transportation on rails, but because of a small population, the rails were laid on the surface rather than underground. (When E. H. Harriman was contesting with Henry Huntington for control of the Pacific Electric, he announced his intent to build a subway, but the economic justification did not exist and the plan was abandoned during the business panic of 1907.)

From early days the industries attracted to Los Angeles have had extraordinarily high space requirements per worker and few blue-collar jobs were suited to stacking. The city's oil fields were an early example. Later came the movie industry, which required large production lots, especially in its early and peak years. Since World War II aircraft manufacture has been the largest industry in the area. Few greater contrasts in space requirements per worker can be found than between the manufacture of garments and airplanes.

The interurban network, as we saw in Chapter 2, created the basic structure of the Los Angeles metropolis before the automobile came into common use. Later, when the freeways were built, they largely followed the old routes of the Pacific Electric. The growing population took advantage of the interurban to enjoy spaciousness in residence (which, along with climate, may help to explain the city's rapid growth). It is probable that the interurban, which also carried freight on some routes, was a factor in the development of industries that had large space needs. The city of New York grew up crowded. In a period of major growth it had relatively light transportation needs because homes and jobs were close together. Los Angeles, developing in a later technological era, grew up spaced out. An electric rail system helped to disperse the packed population of Manhattan Island (in 1970 it was down to two-thirds of what it had been in 1910, and still falling), but another electric railway gave Los Angeles from the outset a high ratio of space to people.

The automobile superseded the electric interurban for a variety of reasons, but these two were particularly important: It made it practical for homes to be built on land lying between rail routes but beyond normal walking distance from a trolley stop. The automobile was also the most practical means of reaching dispersed job locations.

In a symbolic sense, the triumph of the automobile occurred even while new rail lines were being laid. In Henry Huntington's time, the social equivalent of a private jet airplane was a private railway car. Huntington had a private trolley car. Tracks were laid to a side entrance to the mansion on his suburban estate, and each workday morning at his doorstep he boarded his luxuriously furnished tram for the journey to his downtown office. Then in 1913, the man who had done the most to build a

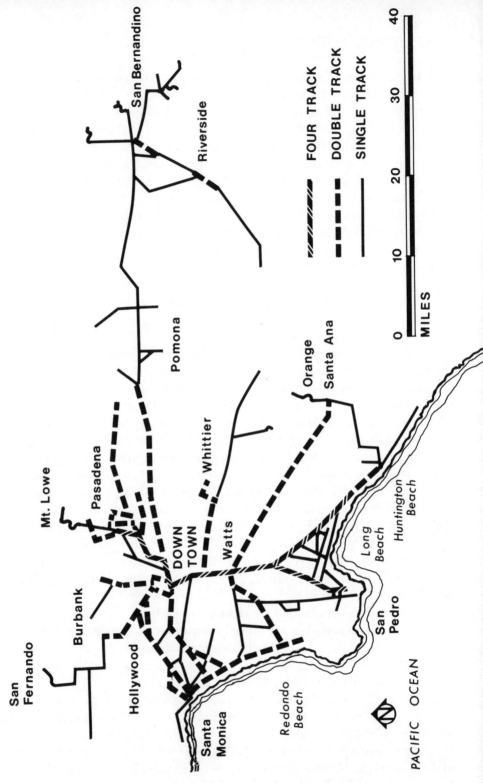

Figure 8. *How the Pacific Electric Railway Shaped the Metropolis of Los Angeles: Map of Routes About 1920*

fabled interurban rail system gave up his private tram and began commuting by automobile.

Possibly the time has come when Los Angeles and its suburbs again need an electric railway—this time underground. A goal of doubling downtown employment, however, is not a persuasive justification to nonresidents who, under existing rules, would pay most of the cost. But if the federal government, recognizing the superior interest of nonresidents, should say that if Los Angeles wants a subway it should pay the cost, what answer can be given to New York, which has high costs in merely keeping its subways in running order? The harsh squeeze on New York, which is already unpopular with the rest of the nation, is that it must either receive a disproportionately high share of federal aid for mass transit or be denied the assistance which may be critical to its future.

The best solution for all parties—including other communities with transportation needs still different from those of either New York or Los Angeles—is a different system of financing. In urban transportation, as in other areas of federal aid, the recovery of cities can be pursued most effectively if a sharp distinction is drawn between true subsidies, to be given only for recovery purposes, and funds of local origin which, as a universal x per cent of the federal *individual* income tax, would be returned automatically to local governments. While a confident judgment must be deferred until more data are at hand, it seems likely that the return of local-origin revenues, at an x rate to be established by the Congress, would be sufficient to enable all metropolitan areas to meet their transportation needs without a subsidy from the rest of the nation. Provided that the cities of New York, Newark, and Jersey City received adequate recovery assistance, the metropolitan area of New York should fare quite well by such change in the method of financing urban needs.

It may also be expected that when communities recognize that *their* money alone is financing their transportation, they will quickly discover the merits of reducing the per capita demand.

5. YOUTH'S COMING TO BELONG

Suddenly So Many More

"An orange passing down the throat of an ostrich" is the vivid metaphor of Theodore H. White for the great bulge in the number of young people. The bulge has been, and still is, a painful strain on the gullet.

The bulge began to swell right after World War II. Those first babies are approaching middle age. But the birth rate was at its peak in the late fifties and those who entered the world then are still teenagers. There will not be so many youth again for at least several decades.

There were 11 million youngsters in the 10 to 14 age group in 1950. Twenty years later the number had almost doubled, but there were not many more children under five than there had been when the 1950 census was taken. Now, in the middle of the seventies, when the number of youth is at its maximum, the number of preschool children is back to where it was a quarter of a century ago, and still falling.

We were not prepared for the big surge in the number of young people. The turbulence that we saw in the sixties has been many-sided and has had many causes, some of which we perceive dimly, if at all. Probably the way the young were reared by their parents has been the most important of all, but high on any list must be the sudden arrival of so many young people pressing for a fair place in society.

Still a bit staggered by the force of the recent tumult, it is difficult for us to remember that only a generation ago the ranks of youth were

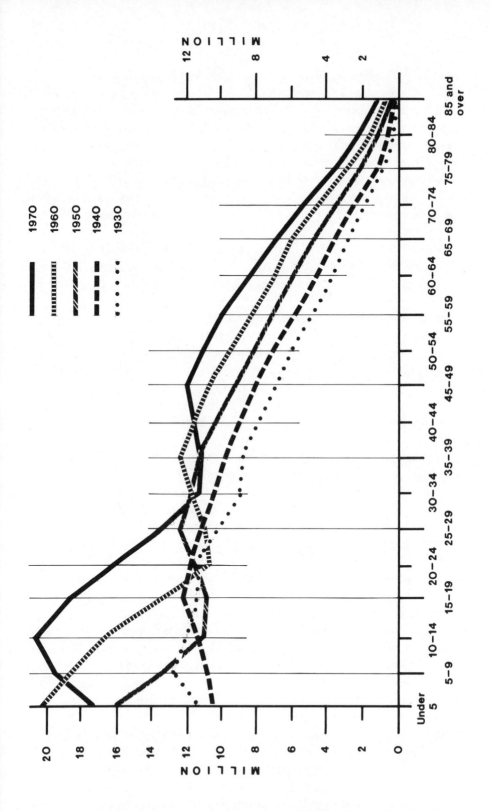

Figure 9. *U. S. Population by 5-Year Age Groups, 1930, 1940, 1950, 1960 and 1970*

shrinking. A decline in the number of births had begun in the twenties and the Depression years brought a larger fall-off. Our institutions and the national economy were still adjusting to the dip when the *tsunumi* struck. In the accompanying chart profiles in 5-year age groups for five census periods—1930 to 1970—show the modest dip and huge swell. During that time the population rose from 123 to 203 million.

Notice in particular two peaks in the number of young people. The earlier one appears in the 1930 profile for the 5 to 9 age group—those who had been born in the first half of the twenties. As they grow older, that group is seen at 10-year intervals as the crest of a rolling wave. By a coincidence, the number of deaths among them has been balanced by approximately the same number of immigrants of the same age, so that in five census counts the total number of people who were born in the early twenties, native-born and immigrants, has remained nearly constant.

The wave of twenties-born people, clearly evident in the chart, is a minor one compared to the upswing in births that peaked three and a half decades later. The crest of the second wave may be seen in the under-5 age group in 1960 and in the 10 to 14 group in 1970. When the full force of this wave hits the labor market it will temporarily make a reduction in unemployment more difficult, and in the third decade of the next century it will put the heaviest load yet on the then already burdened social security system.

Getting into and staying in the ranks of the gainfully employed is the biggest hurdle to young people trying to make a place in our national life. The rate of unemployment is always highest among the newest entrants to the job market, who do not yet have skills, seniority, or dependents; their rate of job turnover is high, often by their own choice. What is disturbing is that the unemployment rate among them has consistently risen.

Elsewhere in this book it is argued that no matter what else we may do, the recovery of cities will probably be retarded unless we bring the overall unemployment rate below the 4% which has come to be considered—too complacently—as equivalent to full employment. It will be easier to do this when a better age balance returns to the labor force. In the past fifteen years or so our national economy has done remarkably well in absorbing as many new workers as it has. Until quite recently, the main employment problem has not been a stagnant economy, but a lopsided proportion of beginners in the labor force.

Let us imagine for a moment that in 1974 the proportion of workers under 25 in the labor force was the same as it had been in 1950. Let us imagine, too, that the rate of productivity and the output of goods and services were unchanged (output not being reduced because of an assumed smaller population). Under such conditions there would not

| UNEMPLOYMENT RATES BY AGE GROUPS, IN 5-YEAR AVERAGES | | |
Period	Age 16-19 %	Age 20-24 %	Age 25 and over %
1950-54	9.8	6.1	3.3
1970-74	15.8	8.8	3.2

Table 11: This table compares 5-year averages in order to minimize the
distorting effects of fluctuation in annual rates.

have been 5.6 million unemployed in 1974. Instead, there would have
been a labor shortage of more than 1.2 million, which hypothetically
could have been supplied by more women working or by immigration.
We should not mistakenly suppose that we would have had fewer goods
and services in a smaller population. An end to poverty would result in a
higher per capita output than any we have yet known.

It is important that we recognize that the lopsided proportion of youth
today is an abnormal situation which affects not only employment
opportunities but the growth of youthful crime and the frequent failures
of city schools. It is also a temporary problem, and we are now apparently
about midpoint in its duration. The problem is abnormal; it is not realistic
to suppose that all of this bountiful supply of young workers can be
employed in a normal way. Private employers cannot justly be blamed for
not hiring more inexperienced young workers than they need. Even
when a factory or an office is working at full capacity there is room for only
so many beginners.

We can absolve industry from responsibility for so many idle youth.
The federal government cannot be exempted from it. Within the
executive and legislative branches there is an abundance of agencies and
committees which might legitimately have made it their business to
ponder the special problem of an excess of young workers and to have
proposed solutions. On the executive side, there are or have been such
agencies as the Departments of Labor, Commerce, Health, Education
and Welfare, and the late Office of Economic Opportunity. On the
congressional side, there are the committeees on Labor and Education. It
is also fair to ask, with respect to this critical issue, where were two bodies
that had been created to identify problems that may be missed by the
bureaucracies and the specialized Congressional committees: the White
House Council of Economic Advisers and the Joint Economic Committee
of the Congress?

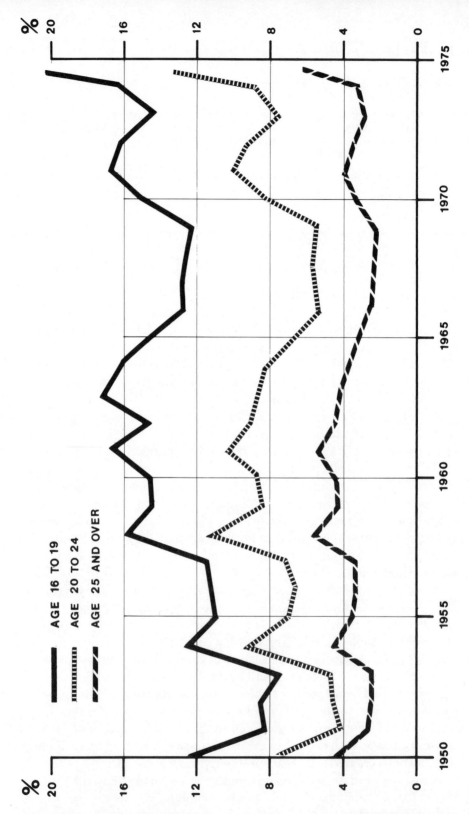

Figure 10. *Unemployment Rates of Youth and Older Workers, 1950 to Mid-1975
(Annual rates, 1950-1974; first six months, 1975)*

Apprenticeship in Crime

The lack of foresight has been disastrous. No sensible person will claim that the increase in crime has been due solely to economic conditions, but the parallel rise of unemployment and of crime among youth is too consistent to be dismissed as a mere coincidence. Young people have a compelling need to belong somewhere. If the promise of gainful employment is dim, they can find adventure, money and status of a sort from an apprenticeship in crime. It is an outlook which spreads quickly to younger brothers and sisters.

In inner cities the apprenticeship begins early and reaches a high proportion of the youth. Reminders of the grim truth are soon evident in a visit to any city.

To gain admittance to the barber shop of a major St. Louis hotel, a customer must show his face in the glass panel of a locked door. The barber—there is only one now in a shop that once employed six—explains the unusual security precaution: He is weary of being robbed by armed youngsters. He is the proprietor and would like to quit but cannot find a buyer for his business, even though it is only two blocks from city hall.

In Detroit a long queue of curious young people await admission to a downtown cinema in which the attraction is a movie portraying the city as "the murder capital of the nation" (a morbid distinction since lost to Atlanta).

On a sunny day students are lounging on the entrance steps of Central High School in Minneapolis. A shattering noise drowns out their banter and a boy crumples from the blast of a sawed-off shotgun. The teenage gunman jumps into a waiting car and is sped away. He is recognized, and when arrested says he was getting even for an unpaid debt. But his aim was poor. He hit, not his intended victim, but a student he didn't know.

In the same neighborhood a few days earlier young hoodlums attacked and killed an elderly cab driver. The police found ten known witnesses but none would talk. Soon after the murder a message had been painted in big letters on a brick wall: "Snitchers will be killed."

On the evening this warning was seen on TV screens in Twin Cities homes, the mayor of St. Paul presided over an angry meeting of parents at the Como Park Junior High School. As reported in the press, the meeting had been convened at the demand of parents to hear their complaints of "assaults on their children, strong-arm thefts of money and lunch tickets, extortion and sexual approaches to their daughters." The director of the city's Human Relations Department told the parents that he shared their alarm and recalled that when in response to earlier complaints about robberies on a school bus he had assigned an aide to ride the bus, she herself had been confronted by a thirteen-year-old girl who demanded her purse.

These incidents of violence in schools and school buses should be noted because they are part of a record widely reported in the local press. Shootings, it must be added, are rare. The shooting described here was only one in five years. But every one is remembered a long time by parents and teachers.

The heavy burden which crime imposes on cities is typified by the experience of Baltimore. In 1970 the city spent $69.23 per capita on criminal justice: police, jails, prosecutors, courts, counsellors and parole officers. The suburban average was $20.52. In the city there was one fulltime police employee for each 196 residents. In the rest of the metropolitan area the ratio was 1 to 728.

Urban crime in general—the increase of crime in suburbs, for example—is a problem too big to be considered here. Our specific focus is the influence of inner city living on an early beginning in crime. For this purpose, analyses made by the police departments of St. Paul and Minneapolis are among the best to be found. In St. Paul, 74% of all persons arrested in 1972 for nontraffic offenses were under 25. Half were juveniles and 21% of all were under 15. Aside from traffic arrests, more children 12 years of age or younger were arrested than persons 45 and older.

Juveniles accounted for three-quarters of the arrests for auto theft in St. Paul, two-thirds of those for burglaries, one-quarter for robberies and aggravated assault, over one-quarter for forcible rape, and one-sixth for possessing weapons.

St. Paul's records excel in their analysis of offenses according to age, but Minneapolis provides the best data for relating young crime to the neighborhoods in which arrested juveniles live. In April, 1970, when the decennial census count was made, 3,279 persons aged 10 to 17 lived in 15 particular census tracts. All but one of these are in the inner city area. In the next ten months city police arrested 1,067 youngsters in this age group who lived in these census tracts. The particular 15 tracts are worthy of note because in each of them at least one out of four juveniles was arrested in those ten months. In one tract three out of four juveniles were booked by the police. Nine other tracts were in the 20 to 25% range, and in 58 of the city's 127 census tracts at least one out of ten persons under 18 years of age was arrested for some offense against the law.

As might be expected, most of the young offenders lived in neighborhoods characterized by a low median family income and a high proportion of children in one-parent homes (although this was not universally true). A dominant characteristic was a sharp population decline. In all tracts but one, the loss of population during the sixties was one-sixth or more. In the aggregate, the population of these tracts fell by a third.

A major shrinkage of population in a neighborhood does not necessarily cause juvenile delinquency. Mostly, it is a reflection of conditions which cause people to move, including to some extent the prevalence of juvenile crime. Yet, nearly all persons consulted in Minneapolis and several other cities, who were familiar with such neighborhoods, considered heavy population losses to be a contribution to juvenile delinquency because they interfered with the creation of stable

JUVENILE ARRESTS IN CERTAIN MINNEAPOLIS CENSUS TRACTS CORRELATED WITH OTHER CHARACTERISTICS IN 1970

Tract No.	Juveniles aged 10-17 who were arrested in 10 months	Population change 1960-70	Median family income	Children under 18 in a one-parent home	Blacks as a % of total population
	Rate per 100	*%*	*$ Thousand*	*Rate per 100*	*%*
34	75.6	−60	3.3	18.5	29
57	60.6	−34	6.2	16.4	1
60	35.4	−40	6.7	10.1	5
78	35.3	−27	8.7	12.4	6
63	31.7	−21	8.6	5.8	2
33	30.5	−24	5.3	21.2	76
61	28.1	−31	5.3	11.4	7
79	27.7	−17	7.1	10.9	3
95	26.8	− 2	8.0	9.5	25
29	26.5	−27	5.6	14.1	13
35	25.8	−72	4.3	25.7	15
52	25.6	−37	5.8	19.6	3
58	25.4	−55	6.4	14.1	3
72	25.3	−17	7.1	9.9	2
54	25.0	−35	5.8	15.3	1
FOR COMPARISON					
25	3.4	−11	9.6	7.5	0
113	2.4	+ 1	14.0	2.1	0
City-wide	9.3	−10	10.0	6.8	4

Table 12

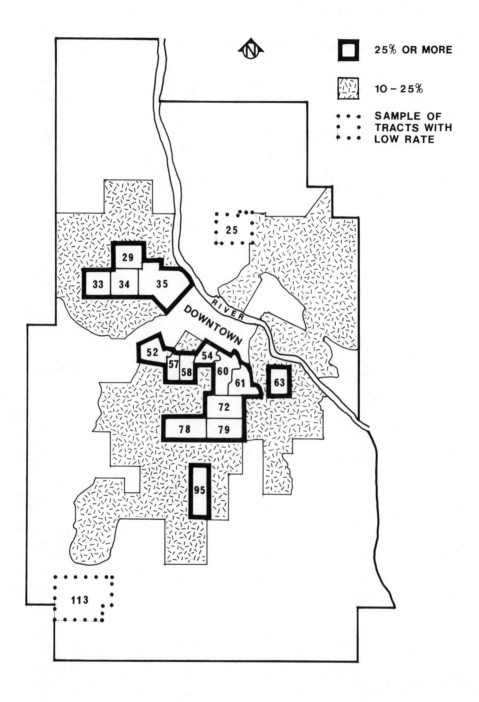

Figure 11. *Distribution of Juvenile Arrests in Minneapolis, 10 Months, 1970-1971*
(Numbers identify census tracts)

neighborhood relationships. The rate of juvenile arrests and other neighborhood characteristics of the 15 census tracts are shown in Table 12.

There is another side to the dismal story. In more than a quarter of the city's census tracts, the rate of juvenile delinquency is low, measured by present standards—under 5% during the 10-month period for which data were compiled. Two tracts are fairly typical of this group.

Tract 25 is in the working-class northeast sector of Minneapolis. It is close enough to downtown to be considered part of the inner city, but the residents do not think of their neighborhood that way. Breadwinners are predominantly skilled workers. Median family income at $9,581 (in 1970) was a little below the median for the city as a whole. Quite a few tracts with a higher median income had a substantially greater rate of juvenile delinquency. Religious and ethnic cultural influences remain strong, as does parental influence, and clearly they have had a large bearing on the conduct of children reared in such homes.

Tract 113 borders a suburb in the southwest section of the city. Here the breadwinners are predominantly executive and professional people. Median family income was $13,957, fourth highest in the city. The rate of juvenile delinquency is one of the lowest.

On most political issues there are large differences between the people who live in Tract 113 and those in Tract 25, but in their alarm over the prevalence of crime in the city and in their fear that peer influences may prove more powerful than family influences, they think and speak alike.

The Uphill Struggle of Schools in Inner Cities

Universitas BIBLIOTHECA Ottaviensis

The Minneapolis public schools rank among the best in big cities. Even in comparison with most suburban schools in the Twin Cities metropolitan area, their overall record is good when measured by conventional criteria. However, in their effort to educate inner city children they encounter stubborn obstacles not greatly different from those found in other inner cities. For an examination of city schools, let us remain in Minneapolis.

The basic facts concerning the Minneapolis public schools are these:

Enrollment in the 1975-76 school year was 53,999, 23% fewer than seven years earlier. Another 10,213 attended parochial or other private schools. Teaching was also provided in hospitals and other institutions for handicapped children and pregnant girls. About one school building out of ten had been in use 80 years or more.

An elected school board of seven members, serving staggered six-year terms, levies its own taxes and issues its own bonds. About 40 cents of each dollar of local property taxes is used to support the schools. The 1975-76 budget was $83 million, plus $8 million in federal grants.

Expenditures per pupil were high in Minneapolis in comparison with most suburbs. In a survey of 48 school districts in the metropolitan area in 1971-72, the Twin Cities Citizens League found that the Minneapolis average expenditure was $981, exceeded only by St. Paul with $993 and by three upper-income suburbs. The highest suburban expenditure was $1,118 and the lowest was $571. The median for the metropolis was $776. Minneapolis led all school districts in the ratio of professionals and paraprofessionals per pupil.

In 1950, 60% of Minneapolis families had incomes above the median for Hennepin County. By 1970 the proportion had fallen to 36% and each year it is less. More than one out of four of the city's school children come from families which receive government aid for dependent children; in some districts, the proportion is three out of four. About a fifth of the students come from families officially designated as minorities: blacks, Indians, Orientals, and persons of a Hispanic culture. The proportion is rising.

When the Congress in a major way made aid to elementary school education a federal responsibility by enacting the Elementary and Secondary Education Act of 1965, the legislation was accompanied by many glowing predictions that an infusion of federal money would soon overcome the unequal opportunities of poor children to obtain a good education. Now, in a pendulum swing away from overconfidence, it has become fashionable to say that more money doesn't really make much difference.

The experience of the Minneapolis school system supports what many people have believed all along (except that their opinions, being moderate, were seldom newsworthy), namely, that money devoted to reducing the number of students per teacher can help a great deal, but nothing will wholly compensate for a child's poor start in a family indifferent to learning.

Federal aid under Title I of the 1965 Act may be used in "target schools" to provide remedial training for children who are one or more years below their grade level in reading and math. In recent years about one out of six students in Minneapolis public schools have received such training. School officials, careful not to make extravagant predictions, are nonetheless confident that important gains are being made in raising the educational performance of students from poor families as a result of special training for teachers and teacher aides and use of materials developed within the Minneapolis school system.

Even before federal aid was available, Minneapolis had maintained a good performance in inner city schools. Central High School, located in a low-income, high-crime area has a tradition of achievement. In 1972, 44% of the previous year's graduates were enrolled in college; the average for all city high schools was 46%. Central High graduates, enrolled in the University of Minnesota's Institute of Technology, had a freshman grade average of 2.67—.12 points higher than the average for all freshmen. Those attending the College of Liberal Arts, however, lagged below the average. Another part of the picture—one largely beyond the ability of schools to alter—is that the unemployment rate among inner city youth is three times the city-wide average.

Only a part of the federal aid the city's schools receive is used to give remedial training to students from low-income homes. As in many other communities, the school board has been buffeted by differences among parents about educational methods. In some upper-middle-class neighborhoods where people tend to speak of *lifestyles* there has been a demand for innovation and experimentation. But in the working-class Northeast and in similar neighborhoods residents speak of a *way of life*, which to them means enduring values, not something so transient as a style.

To satisfy parents who want innovation, and with the aid of $5 million in grants from the Experimental Schools Program of the U. S. Office of Education, the school administration has reserved four elementary schools and one junior-senior high school in and near the university district for experimental methods. The four elementary schools have been designated the Contemporary School, the Free School, the Open School and the Continuous Progress Elementary. Students from any part of the city may attend, and the programs have been popular enough that there is a waiting list of students who wish to enroll.

In deference to both the *lifestyle* and the *way of life* parents, the school administration employs two different languages to describe educational aims and methods. Conventional English is used for the traditional schools. In contrast, according to a promotional brochure for the alternative schools, students who attend them are not taught. Instead, they "cope" and "relate" and "function in the options open to them." They do so in settings which are either "structured" or "unstructured" and in the presence of "facilitators," who at headquarters are carried on the payroll as teachers.

A Proposal for a Youth Opportunity Corps

For perhaps another decade and a half, an abnormal proportion of young people will exceed the capacity of private employers to offer them work. In the nineteenth century, when large families were common, a high ratio of youth to their elders could be leveled out by the advancing frontier. Such an outlet is not available in a highly urbanized society. But we can create one, no less than the federal government once did with the Homestead Act of 1862 and with bonuses of free land to railroad builders who helped to open up the West.

The best answer to youthful idleness and the concomitant apprenticeship in crime is to create a government-supported youth corps. Constructive public service, along with a sense of adventure and of belonging, a bit of pageantry to nourish the spirit—all would do no harm, and might fill a void now served by drugs.

A visitor to the Watts district of Los Angeles on a Saturday morning can find young children applying white paint to utility poles as high as they can reach. The painted poles have become a Watts symbol, and the children who keep the paint fresh belong to the Community Cadet Corps, open to youngsters aged seven to thirteen. The corps is sponsored by the Watts Labor Community Action Committee, which initially got its money from Los Angeles trade unions. Since then, the committee has received other private donations and some government grants. Although the great foundations have not distinguished themselves by fostering an understanding of the present youth problem, the Ford and Rockefeller foundations did make grants to the union-sponsored organization after it had proven itself.

When the paintbrush kids grow older they may join the Neighborhood Youth Corps for boys and girls aged fourteen and fifteen. At sixteen they become eligible for the Elite Youth Corps. At meetings of organized youth in this all-black district one may hear such words as "work experience," "self-improvement," "self-discipline" and "pride"—spoken, not in derision, but respectfully. On gala occasions, which sponsors of the corps know to be needed, members don simple uniforms, march to music and carry banners. Like a Shriners parade? Why not? It helps the youngsters to feel that they belong.

Forty miles from downtown Los Angeles the sponsoring committee operates the Urban Residential Educational Center where school dropouts grow vegetables and are trained in automobile repairs, the culinary trades, horticulture, and building maintenance. The Los Angeles Chamber of Commerce, which conducts an impressive job placement program, has helped graduates of this center as well as many other youth to find employment.

But giving a sense of belonging to idle youth, who are surplus to the production needs of a market economy, is obviously too big a task for volunteer community organizations. While the transitional problem exists, there must be a federally supported effort to overcome it. The purposes to be served are easily defined: Transitional employment in some needed public service; vocational training for future self-reliance; a cultivation of civic values that may have been missed at home or at school; a nourishment of ambition; adventure and a lift to the spirit. Later, with such preparation, today's inner city youth will be well-suited to relocate in communities where blue-collar jobs grow most strongly.

A junior auxiliary, a cadet corps, would also be useful. Even while children are still in school, there is a need to help them to "relate" to a larger world. The protagonists of innovation in educational methods too often repel by their excesses—there is excess, surely, in the private language in which teachers must be known as "facilitators"—but beneath the froth some of them have hold of an important truth which they share with the sponsors of the paintbrush kids of Watts: Children need to be introduced to responsibility at an early age. Early responsibility came naturally in a rural society, but we have not yet learned to recreate it in either cities or suburbs.

I like to recall, when this thought is in my mind, the story of Thomas Savage. He was thirteen years old when he arrived in America with the first settlers at Jamestown. He was probably an orphan and was thought to be indentured to his protector, Capt. George Kendall. In that terrible year of 1607 half of the colonists perished between May and December from disease and hunger. While Capt. John Smith was away on an exploration journey inland, Kendall, who was one of his associates in the leadership, was executed by a rival faction which seized control of the colony and held it briefly.

Young Thomas was now wholly alone. The colonists decided to place him in an Indian tribe so that he might learn the language, and in exchange a son of Chief Powhatan came to live with the Europeans. Thereafter, until he was grown and had settled new land in Accomack County, Thomas Savage was an indispensable link that enabled colonists and Indians to communicate with each other.

For all our sophistication, we are less able to help the young find a challenging place in society than the first colonists were.

6. THE DIMINISHING IMPORTANCE OF RACE

But, Still, the Persistence of Black Districts

A great many blacks moved from one urban residence to another during the sixties—enough to tell us what to expect in racial residential patterns for some time to come. In large numbers they moved from the inner city to parts of the outer city and in much smaller numbers from the city itself to some suburbs. However, in the metropolitan area of St. Louis the increase in the number of blacks outside the city was greater than within it, and such was almost the case in the Los Angeles area. The main story, even in suburbs where blacks settled, was an expansion of black districts or the beginning of new ones. There were the beginnings of true residential integration, but to a minor extent only.

It depends, of course, on what is meant by *true.* A precise meaning of integration is not easy to establish. If it is merely the absence of *de jure* segregation, it prevails now. That has been accomplished by federal laws which prohibit practices that interfere with freedom of choice in buying or renting a home for reasons of race. Many neighborhoods which were once all-white now have an occasional black family. The presence of an occasional black, however, is less than an impressive integration of blacks and whites.

If the test is simply statistical, integration has spread widely in many residential districts in cities and in some suburbs. It is easy to find census tracts (which vary greatly in size but contain an average of four to five thousand persons) which were once white and now have many blacks. But what we see in census data is a single frame in a moving picture—a still photo of what was true on a day in April in 1970. When we look carefully we find, in most cases, not stable integration, but a white-to-black transition.

A true integration, surely, is both substantial and stable. Perhaps the best test is to be found in the expectations of blacks and whites who share the same neighborhood. If most of them expect a substantial racial mix to continue because they themselves will be part of it, then a genuine and lasting integration has taken root.

An expectation of this kind prevails in the new city of Columbia, Maryland, near Baltimore. The city, which was started in 1964, had a population of 37,000 in 1975 and about one out of five was black. The blacks are not concentrated in one or two areas but live intermingled with whites throughout the city. Reston, Virginia, is another new city in which a similarly successful integration has taken place, although on a lesser scale. A Columbia-like pattern may be developing in several Baltimore neighborhoods where census data show a mix of blacks and whites at the same age level—young adults with children—and who appear to have about the same income prospects. And so, too, with some neighborhoods in the other cities that were studied. But looking at the evidence realistically, it must be said that the increase in true residential integration has been quite slow. Some evolving patterns indicate the possibility of a faster pace.

Morris Milgram is high on the list of Americans who may be considered experts on residential integration. Milgram has been a leader in developing integrated housing. In the Jan. 6, 1975 issue of *The New Leader,* he wrote:

> My experience in developing about three dozen interracial communities around the country has been that locations far from areas of minority concentration, and well beyond the path of black expansion, are ideal, if the rise of future ghettos is to be avoided. Communities developed under these conditions generally stay integrated with black minorities, even in cities whose populations are largely black.

Not many developers share Mr. Milgram's idealistic commitment to residential integration. If earning more money were his primary purpose, he could find less difficult ways to do it. But he must protect himself and his associates from *losing* money. Consequently, he is careful to choose sites "far from areas of minority concentration and well beyond the path of black expansion."

The Several Patterns of Black Expansion

In our search for a better understanding of the evolution of metropolitan settlements, we need to know more about the black expansion which Mr. Milgram has found may engulf integrated neighborhoods after they have been created. Actually, there are several patterns. This was evident from the results of a detailed examination of population changes by race in Baltimore, Fort Worth, and Minneapolis (along with a lesser examination in Detroit). I shall deal with Baltimore in this chapter, because the patterns found there were similar to those in the other cities—even in Minneapolis, with its small percentage of blacks.

Table 13 covers the ten cities of our study and in this instance a 20-year period.

	Proportion of blacks in city's population		20-year change	
	1970 %	*1950* %	*Blacks (000)*	*Whites (000)*
CHANGES IN RACIAL COMPOSITION OF TEN CITIES, 1950-1970				
Baltimore	46.4	23.7	+195	−239
Detroit	43.7	16.2	+360	−699
St. Louis	40.9	17.9	+100	−355
Dallas	24.9	13.0	+153	+257
New York City	21.2	9.5	+919	−915
Fort Worth	19.9	13.2	+ 41	+ 73
Los Angeles	17.9	8.7	+332	+503
Minneapolis	4.4	1.3	+ 12	−100
St. Paul	3.5	1.8	+ 5	− 7
Kenosha	2.4	0.2	+ 2	+ 21

Table 13

In the 20 years between 1950 and 1970, the percentage of blacks in nine out of the ten cities of our study more than doubled. (In the tenth, Fort Worth, the gain was by one-half.) There were similar increases in the proportion of blacks in other major cities, as well. Distinguished demographers were predicting only a few years ago that by the mid-eighties as many as 20 major cities would have a black majority. Some said 30 cities.

It is now almost certain that even the more moderate forecasts were far too high. In 1970 three cities had a black majority. They were Washington, D. C., 71%; Newark, 54%; Atlanta, 51%. Baltimore,

Detroit, and St. Louis in our study, and seven others with a population of 250,000 or more, had a black population of at least 30%: New Orleans, 45%; Birmingham, 42%; Memphis, 39%; Cleveland, 38%; Philadelphia, 34%; Chicago, 33%; and Dayton, 31%. All told, only 13 cities. And it is unlikely that even in all of these the percentage will reach 50%.

The forecasts overshot the probable result for two reasons. First, migration from rural areas, including blacks, has slackened, as we noted earlier. Second, black districts are not stopping at the city line. Nonetheless, there will certainly be substantial increases in the proportion of blacks. More whites than blacks continue to leave the cities and the majority of whites who have stayed behind during earlier migrations to suburbs are not at the childbearing age.

EFFECTS OF NATURAL INCREASE AND MIGRATION ON THE RACIAL COMPOSITION OF BALTIMORE'S POPULATION, 1960-1970

	10-year change per 1,000 whites	*10-year change per 1,000 blacks*
Births	+161	+318
Deaths	−126	−117
Natural increase	+ 35	+201
Net migration	−249	+ 95
Total change	−214	+296

Table 14

Here is one of the major reasons that blacks move outward within cities: There are more of them to be housed. For every ten blacks in Baltimore in 1960 there were thirteen in 1970; two of those from natural increase. And for every ten whites there were only eight a decade later.

A larger black population, however, was only a part of the story. Like many whites, many blacks made move-ups in the quality of their housing. In large part, the move-ups by members of the two races were linked in tandem—that is, whites moved to suburbs and blacks moved into the houses they left. Stated this simply, it is a familiar story. But what happened was not simple, and when we look carefully we find results and trends which do not fit the usual interpretations. *White flight,* for example, rolls easily from the tongue, but the glib rhyme races beyond the facts.

For a long time there have been four principal concentrations of blacks in Baltimore. The two largest are known as Inner City West and Inner City East. Each flanks a slender spine of distinguished old houses

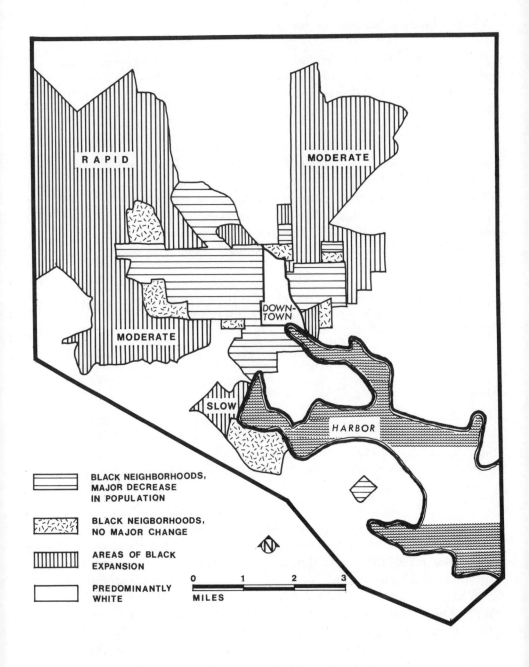

RAPID

MODERATE

MODERATE

DOWN-TOWN

SLOW

HARBOR

BLACK NEIGHBORHOODS,
MAJOR DECREASE
IN POPULATION

BLACK NEIGBORHOODS,
NO MAJOR CHANGE

AREAS OF BLACK
EXPANSION

PREDOMINANTLY
WHITE

0   1   2   3

MILES

N

Figure 12.   *Changes in Residential Patterns of Blacks in the City of Baltimore,*
1960-1970

extending north from downtown and which are occupied by well-to-do whites. A third, much smaller, grew up around Morgan State University, once an all-black institution and still mainly so, in the Govans district in the north central part of the city. It is a middle-class area which was rural land outside the city when the college was founded. Still smaller is the black community in Cherry Hill, near the city's southern edge. Bounded by the harbor, the Patapsco River, and railway tracks, it is a natural enclave in an industrial area. It is also a major site of public housing.

By 1970 the number of blacks who were living in neighborhoods where few blacks had lived ten years before equaled two-fifths of the entire black population in 1960. The dominant pattern in this change was an extension of existing black districts, like a new wing added to a house. Quickly and massively white districts became black. Most of this expansion took place in the west and northwest, and, in contrast to the poor housing from which it started, the new wing consisted mainly of middle-class neighborhoods which were preserved as such. It was a continuation of a trend that was already evident in the fifties. The pattern included also some neighborhoods extending from Inner City East, and accounted for about 80% of the blacks who made identifiable move-ups in housing quality during the decade.

A second pattern was also a white-to-black transition in middle class neighborhoods, similar to the first except that it occurred in a different part of the city—in the Morgan State University area and outward from it—and it moved more slowly and was thus much less complete. This pattern included about 10% of the blacks who made identifiable move-ups. While it is too early to venture a prediction, a large part of the second transition could end up as integrated neighborhoods, not from any evident planning, but simply because the transition may come to a stop.

A third pattern was created by young and relatively affluent whites and blacks moving into new apartment buildings as renters. One such new housing development was on the edge of downtown. The others were near the city's eastern, northern and western boundaries. Whereas the first two patterns were characterized by a black replacement of whites, this one was a case of whites and blacks sharing the first occupancy of new housing, such as happened on a larger scale in Columbia. The white participation was a deliberate choice rather than a resigned acceptance. This pattern accounted for about 2% of the blacks who made identifiable move-ups within the city. It is too early to know whether or not it will endure. It does not have the stabilizing influence of home ownership, and many of the tenants may be expected to relocate when their families grow larger.

Another 8% of the blacks who relocated—less than 3% of the city's black population—dispersed to neighborhoods which remained white except for the few blacks scattered within them. It was an integration which is perhaps best described by the French word *petite.*

We find in the last three patterns developments which are clearly different from the old pattern of segregation. They are more interesting for the characteristics they show than for the particular proportion of the black population they represent. They are still evolving. It is not yet clear how they should be identified. For the time being, let us simply call them happenstance, provisional and petite types of integration. They do not meet our definition of true integration—that it be both substantial and stable—but they could develop into it.

Mythology and Fact

To make the analysis described in this chapter, Baltimore's 201 census tracts were ranked in the order of the amount of the average monthly rent in each tract as shown by the 1970 census. The population of each tract, by race, was then recorded for 1960 and 1970. Visits were made to most neighborhoods. Major new housing construction and conversions of residential land to other uses were identified by tract. A correlation between rents and average values of owner-occupied homes showed rents to be a reliable measure of the changes which are reported. By trial and error it was found that four particular average rent levels gave the clearest picture of population shifts from low-rent to higher-rent tracts. The findings are shown in Table 15.

Although the measure of population movement by levels of rent is a departure from customary ways of showing relocations, it has the merit of reflecting what people are able and willing to pay for housing. Thus, we see in the table a dramatic illustration of the shrinking demand for the poorest housing, which was earlier identified with the falling population of inner cities. Baltimore, it will be recalled, had only a modest population loss for the city as a whole, but in those census tracts where the average rent in 1970 was under $90 a month, the combined population loss was three times the city's loss. Where the housing was cheapest—under $75 a month—the population fell by an average 25%.

There are aspects of the outward movement of the city's blacks which, to me, remain a puzzle. The main determinants, however, are clear. First, because of a 30% increase in population they needed to expand somewhere, within the city or outside it. Second, those who could afford it were in the market for more spacious housing in better neighborhoods, and there was a large and increasing number who could afford it. Third, because of their race, they had less freedom of choice in relocating than

DISTRIBUTION OF BLACKS AND WHITES IN BALTIMORE IN 1960 AND 1970 ACCORDING TO THE AVERAGE MONTHLY RENT PREVAILING IN 1970 IN THE CENSUS TRACTS WHERE THEY LIVED

	Average Monthly Rent in 1970			
	Under $75	$75 to 90	$90 to 105	Over $105
Living in the tracts in 1960				
whites	102,807	176,767	96,016	233,239
blacks	147,602	93,634	74,863	11,233
Living in the tracts in 1970				
whites	73,716	145,165	66,374	194,104
blacks	113,912	96,220	116,945	98,738
Change, 1960-70				
whites	−29,091	−31,602	−29,642	−39,135
blacks	−33,690	+ 2,586	+42,082	+87,505
Total change	−62,781	−29,016	+12,440	+48,370

Table 15

whites at a comparable income. Fourth, even in the short span of a decade the restraints on their freedom of choice were significantly eroded by the powerful surge of the civil rights movement in which blacks gained moral authority, legal protection, and political strength, while many whites were led by conscience to support their moral and Constitutional claim to equality. Fifth, apart from racial discrimination, there were circumstances which made it more difficult for blacks to find housing in some parts of the city than in others, whatever their preferences might have been.

These determinants, taken together, help to explain why the black expansion was large and irregular. But they do not tell us enough. We must look further. Let us begin such inquiry with a passing glance at some popular mythology. A flamboyant cliché, which is repeated even by responsible people, holds that suburbs are "a white noose around black cities." How well does it fit the case of Baltimore? In truth, the "noose," if such it is, lies not so much around the city as within it. As the accompanying map shows, districts which were overwhelmingly white and remain so form the city's northern, eastern, and southern tiers and comprise also pie-shaped wedges which reach almost to the city's center. It is a "noose" of a strange contour which in the north central part of the city makes a deep dip to leave outside it the Johns Hopkins University district, which bends again to exclude the southeast's working-class neighborhoods, and bends once more to leave outside the impoverished, but white, Steuart Hill district in the southwest.

A similar cliché holds that cities are being *resegregated.* What apparently is meant is that the proportion of blacks is increasing. A renewal of segregation cannot occur unless there has been a prior condition of integration. To suggest that Baltimore was more integrated when it housed fewer blacks is a careless use of language. Until not long ago nearly all residents lived in neighborhoods which were all-white or all-black. Racial segregation was even decreed by a zoning ordinance in 1910 as a way of keeping the growing black population within approved areas. (Baltimore is believed to have been the first city to use zoning for that purpose.) Although progress toward integration is slow, there is no observable trend backward except for the possibility that the racial mix such as now found in the Morgan State University area could be engulfed by the white-to-black transition which created it. However, there is also a possibility—perhaps equally as strong—that a large integrated area may result because the transition may run out of steam. Both the ideas of the white "noose" and of "resegregation" of neighborhoods are wide of reality in cities that were studied.

We cannot adequately understand the several patterns of black expansion without also understanding the nature of the change in *both* black and white populations in the affected neighborhoods. A fascinating aspect of the low-rent tracts (under $75 a month) is that virtually no white-to-black transition took place in them. There are 49 census tracts in this group; in only three did blacks replace whites to a significant degree, and that by less than 2,000 altogether. Otherwise, both white and black neighborhoods kept the same racial character while losing population heavily. Housing was abandoned in both white and black neighborhoods, but a large part of the population loss resulted from less overcrowding and the departure of maturing children. We know this by interpreting the figures on the average number of residents in a household, and what ages they are. In 1970 the neighborhoods with the lowest rent housed 15% of the city's whites and 27% of the city's blacks.

In the course of interviews in the cities I studied, I often encountered the notion that population declined because homes were being torn down for urban renewal or freeway construction. In one city with heavy losses (not Baltimore) I heard this explanation from a high-ranking city official. Actually, houses which were vacated in other inner city neighborhoods were more than enough to provide shelter for the people who were displaced. There were some displacements of people but they were a small part of the total. In Baltimore, for example, new office buildings for the state government replaced some century-old hovels, and the change in land use was hotly assailed at the time for depriving people of their homes. Those who were obliged to move were indeed inconvenienced, but most were not obliged to move far or to accept less satisfactory housing.

Abandonment of houses has been modest in Baltimore in comparison with Detroit and St. Louis—in one medium-sized district in St. Louis the rate of abandonment in 1973 was 12 houses per week—but there have been enough that the city has acquired many through tax default. In an effort to restore them to use, the city government has adopted a practice which started in Wilmington, Delaware, and which by stretching the meaning of an old word is called "homesteading." A house is sold for a token price—a dollar or two—to buyers who agree to repair and occupy it. Some other cities have also adopted "homesteading" and the U. S. Department of Housing and Urban Development has created a special office to promote the practice. It does serve to save some houses from further decay, but it does nothing to change the conditions that led to their being abandoned in the first place; it may simply shift abandonment from one neighborhood to another. As long as inner city residents are able to move up to better quality housing, and the houses they vacate are not in demand by new arrivals, the program has the aura of King Canute ordering the tide to retreat.

Two thirds of the move-ups by blacks to better housing, as shown by the rent analysis, took place in census tracts where the average monthly rent in 1970 was above $105 a month. Not quite a third were in the $90 to $105 bracket; 2% were in the $75 to $90 range. What can we learn about the whites who left these homes to be occupied by most of the relocating blacks? The white population declined in each of the four rent categories by these percentages:

Under $75	28%
$75 to $90	18%
$90 to $105	31%
Over $105	17%

Were these losses a case of *white flight*? It is generally agreed that many whites moved from their former residence because they did not want blacks as neighbors, or at least felt that the proportion of blacks was reaching the "tipping point" at which most other whites would leave. The speed with which the racial change took place in some neighborhoods makes it evident that a substantial number of whites must have been influenced by these considerations. If you have a taste for hyperbole, then say that they *fled*.

But before drawing final conclusions, consider some other factors: First, in those scattered neighborhoods where the average rent was in the range of $75 to $90 a month, the black population rose by only 2,600 while the white population fell by nearly 32,000. Would so few blacks put 12 times as many whites to flight—to other city neighborhoods, at least, if not to suburbs?

Second, the departure of whites and the arrival of blacks did not wholly coincide. The departing whites were broadly in three age groups. One consisted of families with school-age children who were replaced by similarly constituted black families. Members of this group comprised much of the exodus to suburbs when the proportion of blacks in their neighborhood reached the "tipping point." A second group had already left many neighborhoods before blacks began to arrive. They were young people who had been reared in the neighborhoods, but who moved to suburbs to rear their own children. This was true in cities all over the nation, even those that, like Minneapolis, had very few blacks. The city did not compete with suburbs to hold them, and their trickling departure helped to prepare the way for the later white-to-black transition. When they left, the neighborhood population declined briefly, to jump again when blacks with children began to replace parents of that second group. Some parents moved also, to suburbs, to Florida, or to local retirement homes. Some died, some still hold on in the old neighborhoods.

Finally, when we look deeper into what happened in the higher rent neighborhoods we find that in the range of $120 to $135 a month, the white population *rose* by 6% and in the neighborhoods where the average rent was above $135 the white increase was 16%. During the sixties a net of 16,000 housing units were added to the city's housing stock and many of them were built in these neighborhoods. Thus, in the districts where the city improved its ability to compete with suburbs, it increased the white population while attracting blacks as well. In the $120-$135 rent bracket the increase was about 2,200 whites and 1,200 blacks. In even higher rent areas, 4,500 whites and 870 blacks were added.

We have here, then, an instance of racial integration which, for the sake of prudence, I have called provisional. No matter how cautiously it is assessed, however, it does not fit the popular mythology.

Why Some Neighborhoods Were More Ready for Change Than Others

A tantalizing question remains. Why was the black expansion massive in the west and northwest extension of Inner City West, modest in the reach of Inner City East and the Morgan State University area toward each other, and lightly sprinkled in most neighborhoods? Some partial answers are possible.

There is impressive testimony that many real estate brokers and apartment building managers steered blacks who were seeking housing away from mainly white neighborhoods to neighborhoods where transition was advanced. Baltimore Neighborhoods, Inc., an interracial fair housing organization, made an extensive study in 1972 of discriminatory practices, including the dispatch of "sandwich" teams of a white, a black and another white to randomly selected apartment buildings. It found that in about half of the cases where such tests were made the black was discouraged from making a rental application while the whites before and after him were encouraged. The authors of *Racial Steering: the Dual Housing Market and Multiracial Neighborhoods* (Musa Bish, Jean Bullock, and Jean Milgram) credit the Real Estate Board of Greater Baltimore with national leadership in seeking to establish equal housing opportunities, but the practice of steering persists despite condemnation of it by the Board. Sometimes resistance to black settlement in white neighborhoods was not confined to steering. Some blacks who moved to the Hampden and Stadium districts were physically assaulted.

Dr. Homer E. Favor, Dean of Urban Affairs at Morgan State University, who was kind enough to criticize this chapter in its first draft, makes a persuasive case for his contention that racial discrimination has resulted in blacks having to pay higher rents than they would in a fully open market. How *much* higher is probably impossible to establish, but the fact that the market was restricted does suggest some overpricing. In some indeterminate degree, therefore, Table 15 is distorted insofar as it weighs whites and blacks equally in the rents that they paid. The distortion, however, does not alter the fact that many blacks made a move-up in housing quality; other figures back that up.

Another element in the several patterns of black expansion is that some neighborhoods were more vulnerable than others to the pull of the suburbs, and the most vulnerable of all were the middle-class neighborhoods in the west and northwest, which changed quickly from white to black. White residents who had settled there were relatively affluent. As Dean Favor has observed, the direction of prevailing winds—from the west and northwest—made this area a preferred site in a heavily industrialized city. The terrain is also higher and more varied than land near the harbor.

However, the area had been developed before the automobile era and in its early years. Although the houses are of good quality, they are rowhouses in contrast to the newer detached houses which are common in the city's north and northeast, including the Morgan State University area. Population data for the neighborhoods indicate that maturing children started relocating in suburbs early in the postwar period. The opening of the Jones Falls Expressway made it easy for them to commute to downtown from their new suburban locations.

The largest concentration of blacks was in the adjacent Inner City West. Severely overcrowded, they needed to expand. Also, the incomes of many were rising and there was a pent-up demand for better housing by middle-class blacks who perforce had been confined to the inner city until the restraints began to erode. The west and northwest neighborhoods were thus the natural meeting place of the greatest supply and the greatest demand. This circumstance in no way mitigates the ugliness of racial discrimination but it does help to explain, better than any other observable factor, the difference between the rapid transition in these neighborhoods and the slower-paced transition in the north central area.

There were other neighborhoods where, race prejudice aside, conditions were not favorable to a significant increase in black residents.

There is not much cultural exchange between the university people around Johns Hopkins and the factory and dock workers of Highlandtown and Highlandville in the southeast, although they have much in common. Those in one district find leisure-hour satisfactions in faculty parties, lectures and cultural events sponsored by the nearby Art Museum. The Southeast spends its leisuretime at bowling, neighborhood church socials, and sing-alongs at local taverns. Both types, however, reflect ingrown social interests. These and the proximity to their work have made the university district and Highlandtown and Highlandville relatively stable. These districts remained nearly all-white. (Many maturing children in the southeast neighborhoods, however, move to the suburbs, and the population is falling.)

The supply of housing available to blacks was restricted, as we have seen, by racial discrimination. The geographic distribution of the supply also varied widely for reasons independent of race—reasons which were similarly observed in Fort Worth and Minneapolis. So much for supply. How were the patterns of black expansion influenced by the nature of the demand? Were all neighborhoods in the same price range equally appealing to blacks who could afford to relocate? We can be confident that they were not. To suppose that they were is to treat the relocating blacks as abstract units of economic demand uninfluenced by such factors as convenient access to work, to friends and kin, and to the churches and other institutions important to their lives.

We are obliged to conclude that blacks voluntarily congregated in neighborhoods where their common interests could be satisfied and that this was one of the several major influences which shaped the patterns of their expansion, even if there is no practical way to measure it. Certainly it is not unique to blacks. Some German neighborhoods in St. Louis have

RACIAL CHANGE IN FOUR CATEGORIES OF BALTIMORE NEIGHBORHOODS, 1960-70

	Rapid White-to-Black	Moderate White-to-Black	Provisional Integration	Petite Integration
	West and Northwest Area	Morgan State University Area	Scattered Areas with New Housing	Highlandtown and Highlandville
Population				
Total in Category, 1970	90,490	22,682	26,662	50,613
Change, 1960-70 %	+28	+ 4	+70	−16
Blacks as % of total				
1960	6.4	5.8	1.1	0.9
1970	87.4	31.6	10.1	1.6
Housing, 1970				
Average monthly rent	$110	$122	$140	$74
Rental units as % of total	59	34	64	38
Persons per housing unit				
All	3.60	3.09	1.98	2.84
Whites	2.62	2.79	1.92	*
Blacks	3.81	4.25	2.88	*

*Not available

Source: Based on data from the U.S. Bureau of the Census

Note: The census tracts which comprise each category are listed in the appendix. The higher number of blacks per housing unit may represent some doubling up.

Table 16

an ethnic continuity of a century and a quarter even though they were relocated from the old city to the Baden and Bevo Mill districts. The periodic relocation of Jewish neighborhoods can be traced in most cities. In Minneapolis the principal Jewish neighborhood shifted from the Seward district to the Near Northside about the time of World War I (when its former residents moved to the new Calhoun-Isles district) and relocated again in the suburb of St. Louis Park during the fifties. In each instance the relocation was accompanied by the building of new nearby synagogues.

The ethnic composition of such neighborhoods is progressively diluted as members of succeeding generations disperse, but the persistence of ethnic neighborhoods is nonetheless a widespread phenomenon of American life. Even after the shame of racial discrimination has been confined to history, we must expect that many blacks will choose to live in mainly black neighborhoods. Perhaps people who are continually reminded that they are a minority sometimes wish to have the feeling of being a majority.

The Potential Evolution of the Minor Patterns

It was said earlier that the white-to-black transition in all but one or two neighborhoods of the north central part of Baltimore may not reach the stage of a full transition. It may become a lasting happenstance integration. A speculation by the city planning department provides an interesting background for examining such possibility. A published planning document known as *MetroCenter/Baltimore Technical Study* gives this view of the black expansion (MetroCenter, it will be recalled, is the official name for a proposed major expansion of downtown):

Many blacks feel that they must develop the capability to do their own thing, and not depend on "trade-offs"; that MetroCenter programs take funds away from them, and are against their interest; and that "regional" considerations mean *white* considerations. In the meantime they anticipate taking power.

The white business and civic leadership of Baltimore saw this situation coming years ago—that of a black-controlled city holding MetroCenter hostage in the fight with suburban counties for federal and state funds. But their action to stabilize integrated neighborhoods and open up suburban areas to blacks was largely ineffective. Although some areas were integrated for a time, the pressures for change were too great and the suburbs were never really opened up. In the process, blacks purchased good housing in good neighborhoods and substantially improved themselves and their children's situation.

The authors of the document then proceed to speculate that "perhaps one third of the projected Baltimore City black population could be attracted by better suburban housing if the housing and job opportunities were open to them," and that "if a white moved away—perhaps back to the city—for each black that moved into the suburbs, the proportion of blacks would be about 23%, still slightly less than the metropolitan average."

They conclude, however, that the wistfully contemplated exchange is impractical because it would be thwarted by "a portion of the black political leadership" who consider that "suburban housing for blacks is against their interest" (i. e. black political control of the city) and by white suburban politicians who would balk at the city "sending them relatively poor blacks in return for white middle-income residents."

A barter of people as thus described is properly dismissed as impractical. However, there have been some modest developments which were not considered in the planning document. Black expansion in the suburbs has been slow in comparison to the white expansion, but it is occurring. In 1970 there were only one-sixth as many blacks in the suburbs as in the city, and the rate of black increase in the suburbs during the sixties was 16% compared to 30% in the city. The black share of the total was still only 7%, compared to 6% in 1960, and much of it was concentrated in black districts such as the Liberty Heights corridor. Since 1970 black expansion into the suburbs has grown, apparently at a stronger rate. Most of the settlement in Columbia has been since then. Many blacks work in professional and clerical jobs in the big Social Security offices in Woodlawn, just west of the city, and some are finding convenient suburban homes. The planning document, preoccupied with promoting more downtown congestion, also overlooked the gain in white population in those neighborhoods where the city regained the ability to compete with suburbs on even terms.

The dispersion of blacks into once all-white neighborhoods, although modest, still continues. The growth of a petite integration in both suburbs and the city's suburbanlike districts has the effect of reducing the black demand for housing in the north central area, and there is at least a fair prospect that the white-to-black transition in the west and northwest will not be repeated there. Contrary to the simplistic generalizations, the direction of change in racial residential patterns in Baltimore and its suburbs is clearly toward a larger integration.

More important, surely, than any other influence is the prospect that the importance of race will continue to diminish as blacks reduce the gap between themselves and whites in education, employment opportunities, and income. A symbol of the revolutionary change that has already taken place was the election in 1974 of Thomas Bradley, a black, and Coleman Young, a black, as mayors of Los Angeles and Detroit. In the same year blacks were elected as mayors in Washington, D. C., Atlanta and several smaller cities, and as lieutenant-governor in California and Colorado.

The time approaches when Baltimore will have a black mayor and a black majority in the city council. If the city undertakes a recovery program, it is likely that a black political leadership will be in charge during most of the years which will be required for the recovery to be completed. The black leadership will find that Baltimore's recovery problems will not differ in kind very much from those of St. Paul and Fort Worth—which is to say that they will be more difficult than in Dallas and probably less than in Minneapolis, St. Louis, and Detroit.

7. HOW HOUSING HOPES WERE SKEWED BY WELFARE NEEDS

HUD Leads a Retreat

Ever since a federal housing policy had its beginning in emergency public works construction in 1934, three primary purposes have been intertwined.

One was to increase and improve the nation's supply of housing, and it is this purpose which has had the most far-reaching effect. The expansion of the nation's housing stock has meant not only more and better homes but also, after the worst shortages had been overcome, more reasonable prices and rents in relation to the family budget—an achievement which inflation obscures. Many others benefited, too. The increase in supply created jobs, profits for builders and mortgage bankers, interest earnings for savings depositors and—because housing construction draws materials and supplies from many other industries—a lift for the whole economy.

The second primary purpose was to remove housing and other structures which had become obsolete or were badly deficient to begin with. It was called slum clearance in the Housing Acts of 1937 and 1949, and urban renewal following the Act of 1954. The Act of 1949 was notable for its proclamation of a goal of "a decent home and a suitable living environment for every American family," and in time a variety of community improvement purposes were added. The whole, including urban renewal, now goes by the name of community development.

The third purpose was to enable persons of low income to obtain decent housing otherwise beyond their reach. This purpose, like that of community development, has been promoted by a variety of federal subsidies, none of which has proven to be wholly satisfactory. When the first specific housing legislation was enacted in 1937, the subsidy was a capital contribution for housing construction by newly created local housing authorities who would then own the finished structures. In recent years the federal government has been obliged to provide operating subsidies as well to save many public housing projects from being closed.

The other principal techniques of subsidy are interest-rate subsidies for private developers and federal financing for local authorities to enable them to lease privately owned housing and rent it to eligible tenants. A large increase in interest-rate subsidies, which reduced the cost of interest to a nominal sum, was a major feature of the Housing Act of 1968, which ranks with those of 1937 and 1949 as landmarks of housing legislation. The Act of 1970 authorized the Department of Housing and Urban Development (HUD) to experiment with direct cash allowances.

Now, after forty years, many critics of the nation's housing policy, including the federal department responsible for administering it, express doubt that it is useful to link the three basic purposes in a national policy. Give people in need enough cash assistance to rent a decent home, it is said, and housing supply will take care of itself.

Without awaiting the outcome of the experimental program, HUD at the beginning of the Nixon second term proclaimed a preference for direct cash assistance and denounced all other subsidy programs as wasteful and inefficient. It did not, however, indicate support for cash assistance on a scale that would, any more than earlier subsidy programs, provide a decent home for all who lack one. Mortgage guarantees provided by the Federal Housing Administration since 1935 and community development subsidies would have been continued.

A switch to direct cash assistance would have converted housing subsidies into a shelter version of the food stamp program. The Congress did not accept the proposal but neither did it decisively reject it. As a consequence of the controversy which arose when the President impounded housing subsidy funds, no housing legislation was enacted in 1973. The Housing and Community Development Act of 1974 marked time on the issue pending the outcome of the experiment and a more careful consideration of what the long-term consequences might be. The function of the Congress, former Senator Sam Ervin has said, is not to be efficient but to be deliberate, and it was in this spirit that the Congress received a hastily prepared proposal.

Cash allowances for housing are not a new idea. They were considered when the Housing Act of 1937 was being debated and again by a presidential study commission in 1953. The revival of the idea, however, has a new significance because it expresses a subtle change in national outlook which has taken hold in the last decade or so. The new outlook, quite different from the vision of America which prevailed in the Truman era, is that a large segment of the population will be indefinitely dependent upon public assistance. Self-reliance is assumed to be impractical for a large minority.

This outlook dominates the policy planning of HUD and HEW (the Department of Health, Education and Welfare), the two government departments most directly responsible for aid to the poor. The dismal outlook was solidified as the basis for government policy during the Nixon administration, although it had taken root earlier in the social science sector of the academic community with which the administration was generally in conflict.

Whereas HUD—at least during the abbreviated Nixon second term—has aspired to the role of a junior welfare agency unencumbered by any responsibility for increasing housing supply, many in HEW favor the consolidation of all public assistance, including housing subsidies, into a single cash allowance. These are differences about techniques. What is far more important is the fact that the basic outlook of policy planners in both agencies works against the recovery of cities.

To see why this is so, we will examine, in this chapter and the two that follow, the major aspects of existing housing policy, beginning with its origins and evolution over four decades. We will look at a momentous achievement and a dramatic failure. We will also probe the intellectual horizons of proposed policy changes as set forth in a HUD study, in congressional hearings and in a two-volume set of papers prepared by scholars for the Housing Subcommittee of the Committee on Banking and Currency of the House of Representatives. Finally, we will explore the fundamental question of what vision of America a housing policy should serve.

The Emergence of Housing as a Political Issue

Housing in the Seventies is an elaborate study which was hastily undertaken by HUD to support its already announced opposition to the kinds of housing subsidies which the Nixon administration had inherited and administered for four years. An introductory section is devoted to historical perspective and is extraordinarily shallow in content. Its conclusion is that the nation's housing problem originated "primarily as a result of the Great Depression."

The nation's housing problem, as we noted earlier, had been growing worse for more than three quarters of a century before the Depression, pausing only during the twenties. By present standards at least, much housing was unfit when built, and deteriorated further because of overcrowding during the mounting tide of immigration before World War I.

The first of several municipal laws by which New York City sought to impose minimum standards for its crowded tenements was enacted in 1867. A model tenement was built in 1880 by the Improved Dwellings Association, one of several philanthropic organizations which sought to correct disgraceful slum conditions. In the late eighties Jacob Riis, a police reporter, aroused the conscience of the city with his vivid accounts of slum life, which he later incorporated in a famous book, *How the Other Half Lives.*

Earlier in the same decade a young state legislator, Theodore Roosevelt, had accepted the challenge of young Samuel Gompers, president of the newly organized American Federation of Labor, to accompany him on a tour of sweatshops in the city's slums. What Roosevelt saw made him a champion of legislation to regulate housing for the poor. At Gompers' behest, he also agreed to co-sponsor a bill to create a state minimum wage. As President, he established a commission to study possible federal action to improve housing conditions. The report was published in 1908 but was ignored by the Taft administration.

The use of public funds to build new housing as a replacement of slum housing was made into a lively political issue before the Depression. The occasion—the first, so far as I can discover—was the election of a mayor of New York City in 1929. The proposal was made by Norman Thomas, the Socialist candidate, and so successfully did he press the issue that the Republican candidate, Congressman Fiorello H. La Guardia, reversed his position in mid-campaign and virtually accepted Thomas's position as his own. I was then a youthful assistant to Thomas and was familiar with Thomas's development of campaign issues, although I made no contribution to them. With one exception the account given here is abstracted from the microfilm record of *The New York Times*'s coverage of the campaign.

What Thomas said then carries a sense of *déjà vu* four and a half decades later. His campaign embraced nearly all issues which mayoralty candidates discuss today, and although both he and La Guardia lost to the incumbent, James J. Walker, Thomas won the votes of many Democrats and Republicans. "It has become respectable to support Norman

Thomas," said the *Times*, which was one of three of the city's dailies to endorse him for mayor.

Thomas's approach to the housing problem was a break with prevailing policies. More than six decades had passed in futile efforts to eliminate disgraceful housing through municipal inspection. Jacob Riis, Teddy Roosevelt, and many others had excoriated the city's slums, but still they remained. Let the city demolish the unfit housing, Thomas said, and "provide not only decent homes for our people but work for the unemployed."

Thomas's housing proposal touched deep feelings. There was an unmistakable fervor in the response of campaign audiences. La Guardia picked up the housing issue and promised to appoint more housing inspectors to compel landlords to eliminate unsanitary conditions. Then, in a tense, unscheduled debate which came about when La Guardia appeared unexpectedly at a Thomas campaign meeting, he appealed to Thomas to withdraw and to support him. Thomas declined, citing their differences on housing, public ownership of subways, and tax policy.

A week later La Guardia, a master of colorful language, declared that the time had come for the city to end the "obsolete, barbarous rookeries which are disgraceful and unnecessary scabs upon the face of the community." If he became mayor, he said, the city would "set itself to slum clearance and housing projects on a large scale," unless private capital was forthcoming for the task. The qualification that private capital might be available was a gesture. For practical purposes, he now agreed with Thomas.

One part of this account cannot be gleaned from the reporting of the campaign by *The New York Times*. It was something that did not happen, and odd as the omission now seems, it did not seem odd then. *Thomas did not propose a housing subsidy.*

There were several reasons for this. The devastating blow of the Depression had not yet struck. Its intensity could not even be imagined. Only in the final two weeks of the campaign did the sudden drama of Wall Street begin to overshadow other news. At that early stage it was only an investors' crisis which in the words of the *Times* was heard on Broad Street outside the Stock Exchange as a "weird roar" caused by hundreds of traders shouting panic-inspired offers to sell.

A more basic consideration was his political philosophy. As a Socialist he was an advocate of public ownership to an extent greater than the American people have ever been willing to accept, but he had deep misgivings about long-term public ownership of property affecting people as intimately as their dwelling place. He preferred cooperative ownership of multi-unit residential buildings, as the nearest equivalent of private ownership.

A few years earlier the Amalgamated Clothing Workers had sponsored a successful cooperative housing venture in the Bronx which he viewed as a desirable model. To replace the slums, the city would need to be the initial owner of the new housing, as he saw it, but the housing would then be sold to cooperative associations of tenants, and their payments would go into a revolving fund for the construction of more housing.

For the building and initial management stage, he favored a municipal agency modeled on the Port Authority of New York, which owned and managed harbor facilities and bridges and would have the same responsibility for the highway tunnels about to be dug. The capital needed for the revolving fund would come from the sale of bonds.

Thomas and his advisers were not indifferent to the circumstance that many poor people could not, on the income they then had, invest in a housing cooperative. But they thought that the construction and operation of a housing project should be divorced from public supplements to individual income. The elderly should receive adequate old age pensions (this was before the enactment of Social Security legislation), the unemployed should be given jobs in public works, and those who for one reason or another could not support themselves should directly receive assistance adequate to their needs.

The idea of an indefinitely dependent welfare class was abhorrent to Thomas, whose long public career was devoted to the proposition that poverty could be wholly ended. He favored a role for government which would assure emergency and transitional assistance to people who were in need—but as an aid to self-reliance and never as a substitute for it.

An indirect confirmation of Thomas's rejection of a rent subsidy may be found in his view of the city budget, an incident which is especially piquant in light of later costs of municipal government. During the four years that the elegant Jimmy Walker had been mayor, the budget had risen by 30% to $565 million—an increase which Thomas denounced as wasteful and extravagant. In this respect he was in the tradition of Socialist mayors such as Milwaukee's Daniel Webster Hoan and (later) Jasper McLevy of Bridgeport, Connecticut, who were repeatedly elected by voters who rejected their socialist convictions but liked their fiscal responsibility and rigorous honesty.

A footnote on the cost of government and inflation: The New York City budget that shocked a Socialist mayoral candidate projected a per capita expenditure of $82 in 1929. In 1974 dollars this was the equivalent of $274 (a 1974 dollar had the value of 30¢ in 1929). In 1974 the city's budget amounted to $1,630 per capita.

In this story of turning housing into a political issue, a sequel remains to be told. Four years later La Guardia again ran for mayor and was elected. One of his first acts was to create the New York City Housing Authority and to begin badgering the Roosevelt Administration for the aid with which First Houses were started within a year of his election.

The Evolution of Policy in Four Decades

First Houses is the plural name of the first public housing project in the United States. It is a project of modest size: 116 apartments which replaced a lesser number in several decrepit tenements on New York's Lower East Side. The rent charged to the new tenants was equivalent to what they had paid to private landlords. When the fortieth anniversary of the project's ground-breaking was celebrated in late 1974, with Mayor Abraham Beame and other local and Washington dignitaries participating, the present condition of First Houses was described by one of the speakers as "nearly immaculate." Among the celebrators were a man and wife who had lived in the project since it opened—a testimonial to the stability which has characterized it.

First Houses and other projects containing some 22,000 housing units were built directly by the federal government, with uncertain constitutional authority, between 1934 and 1937 as part of an emergency public works program. If a local community created a public housing authority, as New York City did, the new housing was given to the local authority to own and manage. Otherwise, the federal government was the landlord.

In 1937, in conformance with specific legislation to authorize federal assistance for the construction of public housing, the federal government exchanged its roles of developer and landlord for those of patron and banker. The new U. S. Housing Authority lent local authorities 90% of the development cost of public housing projects, one third of which was repayable with interest over a 60-year period. Later it was 40 years.

During World War II most new housing construction was limited to shelter for workers in suddenly expanded war production plants, and after the war government-assisted housing dwindled almost to nothing. However, mortgage guarantees provided by the FHA and the Veterans Administration gave a huge stimulus, as we have seen, to privately financed construction. Everyone who borrowed in order to purchase a home benefited at least indirectly from the liberalized credit terms which the FHA initiated.

The Truman administration, with powerful support from Robert A. Taft, Sr., the leader of conservative Republicans in the Senate, revived housing for persons of low income, and for the first time a national housing goal was set. A single sentence in the Housing Act of 1949 expressed the three intertwined purposes.

The general welfare and security of the Nation and the health and living standards of its people require housing production and related community development sufficient to remedy the serious housing shortage, the elimination of substandard and other inadequate housing through the clearance of slums and blighted areas, and the realization as soon as feasible of the goal of a decent home and a suitable living environment for every American family, thus contributing to the development and redevelopment of communities and to the advancement of the growth, wealth and security of the Nation.

A decent home and a suitable living environment for every American family. The goal is worthy of association with the majestic promises of the Declaration of Independence and the Constitution. The nation had come a long way in social purpose since 1867, when a city had first legislated minimum housing standards—indeed, a long way in just two decades since government initiative to ensure the building of decent housing had been made a political issue.

For those who enjoy the flavor of irony in historical events, there was a particular piquancy in the championship of public housing by Robert Taft, whose father, as President, had interred a modest move toward a federal housing policy twenty-five years before a second Roosevelt made shelter a concern of the federal government. When continuance of public housing was touch-and-go in 1949, Taft's support was decisive and for that reason so were his views on the limit to what could be undertaken. Charles Abrams recalled Taft's role as follows in his book, *The City Is the Frontier,* published in 1965:

> Senator Robert Taft, who had been the measure's most forceful advocate, would not allow himself to be distracted by those who had pressed for enlargement of purpose beyond housing, for the good senator was a Christian at heart to whom "no room at the inn" was a gnawing deficiency in a great and progressive society.
> "I do not believe that public housing is socialism," Senator Taft told me in an interview, "if it is confined to the furnishing of decent housing only to that group unable to provide housing by its own means. We have long recognized the duty of the state to give relief and free medical care for those unable to pay for it, and I think shelter is just as important as relief and medical care."

The "enlargement of purpose beyond housing" to which Abrams referred meant slum clearance for nonresidential use, such as was approved as urban renewal in the Act of 1954. But the Taft statement which Abrams quoted also made it clear that if a housing bill were to pass, the purpose would need to be confined to the provision of shelter to "that group unable to provide housing by its own means." Aid for that purpose, in Taft's view, was not socialism. Anything more would be.

Norman Thomas had hoped that the powers of government would be used to undertake a complete replacement of unfit housing, much as the federal and state governments, beginning in the mid-fifties, organized the construction of a new set of interstate highways. Before the Depression he had believed that this could be done independently of welfare programs and that new multi-unit housing could be sold to cooperative associations of owner-occupants. His approach probably never had a chance. Senator Taft could make a subtle distinction between public housing which would be an acceptance of socialism and other public housing which would not be. In this he was not alone. All of us are constrained by habits of thought, some of which are peculiar. We are not troubled by public ownership of roads since we do not regard the practice as socialistic. Up to a point, even some public ownership of housing can be accepted if it can be judged not socialistic. But a government undertaking to replace slum housing on a scale comparable to the Eisenhower administration's highway construction program would be socialistic and unacceptable, even if government ownership of the housing were temporary, pending a sale to cooperative or condominium owners.

Within this national frame of mind it was easier for the Congress in 1949 to approve instead some government-owned housing coupled to welfare aid, in the form of a subsidy for land acquisition and construction. This approach had practical advantages. It had the appeal of directness. The needy lacked decent shelter. Then build it for them, as one would give medicine to the indigent who are ill or food to those who are hungry. Also, the precedent had already been established in the thirties when public assistance had been necessary on a large scale.

Critically important was the fact that the subsidy element limited the scope of the housing program to supplying the needs of those who required public assistance, and this limitation was important to a large bloc of congressmen whose support only Taft could mobilize. A housing bill which combined these characteristics could muster a slim majority and clearly part of a loaf was better than none.

The Housing Act of 1949 is generally regarded as the most important of all housing legislation. With respect to the goal that it set and the fact that it revived a program that had almost ended, the appraisal is justified. That the Act accomplished that much was a notable achievement. The housing actions of the federal government since then merit a less kindly appraisal.

By 1949 there was already evidence that the tempo in the tandem migrations was stepping up, but it could be attributed to a catching up in trends which had been slowed by the war. To have foreseen then the tremendous force which the tandem migrations would gather would have required powers of clairvoyance seldom associated with human behavior. Against the background of a disastrous depression and a costly war, it would have been necessary to have anticipated an unparalleled rise in incomes which would draw millions of city residents to new homes in suburbs. In addition to this gift of prophecy, it would have been necessary to have anticipated the coincidence of a rapid increase in the mechanization of agriculture which would propel millions of displaced farmers and farm hands to the old housing being vacated in cities.

Vigorous though the national economy was in this period, it was not able to absorb all of the new influx of unskilled labor, especially when most of the new blue-collar jobs were being located outside of cities. Public assistance was required on a huge scale and housing policy was increasingly skewed toward welfare needs. Originally, it had been supposed that the only subsidy which public housing would require would be a contribution to the cost of its construction. But as the proportion of welfare tenants rose, operating subsidies became necessary. The Housing Act of 1974 authorized a half billion dollars for one year's needs. At this level, the average operating subsidy is about $40 a month for each unit of public housing.

It is against a background of the powerful impact of the tandem migrations that we should assess the achievements and failures of the nation's housing policy.

A Mighty Achievement

It is easy to forget how far we have come in improving the nation's housing supply in the years since La Guardia damned the slums of New York as "obsolete, barbarous rookeries." Virtually all of the improvement has come within the past three decades, and probably no one has summarized it more aptly than Roger Starr, director of New York City's Housing and Development Administration. He wrote thus in *The New Leader* (Sept. 30, 1974):

> Although no one seems prepared to say so, the American housing achievement since World War II has been mighty, ending the days when a President of the United States could describe a third of the nation as ill-housed. . . . While no one is quite clear about what precisely defines a substandard unit, the simplest test remains dilapidation or absence of full plumbing. By those criteria the third

of the nation found to be ill-housed in 1936 was down to less than 10% in 1970.

Each ten years since 1940 the Census Bureau has conducted a housing census at the same time that it has made a population count. The dramatic change since 1940 is reflected in the accompanying table.

CHANGE IN U.S. HOUSING SUPPLY (YEAR-ROUND DWELLING UNITS) 1940-70

Census year	Total units in millions	Units per 1,000 persons	Units lacking some or all plumbing, % of total
1940	37.3	283	42.5
1950	44.5	294	27.1
1960	56.6	315	15.7
1970	67.7	333	6.9

Table 17

The most impressive gains came after 1950. While population between then and 1970 rose by 34%, an increase rapid enough to place a strain on resources, the number of year-round dwelling units increased by 52%. A mighty achievement, indeed! The 23 million additional units were a net increase and do not fully measure the monumental volume of new construction. In that time a large number of rural houses were abandoned, although the exact number is not known, and a substantial number of old housing units in cities were replaced. That total must be added to the net gain for a measure of total new construction. Moreover, the new housing was generally more spacious and better suited to the needs that housing should serve than the shelter it replaced and much that was retained.

If we could do all this in two decades, then it is clear that in another two we could, so far as physical capacity is concerned, finish the job of providing a decent home for every American family.

As is well known, most of the increase took place in suburbs—a circumstance that is deplored by many writers on urban affairs. Yet, as we saw in the chapter devoted to the tandem migrations, it is a fantasy to suppose that housing construction in this magnitude could have occurred on developed land in so short a time. Had it not been for the fast growth of suburbs, many present residents of outmoded city housing would still be living in rural hovels that were worse.

The improvement of housing in cities was, even so, much better than

many critics grant. When we look at the increase in housing in the ten
cities of our study in relation to population change, the result is startling.
In twenty years, the ten increased in population by 690,000, despite
losses in five, while their housing units rose by 1,120,000. The average
number of units per 1,000 persons went from 311 to 368 (or a fall in the
occupancy rate per unit from 3.2 to 2.7). In the remainder of the cities'
metropolitan areas (predominantly suburban) housing units per 1,000
persons rose from an average of 313 to 318. The change in each of the ten
cities, according to census data, is shown in an accompanying table.

CHANGES IN POPULATION AND HOUSING UNITS IN TEN CITIES 1950-70

	Change in population (000)	Change in housing units (000)	Housing units per 1,000 persons	
			1950	1970
New York City	+ 4	+491	308	370
Los Angeles	+846	+379	354	383
Detroit	−339	+ 7	282	350
Baltimore	− 46	+ 28	293	337
St. Louis	−235	− 25	307	383
Minneapolis	− 88	+ 5	310	385
St. Paul	− 1	+ 14	300	347
Dallas	+410	+162	325	359
Fort Worth	+114	+ 50	320	354
Kenosha	+ 25	+ 9	303	315

Table 18

The part of the table which is the most difficult to accept at first glance
shows an increase of nearly a half million housing units in New York City
while population rose by only four thousand. The figures were
challenged in the preparation of this book, but not for the first time.
Earlier, city officials, eager to show a population gain as a basis for more
federal and state aid, had argued, according to the Census Bureau, that
the size of the gain in housing was proof of an undercount in population.
But the bureau insists that there are no significant errors in the figures.
The increase in housing units per 1,000 persons was actually smaller than
in St. Louis and Minneapolis. A variety of factors help to explain the per
capita gain in housing. In twenty years there was a major increase in the
proportion of elderly persons, many of them living in underutilized
housing, and in the proportion of single young adults occupying city

apartments. Nonetheless, with all allowances made, there was a great deal less overcrowding—almost surely less than at any time in a century.

In a single decade major progress was also made in providing plumbing facilities that had been lacking. In 1960, 9.6% of all housing units in cities lacked some or all plumbing. Ten years later the proportion of such units in cities was down to 3.5%. Consider Baltimore. In 1960, 51,899 housing units in the city were deficient in plumbing—a jolting 18% of the total. By 1970 the number was down to 5,355, or less than 2% of all. From data concerning demolitions and new construction, we know that more than two-thirds of the shift from "substandard" to "standard" resulted from installation of plumbing in old houses. Some people lived better because of it. Yet housing which initially lacked plumbing was so poor to begin with that it is still close to substandard when plumbing is added. When its occupants can afford something better they will leave it. The standard of what people will be satisfied with is itself changing.

Compared to the overall gain in housing supply, the increase in subsidized housing was modest. Between 1949 and the end of 1974 the increase in public housing units was about 900,000. Approximately another 800,000 were added by interest-rate subsidies. A third of the gain, measured by starts, occurred in two years—1970 and 1971—as a result of the boost to subsidized housing given by the Act of 1968. It would be a mistake to minimize the contribution of subsidized housing, but the main route to a decent home has been, as it should be, a rise in family income that makes public assistance unnecessary.

The most important part of national housing policy was the least noticed: the FHA mortgage guarantee program which directly and indirectly supported favorable terms for home purchases.

The Sad Story of Pruitt-Igoe

Along with a magnificent achievement there have been some depressing failures. Any balanced account of public housing must take note of the Pruitt-Igoe project in St. Louis. It should be understood that it is not typical of public housing in St. Louis or the nation. Its story is told because it is the worst.

When one looks at the housing situation in St. Louis one is struck by a paradox. The city government has classified approximately 70,000 housing units as "poor" and considers no less than half of these, or a seventh of the city's total, to be so poor that they are beyond economic rehabilitation and should be demolished. It is curious, then, that many former residents of public housing have chosen to live in them in preference to public housing. About one-sixth of the high volume of vacancies in the city come from apartments built to replace slum housing.

Ever since viewers of TV news programs were shown the spectacular crumpling of a big apartment building when dynamite shattered its base, Pruitt-Igoe has been one of the contagious image-words which shape opinions about urban problems. The building that was destroyed by the St. Louis Housing Authority was the first of 33 slated to be shoveled away as funds are found for demolition and removal. All that remain now stand empty; 11-story question marks symbolizing two nagging questions: Why do so many of the poor in St. Louis choose slum housing in preference to public housing? And why did Pruitt-Igoe fare so much worse than the other projects—for example, the Vaughn project one block away?

Wholly satisfactory answers may not be possible to obtain but the search should begin with a perspective on the total housing picture in the context of a drastic decline in population.

HOUSING UNITS PER 1,000 PERSONS IN ST. LOUIS, 1940-70

Year	Population	Housing Units per 1,000 persons	Occupied Units per 1,000 persons
1940	816,048	309	289
1950	856,796	310	302
1960	750,026	352	332
1970	622,236	383	347

Table 19

From 1940 to 1970 the relative supply of housing increased, but quality deteriorated. Changes in supply and condition are recorded in the accompanying chart reproduced from an admirable study, "The St. Louis Development Program," by the St. Louis Plan Commission.

Public housing accounts for about 4% of the city's housing supply. Between 1942 and 1968 the St. Louis Housing Authority built 7,902 units of conventional public housing and later added about 1,600 units in "turnkey" projects—a variant whereby a housing authority by prearrangement purchases a completed project from a private developer. The largest projects were the Captain W. O. Pruitt Homes, opened in 1955, and the W. L. Igoe Apartments, opened the following year. Although they were built and managed as separate projects, they were adjacent to each other and were identical in architectural design. In accordance with a custom then prevailing in border state cities, one had been intended for white tenants and the other for blacks, but to conform

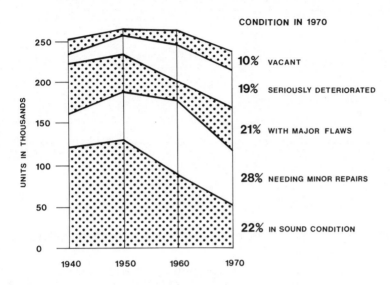

CONDITION IN 1970

10% VACANT

19% SERIOUSLY DETERIORATED

21% WITH MAJOR FLAWS

28% NEEDING MINOR REPAIRS

22% IN SOUND CONDITION

Figure 13.   *Housing Supply in St. Louis, 1940-1970*

with civil rights legislation they were racially integrated at an early date. Usually they were known simply as Pruitt-Igoe. Together they contained 2,738 dwelling units in 33 11-story buildings on 57 acres, and they cost $36,000,000.

In reporting occupancy trends the housing authority has singled out projects built no later than 1963. The ones built after that date are new enough to be well maintained, and have a good occupancy rate.

The occupancy rate for Pruitt-Igoe at the end of September, 1972 was down to 20%. The average rate for the other projects was about 75%. In all of the projects there was a large number of apartments that could not be used until repairs were made, but there was not enough money for this purpose. In 1972 the average monthly rent in all such projects was $39.05. Ten years earlier, when a dollar was worth more, it had been $48.82, but as the proportion of welfare tenants rose, the average rent fell. Public housing had become a major second channel for welfare aid and in a most improvident way. To meet the operating losses caused by the fall in rental income, it was necessary to divert money from maintenance reserves, and soon there was a shrinkage in the number of apartments that could be rented at any price. HUD has given the housing authority $5 million to make repairs, but the authority estimates that

OCCUPANCY DATA FOR ST. LOUIS PUBLIC HOUSING BUILT 1942-63

	1956 %	1966 %	1972 %
Occupancy rate of available units	98	90	52
Tenants' source of income			
Employment only	52	39	22
Public assistance only	31	43	63
Both sources	17	18	15

Table 20

another $25 million is needed before full use can again be made of the big public investment in housing.

Poor maintenance, however, is not a complete explanation of the high vacancy rate in these projects. Some of the worst private housing competes successfully with public housing for a bizarre reason: It is surplus housing that is in the last stage of use before abandonment. The owner no longer makes repairs or pays taxes. In time the city will take possession for nonpayment of taxes but until then any rental income is better for the owner than none. Because of the city's heavy loss of population, a surplus of housing seems likely for some years to come. When public housing was built to relieve a shortage, the consequences of an unforeseen surplus were undreamed of.

Pruitt-Igoe, the most vulnerable of the projects, could not survive the competition. Reasons for its failure have been exhaustively studied. There is a consensus that no single factor was decisive among the variety that eventually brought the project to an end. Rather, there was a cumulative effect which gave Pruitt-Igoe an unfavorable reputation from which it was never able to recover. There were early difficulties in racial integration which, it is believed, might have been averted if the practice had prevailed in the city earlier or if it had been introduced gradually with normal tenant turnover. Eventually, few whites remained despite integration in principle. From an early date the development was populated with a high proportion of families headed by women and dependent upon welfare. Those familiar with the project's early history say that blacks in two-parent families successfully sought assignment to other projects. By tacit consent, Pruitt-Igoe was reserved for the poorest blacks.

It is generally held that Pruitt-Igoe was too large and that its high-rise character was unsuited for families with small children. At one time

10,000 people lived in the project with an exceptionally high proportion of small children.

There is little doubt that the architectural design of the buildings made them unusually vulnerable to crime, most of which was committed by outsiders. Access was through elevators opening directly upon the street rather than upon foyers which could be guarded. Criminal assaults in hallways became so frequent that private deliveries and services were virtually ended. This circumstance may have marked the point of no return. It was certainly a reason why the vacancy rate exceeded all others. By this time private housing was easy to obtain because of the exodus to suburbs and it was considered by many tenants to be safer than public housing.

A high-rise character does not seem to have been a major handicap to other St. Louis projects. Among the more successful, the Vaughn Apartments, which opened one year later only one block from Pruitt-Igoe, consist of 9-story buildings. The Darst-Webbe buildings range from 8 to 12 stories. The Blumeyer buildings, occupied by families with small children, are four stories higher than Pruitt-Igoe. Each of these projects, however, is less than half the size of the project which failed.

A better comparison in size is the Amalgamated-Warbasse cooperative in New York City. It is the fourth in a series of cooperative housing developments which the Amalgamated Clothing Workers began in 1927. This one consists of 2,585 apartments in five 24-story buildings completed on 27 acres in Brooklyn in 1965. Neither a size virtually the same as that of Pruitt-Igoe nor a height twice as great has been a handicap in attracting many families with small children and in maintaining a record of full occupancy.

When actual construction costs are converted into 1974 dollars, the average cost of a housing unit was $26,718 in Amalgamated-Warbasse and $23,804 in Pruitt-Igoe. The former included pro rata costs of a supermarket, a power generating plant, parking areas for 1,106 automobiles and entrance foyers which can be guarded. Pruitt-Igoe had none of these features. The average number of rooms per apartment is 4.4 in Amalgamated-Warbasse and 4.3 in Pruitt-Igoe.

Thus, in project size, high-rise characteristics and unit cost, the two housing ventures are not far apart. Why, then, has one been a great success and the other a dismal failure? Surely a large part of the answer is that residents of Amalgamated-Warbasse are members of a stable community and have an ownership stake in it. They do not directly own the apartment they occupy, as in a condominium, but together they own the whole development, including its supermarket and its power plant. As owners (one vote per apartment) they have a vital interest in maintaining their own apartment and the common-use property in good condition. Most have a background of similar employment and union membership. Family ties are strong. (In the Amalgamated cooperative that began in 1927 there are many families of two and three adult generations in their separate apartments.)

Pruitt-Igoe tenants, on the other hand, were not part of an established community with long-standing ties in common. They shared no stake in keeping the property in good repair as Amalgamated tenants do, and consequently had no reason to take pride in doing so. Had the residents of Amalgamated-Warbasse occupied Pruitt-Igoe before it fell into disrepair and had they been able to become cooperative owners (making some alterations for security against intruders), it seems likely that the ill-fated project would have been a success.

Lost: A Sense of Proportion

The judgment that the high-rise nature of the Pruitt-Igoe apartments was a principal cause of the disaster that befell them does not hold up well when tested by comparisons, but it is symptomatic of a rush to glibness that permeates a broad stream of contemporary thinking about cities.

"Often it is not the more logical ideas that take precedence but ephemeral notions that are more extravagant and easier to grasp," Andrei Sakharov has written in criticism of a carelessness in intellectual standards that is now common both in America and Europe. The criticism by the brave winner of the 1975 Nobel Peace Prize appears in *My Country and the World,* recently published in the West after the text of the book had been smuggled out of the Soviet Union.

In any assessment of the nation's housing problem that is governed by a sense of proportion, the basic facts are these: Since the end of World War II tremendous progress has been made in increasing the supply of housing—an achievement that is especially noteworthy in the face of a massive migration to cities from the countryside. A huge amount of unsuitable housing, nonetheless, still remains, predominantly in cities, and its replacement is a necessary condition for the recovery of cities. For several decades to come many poor families will need some form of housing subsidy in order to have a decent home. If they are to become self-reliant, many who will need housing subsidies will also need to relocate outside of cities, and the subsidies should therefore be used to encourage resettlement. Methods of subsidy should be flexible enough to serve these ends.

When changes that should be made in housing policy are being considered, one might reasonably expect precedence to be given to ideas which correspond to these basic facts. Unfortunately, it is not. Those which presently take precedence, as we may see in the next chapter, provide a melancholy illustration of the truth of Sakharov's observation.

8. THE DIN OF ADVICE
THE CONGRESS HEARS

The Housing Act of 1974: A Case in Point

When Norman Thomas made government assistance to housing a political issue he started a debate that has reached monumental proportions. It is a debate conducted in all but the smallest local governments, in thousands of civic bodies, in a wide spectrum of trade and professional associations. It comes to a head, naturally, in the Congress of the United States when new funds must be sought for existing programs or when proposals to expand or revise existing programs are considered.

In writing the Housing and Community Development Act of 1974, the Congress was amply advised. The Senate's Subcommittee on Housing and Urban Affairs alone heard 109 witnesses on aspects of one or more of 47 bills which 43 Senators had introduced or co-sponsored. Among the witnesses were spokesmen for organizations of state governors, mayors, city managers, county officials, housing authority executives, city planners, home builders, mobile home manufacturers, mobile home dealers, apartment building developers, new community developers, owners of leased housing, mortgage bankers, realtors, title companies, architects, surveyors and mappers, elderly citizens, park directors and environmentalists. Many of them gave the same counsel to the House Subcommittee.

Unlike the Housing Acts of 1937, 1949 and 1968, the Act of 1974 did not initiate new programs or set ambitious goals. In its 108 small-print pages it did three things. It revised existing programs and simplified their administration. In particular, it consolidated seven previously separate programs concerning community development into one, to be funded for a beneficiary local government in a "block grant." Local governments thus obtained a greater flexibility in the use of federal assistance than they previously had had. The welcome consolidation and flexibility entailed a complete revision of the basic 1937 Act plus 180 amendments to 13 other housing acts and seven other acts of Congress having a tangential bearing. Secondly, the Act of 1974 marked time on the intensely controversial issues of the techniques of housing subsidies by concentrating temporarily on leasing as the principal method. Finally, the Act authorized $8.4 billion in program grants to local communities for the next three fiscal years.

Most of the interested parties who testified before the appropriate Senate and House subcommittees confined their advice to these down-to-earth managerial concerns. However, the Congress also received a broad range of recommendations which remain available for consideration in the writing of future legislation concerned primarily with policy changes, as distinct from administrative reform. These are contained in published hearings of the Joint Economic Committee on *Housing Subsidies and Housing Policies,* two thick volumes of papers prepared by experts for the House Subcommittee on Housing at its request, and in a major study, *Housing in the Seventies,* offered by HUD.

The proposals contained in these documents establish an agenda for debate on potential policy changes. Their nature—and their great omissions—have a vital bearing on the potential recovery of cities.

A Cultural Lag in the Social Sciences

The intellectual horizons of these studies do not reach far despite the impressive academic credentials of their authors. On the contrary, the recommendations which are offered bear the distinctive trademark of how-to scholars largely untroubled by nagging questions of where-to, patrolling their familiar precincts of "problem-solving."

The idea that cities might recover appears nowhere in the half-million words assembled for the House Subcommittee, or in the statements submitted to the Joint Economic Committee, or in the HUD study which occupied the forced-draft attention of 135 employees and 17 consultants for six months and which former Secretary James T. Lynn described as a "comprehensive study report evaluating the federal role in housing and finance and proposing alternatives for a new housing policy." (Some of the testimony before the Joint Economic Committee was a criticism of some HUD administrative practices. The comments in this chapter do not apply to that criticism or to papers submitted to the House Subcommittee without recommendation.)

It is not merely that the word *recovery* was not used—after all, there are many ways in which the idea might be expressed—but rather that the idea itself never appeared, even in a flicker. Earlier we defined the recovery of cities as a regained ability to compete with suburbs as a place of residence, and an ability to meet fiscal needs from revenues of local origin, requiring an automatic return to local governments of part of the federal individual income taxes paid by local residents). The academic scholars, consultants, and high administrative officials whose policy views swell these tomes seem to regard the present dependency of cities as a great river which rolls on and on and never meets the sea. None of the advice to the Congress contemplated an eventual end to subsidies or considered ways to distinguish true subsidies from a return of local revenues. The general tenor of the recommendations was that whatever the problem, the appropriate response requires more money with no foreseen end.

A city's ability to compete with its suburbs as a place of residence—the second criterion of recovery—was also not considered in these documents, although not because their scope was too narrowly conceived. There are frequent and favorable references to "comprehensive planning," "metropolitan housing goals," and "management of urban growth." One paper bears the ambitious title, "Goals and Strategies of a National Housing and Urban Growth Policy." The idea of a city's regained competitiveness was not discussed, one must suppose, either because it did not seem to be important or was not thought to be feasible.

However, housing policies which would vitally affect a city's relationship to its suburbs were considered at length. Policies that were recommended pursue one or another of two themes. One theme emphasizes conservation of existing housing stock for the use of people who now live in cities. The other urges dispersal of some significant proportion of low-income residents and members of recognized minorities to suburbs. As presented, each theme contradicts the other. If many city residents are to be dispersed to suburbs at a time when there has been a major fall-off in new arrivals, why, then, try to save housing of the poorest quality which is already in surplus in many cities? The two sets of arguments never come within the same field of vision, even in "strategies for national housing and urban growth."

Actually, each theme has a limited merit. Some housing that is lost to abandonment could be saved through timely maintenance, and should be. But far from all. Many houses and apartments in inner cities will never be occupied by any except the very poor. When poverty is reduced no one will want them. Within a perspective of a city's recovery, this housing should be replaced by that which would attract commuters if they are to be drawn to the city as residents.

There is merit, too, in encouraging some residents of the city to leave it, although not for the reasons which dominate the dispersal theme. Those who can find better opportunities outside the city than in it should be enabled by a housing policy to relocate near their opportunities for *their* benefit, but not to satisfy someone else's notion of a suitable income and racial mix.

Within a perspective of a city's recovery, an accelerated exodus of some city residents in quest of better opportunities need not be feared although more homes will be abandoned. In a large field of vision, the present contradictions between the two themes could be overcome. A housing policy designed to support a city's recovery will simultaneously make it easier for some city residents to move away and for people who now live in suburbs to settle in the city.

The solicited advice that the Congress received was plodding, fragmented and, in the absence of a large vision, bogged down in contradictions. But it was not unrepresentative of urban affairs scholarship. "The reality," wrote the respected Dr. George Sternlieb of Rutgers University, "has outrun the scholarly apparatus." His observation was made in a paper prepared for the House Subcommittee and was confined to the abandonment of housing in cities. But it summed up neatly the weakness of the "scholarly apparatus" with respect to larger urban problems, as well. The development of a theory that would provide a believable explanation of what befell cities, and thereby point a way toward their recovery is a work that is peculiarly appropriate to academic scholarship—and, as we noted in the chapter on "The Evolving Metropolis," is peculiarly missing.

Why the "scholarly apparatus" has not developed a comprehensive theory about cities is in itself an intriguing question. Speculatively, several reasons seem possible. Excessive specialization may be one. The how-to preoccupation of social scientists may be another—a tendency perhaps unduly encouraged by government agencies. Perhaps there is a too casual confidence in the self-sufficiency of social science; a notable characteristic of most writings on urban affairs is their isolation from a study of history.

Whatever the explanation of its cause, the cultural lag within the academic community that Dr. Sternlieb noted limits the usefulness of most contemporary urban affairs scholarship to matters of secondary importance. For observing conditions and events within a cultivated specialty, experts and problem-solving scholars have an eye that is sharp and trained. Their other eye, which might behold the panorama of diverse whole settlements growing and evolving in history—that eye, unhappily, seems to be made of glass.

The Fallacy of the Homeowners' Subsidy

The advice tendered to the Congress by high-ranking experts was distinguished not only by its failures to contemplate the most important issue of all—the potential recovery of cities—but also by some experts' ardent attachment to several fashionable fallacies.

One such fallacy has a beguiling simplicity and has been accepted facilely enough to fit the class of opinions that Dr. Samuel Johnson characterized as "propagated not by reason but caught by contagion." As argued by Anthony Downs, a consultant, in testimony to the Joint Economic Committee, its thesis is that "it is the affluent and not the poor who are the chief beneficiaries of housing subsidies."

Dr. Henry Aaron, a senior fellow at the Brookings Institution, also testifying before the same body, concurred in this view and defined the "subsidies" of the affluent—or more precisely, homeowners, many of whom are not affluent—as "the exclusion of net imputed rent and the deductibility of mortgage interest and property taxes under the personal income tax."

Neither Downs nor Aaron proposed to abolish the tax deductions. Their purpose in citing them as "subsidies" was to justify housing subsidies to people who need them. "Since the affluent are generously subsidized, more generosity is due the poor," they said in effect. Or, as others, less polite, would put it: "Homeowners have their rip-off; renters are entitled to one, too." The case for housing subsidies of some kind is powerful enough to rest on its own merits. It does not need specious reasoning.

How valid is the argument that a tax deduction for interest is a subsidy? The Internal Revenue Code does not distinguish between interest paid on a home loan and interest on money borrowed for other commonplace purposes. If home ownership is subsidized by a tax deduction for interest, so also is automobile ownership if the buyer makes interest-bearing deferred payments. A young man borrows to buy an engagement ring. Does the government subsidize his courtship? Yes, say Downs and Aaron, if they are consistent. By their breath-taking logic, the whole credit system as used by individuals is a vast subsidy.

They apply the same reasoning to a homeowner's property tax, which may be deducted in computations of the federal personal income tax. Yet, real estate taxes have the same deductible status as state and local income taxes, gasoline taxes, and general sales taxes. Nearly everybody pays a sales tax on the purchase of clothing and may deduct the amount of such tax from the net sum on which a personal income tax is paid. Does this mean that the federal government subsidizes the ownership of clothing? In the logic of Downs and Aaron, it does.

A third presumed subsidy, according to Dr. Aaron, results from the failure of the federal government to require a homeowner to add to his taxable income a sum representing the rental income he would receive if he charged himself rent for his use of the home he owns. This, along with certain hypothetical expenses that might be allowed against a hypothetical rental income, is the meaning of "net imputed rent."

It is true that imputed rent is a neglected source of tax revenues. For that matter, there are many neglected sources; at one time the French Government taxed homes according to the number of windows they had, with predictable results for the glass industry. Dr. Aaron, in finding a subsidy in the absence of a tax on imputed rent, stops at home ownership but his logic does not. Beds and chairs (and many other things) qualify for imputed rent as logically as does a house. Are not some houses and apartments rented furnished? Perhaps you have neglected to be thankful for your good fortune, but if you own the bed you sleep in you are getting a government subsidy equal to the tax that is not charged on the income you earn (but do not report) from renting your bed to yourself instead of to someone else. At least as Dr. Aaron defines subsidies, you are subsidized.

Since many who rent a home own their furniture (and since we may safely assume that few homeowners rent beds), we may logically conclude that bed ownership is subsidized even more widely than home ownership. Nearly all bed owners, if a popular theory is true, receive at least two subsidies: an income tax exemption from imputed rent and an income tax deduction of the sales tax paid when the bed was purchased. If it was bought on credit, which is a practice among many young families, the bed owner receives a triple subsidy just like a homeowner.

But who pays the cost of subsidizing bed (and home) owners? It is not enough to say that the federal government pays because that evades the question of who ultimately pays. In this instance, the government is presumed to collect more from some citizens in order to collect less from others. It could be said that all taxpayers subsidize bed owners but that would simply mean that bed owners are paying a large part of their own subsidy. In that event we should distinguish between a gross subsidy and a net subsidy. However, Dr. Aaron and others who hold that homeowners are the beneficiaries of subsidies do not make this important distinction, which would greatly deflate the significance of their claim. In his testimony to the Joint Economic Committee, Dr. Aaron estimated that total subsidies to homeowners in 1970 amounted to $10 billion without any qualification that they themselves paid a large part of the total. We are thus left to infer that the whole cost of the presumed subsidies was borne by renters.

In 1970 homeowners occupied 40 million housing units and renters occupied 23.5 million. If we accept Dr. Aaron's estimate and apparent meaning, the average renter paid an additional $426 in federal income taxes that year in order to subsidize 1.7 homeowners by an average of $251 each. This was bad enough but consider the case of people who own neither a home nor a bed—a typist, for example, living in a furnished efficiency apartment. We cannot learn the ratio of bed renters to bed owners from census data, but it is obviously quite small. If the reasoning we have encountered is sound, then we must conclude that a relatively few bed renters (if not them, who else?) are obliged to carry the whole burden of subsidizing a pampered class of bed owners.

If the arguments of those who hold that homeowners are subsidized are to be considered seriously, we need from the proponents of this view a precision that is missing in the testimony given to the Joint Economic Committee and in the more extensive treatment that their thesis has received in scholarly publications. Do they mean that the total cost of the presumed subsidies are borne only by those who do not benefit from them, or is the cost spread among all taxpayers? It is a vital point. If they refer only to "net subsidies"—that is, the cost that falls on renters after the cost that homeowners themselves bear has been cancelled out—there is still a case for debate, but the amount of the presumed subsidy is a minor fraction of what is implied in the claim.

The claim is misleading in another sense also, for it is implied that homeowners have been singled out for special treatment. This is not so. Deductions for interest and state and local taxes were provided for in 1913 in the first federal income tax law enacted after the Sixteenth Amendment, which authorized the tax. Such deductions have been approved in every federal income tax law since then. A review of the congressional hearings that led to the 1913 legislation does not disclose any intent to give a special advantage to homeowners. The deductions were not then viewed as a subsidy. That interpretation came much later.

The recent interpretation is broad enough to hold that any object bought on credit, or on which a sales tax is paid, or which can be assumed to carry a very elastic imputed rent, is in some degree subsidized. In theory, a case can be made for such interpretation but it is so broad and so loose that it strips the concept of subsidy of a practical and precise meaning. In a time when reliance upon subsidies has become widespread it is important to restore precision to the concept if we are to be able to exercise reasonably effective control over the proliferation of subsidies. A precise meaning of subsidy is also of basic importance to the recovery of cities. We can begin by thinking clearly about the alleged privileges given to homeowners.

A government subsidy, as we noted earlier in distinguishing it from a return to cities of local-origin funds, is an unearned and non-repayable transfer of economic resources by government from one party to another (and without the association of sentiment that characterizes a gift). With this practical definition as our starting point, we should then ask: Does the federal individual income tax, with its allowable deductions for interest and state and local taxes, cause a significant and consistent transfer of economic resources from renters to homeowners? Superficially, it would seem so. But let us look further.

First, let us quickly dispose of the idea that the total amount of deductions and untaxed imputed rent is a tax saving for homeowners and a cost to renters. Homeowners outnumber renters 5 to 3 and at least five-eighths of the cost of the deductions is thus borne by homeowners themselves in higher tax rates than would be necessary if there were no deductions. Actually, the homeowners' share is considerably larger than that. Mr. Downs's identification of homeowners as "the affluent" and of renters as "the poor" is much too simplistic, but it is unquestionably true that the average taxable income of homeowners, with or without the deductions, is higher than the average taxable income of renters. They pay taxes not only on a larger income but they pay also at higher rates. Thus, the "net subsidy" is significantly less than it would be if renters and homeowners had equivalent incomes.

But even this scaled-down "net subsidy" is an illusion, or mostly so. Renters, as well as homeowners, participate in the "benefits" that result from deduction of mortgage interest and property taxes in computation of the federal income tax. The difference is that renters' "benefits" show up in their rent bill instead of their tax bill.

It happens this way: Landlords, like owner-occupants of homes, are entitled to deduct the cost of interest and local and state taxes. In their case, these costs are a recognized business expense. Additionally, they may deduct a sum for depreciation and some maintenance expenses, which homeowners may not. Consequently, as a group, landlords have more tax advantages than do homeowners as a group. The germane question, then, is whether they can retain these advantages for themselves or, in fact, pass them on in a competitive market.

If a few landlords had a monopoly or near-monopoly on houses and apartments for rent, they could retain their deductions as a monopoly profit. In actual practice, however, the home rental business is competitive—indeed, "highly competitive," as Dr. Aaron said in another part of his testimony. Because landlords, in normal circumstances, must price their rents to meet the competition of other landlords, at least a large part of the tax deductions which they are entitled to take are perforce passed on to tenants. In general, profits from the rental of housing correspond to a moderate return on capital but are not excessive.

This, of course, is an oversimplified statement of a complex phenomenon. It ignores, as out of place in this brief discussion, the various technical qualifications which belong in a professional analysis, but broadly it can be said that as long as there is a significant market interaction between the supply of homes for rent and the supply for sale, the presumed subsidies for homeowners are washed out. When we look for hard evidence of a substantial and consistent transfer of economic resources from renters to homeowners it is not to be found except as it is a consequence of inflation. That, however, is another matter.

Curiously, Dr. Aaron had no trouble in recognizing the effect of a competitive market on rent in arguing in the same testimony for direct cash assistance as the preferred technique of a housing subsidy. His point was that a cash payment to needy tenants would result in an improvement of housing available to them, and he made it this way:

> Evidence suggests that property owners would respond to increased demand, particularly if goaded by the threat of vacancies, by raising rents in order to cover the improvements and better maintenance that tenants would be in a position to demand.

Dr. Aaron, the realistic economist, is a persuasive witness against Dr. Aaron, believer in the myth of a homeowners' subsidy.

The Fallacy of the Cross-Section Community

Several who testified to congressional committees or submitted policy papers argued that it should be a federal objective to promote resettlement in suburbs of some city residents who are poor or are members of ethnic minorities.

Some who proposed resettlement mentioned better access to employment as a reason. But when they did it was a minor purpose cited in the spirit of "if these reasons aren't enough, here's another." No one said anything remotely resembling "self-reliance is better than dependency, both for the individual and society." Some suburbs would be of no help at all in improving access to jobs that could be filled by persons without skills. It is no favor to the poor to provide them with good housing in a location that locks them into indefinite dependency.

In advice given to the Congress the most important needs of the poor were lost in pursuit of a concept of where people ought to live in order to conform to a government-determined mix of residents intended to reflect greater variety in their incomes and ethnic origins. "A broader cross-section of the population" is the phrase used in one paper to describe the result that should be established in suburbs by a national housing policy. The paper was prepared by William L. C. Wheaton, Dean of the School of Planning, University of California at Berkeley, and four associates. The comments which follow apply specifically to this paper and to one by Joel L. Fleishman, Professor of Political Science at Yale University. A major theme of Professor Fleishman was "redistribution of low-income and black families in the metropolitan areas." Both papers were prepared for the House Subcommittee on Housing.

Dean Wheaton and Professor Fleishman, though differing on details, proposed the same basic idea: A substantial number of poor people and members of recognized minorities should be dispersed from cities to suburbs. The dispersal would be governed by a metropolitan housing plan that would establish targets of low- and moderate-income housing units for most political jurisdictions in the metropolitan area. Some proportion of the housing units in each jurisdiction subject to a target would be reserved for persons who are members of ethnic minorities. Dean Wheaton spoke of "quantitative targets" in an "affirmative housing program."

He also contemplated an exemption of some political jurisdictions from quantitative targets for practical reasons and the same bow to practicality may be deduced from Professor Fleishman's paper. Dean Wheaton noted that some "high-income enclaves . . . do not appear to offer services needed by low-income families and have very high land prices." Thus, "little would be gained by attempting to change their policies to accommodate a broader cross-section of the population."

Professor Fleishman would require "federally subsidized developers" to meet minimum "quotas" for black residents in their new developments. He was clear that new housing developments should "include a fair share of the black and the poor" but was ambiguous with respect to requiring a "fair share" in older neighborhoods. In any event, he urged the federal government to establish "clear policy guidelines on the spatial distribution of population by race and class."

Metropolitan housing agencies would be created to prepare metropolitan housing plans and supervise their execution. The ultimate judge of an acceptable cross-section of population to be achieved in targeted communities would be the federal government. As a last resort, in Dean Wheaton's view, "Federally chartered corporations should be authorized and empowered to act to meet established net expectation housing targets."

Although the proposals of Dean Wheaton and Professor Fleishman are characterized by a confusion of purposes and an insensitivity to civil liberties, the proposals reflect a benign intent toward the people they would redistribute. It is clear that they genuinely wish to improve their lot. But they also have other concerns. Some middle-class concessions to the needs of the poor are essential, Professor Fleishman argued, or federal courts may strike down local zoning laws. "The whole structure of suburban zoning may collapse, and with it that fragile barrier against the chaos of unrestrained and unordered growth," he warned. "The goal for low-income suburban housing," he continued, "ought to be the achievement of some kind of balance in a suburban community which assures continued substantial dominance of upper-and middle- income families." An arrangement of this kind, of course, would not exclude blacks and poor people from election to political office if they had the support of the dominant element.

The intellectual error of Dean Wheaton and Professor Fleishman that leads to the idea of government-imposed cross-section communities is a confusion of purposes reflected in the constant coupling of "minorities" and "the poor" as if their housing wants were indistinguishable. Blacks will remain blacks, and one may hope that the time will come when Americans will be wholly indifferent to a person's race. The proper concern about poor people is exactly the opposite, namely, that they should cease to be poor.

For the concept of an imposed *cross-section community* let us substitute two other concepts and note the different consequences for a housing policy. One we will call the *nondiscrimination community* and the other the *opportunity community.* The distinction does not mean that the two are incompatible but it avoids a confusion of purposes.

The requirement for a nondiscrimination community is starkly simple, even if it has not yet been fulfilled universally. It is merely that no one shall be denied residence in any community because of race, religion, beliefs, or for any other reason for which a denial of residence would transgress the principle of equal rights under the Constitution. No community may be exempt for "practical reasons." Meeting the requirement for a nondiscrimination community does not present a housing problem to be corrected by a subsidy. If a civil right is infringed, redress is the responsibility of government agencies charged with the administration of justice.

The opportunity community must fulfill other and more specific requirements. The opportunity community, simply defined, is one which by its location and by the quality of its housing and community services offers those who live in it opportunities for self-reliance and, in the words of the 1949 Housing Act, a decent home and a suitable living environment.

Nothing is more common to the art of persuasion than citing a good example. Thus, one reads the papers of Dean Wheaton and Professor Fleishman and books and articles by others with similar content awaiting the moment when the author will say: "Here, in this community or in this city district, is the racial and income mix I am talking about. This is its history and this is my best guess concerning its future. It is a good model to be reproduced in other communities." One awaits an explanation of this kind in vain, wonders why no example is offered, and senses that perhaps an unflawed model does not exist. The community that is projected without example is as idealized as nymphs in a Botticelli painting.

A vagueness about what an acceptable cross-section community would be, however, was not reflected in doubts about how to achieve it. "Rule 3: Never use a stick when a carrot will do just as well," Professor Fleishman instructed the House Subcommittee in a metaphor adroitly chosen to convey an image of the objects as well as the means of behavior reform. The carrot is federal aid in sufficient volume to provide, in Dean Wheaton's phrase, "leverage value." He proposed a federal "bonus payment ranging upwards of 10% of the local city (suburban) budgets," in addition to grants covering all increased costs attributable to the new residents. Such support would need to be given, in Dean Wheaton's words, in a way that "does not require highly visible local government political or administrative action." High visibility—meaning actions understood by most voters—might cause the support to be rejected, he said.

The two agreed that a stick would be required in any event. According to Professor Fleishman:

> Finally, and probably most important, is the more coercive tactic of conditioning all federal support programs to suburban municipalities on their permitting the building of low-and-middle income housing. While such conditioning is clearly coercive, so is the urgency of the problem.

Dean Wheaton proposed federal actions tactfully described as "indirect incentives" which might be used to obtain local electoral majorities for a good cause. They have the delicacy of a Love-It-or-Leave-It bumper strip. Consider two:

The Post Office, GSA (General Services Administration),
Defense Department, and other agencies could be ordered to cut
back their expenditures in non-complying communities by 10% per
year of non-compliance, a prospect which would generate
interesting and novel incentives.

For one who teaches planning, Dean Wheaton left dangling some
tantalizing planning problems. How would the Postal Service, pursuant
to a federal order, cut back 10% of its expenditures in a non-complying
community? Return to senders 10% of all mail addressed to residents of
the community? Or no mail at all in February and the first week of
March?

And if at the end of a year there was still no compliance? Notch up the
rack another 10%.

A second *incentive:*

The Congress could secure relatively universal local government
action on behalf of equitable housing practices merely by abolishing
or substantially reducing the homeowners' deduction of local
property taxes and mortgage interest payments against the Federal
income tax where the home was located in a city lacking an
affirmative housing program. . . . The denial of the deduction and
notice to taxpayers could be handled by a standard computer
location code in Internal Revenue Service files.

American Civil Liberties Union, where are you?

HUD's Short-Order Study

HUD's entry in the array of advice to the Congress on what the
nation's housing policy should be is a slapdash study, *Housing in the
Seventies,* which reflects its off-the-cuff origin and its performance
under the pressure of an artificial deadline.

It came about in this manner. Early in 1973, as the Nixon
administration was beginning its second term in a provocative
confrontation with the Congress, George Romney, on the point of
retiring as Secretary of HUD, announced the suspension of all subsidized
housing programs. Appropriated funds not required for projects already
approved were impounded. Soon thereafter a White House spokesman
described the programs that Romney had administered for four years as
inequitable, wasteful, and ineffective.

A few days later, James T. Lynn, having been nominated to succeed Romney, appeared before the Senate Committee on Banking, Housing and Urban Affairs in a hearing on his qualifications. In reply to a question, he said that he agreed with the White House objection to the programs. Asked for evidence that the programs had failed, he said he would undertake a thorough reevaluation of all HUD programs and would do so with an open mind. The study got under way in March and its main portion was completed in October.

Later, Senator John Sparkman, then chairman of the Senate Committee, quoted on the Senate floor from a leaked memorandum written by the Deputy Assistant Secretary for Policy Development on the eve of the study's start. According to the memorandum, the official reasons for suspending the programs were "paper thin" and "highly subjective," and "preparation of the administration's position will have to begin from ground zero." In due course the study concluded that the administration had been right in the first place.

Various parts of the study are appropriate to a technical reference work but have little, if any, bearing on a potential revision of housing policy. Other parts, in the judgment of Henry B. Schecter of the Library of Congress, who prepared a detailed critique, are of questionable reliability, perhaps because of the haste with which the study was made. HUD is not without able civil servants who understand the nature of the nation's housing problem, but their knowledge is not reflected in this superficial and loosely reasoned study devoted to the thesis that there is not really a housing problem but only a shortage of income on the part of the poor—a problem that requires nothing more than a program of cash assistance. Senator Sparkman appraised the study aptly in these words:

> This analysis is simplistic, and its policy is seriously defective. The low-income housing problem of our country is not simply an income problem. . . . There just is not enough decent housing in this country to go around, even if every family were given enough money to buy it. Nor is it likely that a program of cash assistance would, in the absence of a production program, assure an adequate supply—at the right places and times—for many years to come.

The Canadian humorist, Stephen Leacock, once described a certain political leader as "a warrior who mounted his horse and rode off in all directions." Together, HUD and the Congress's chosen advisers on housing darted off in almost as many directions as Leacock's warrior, but not quite. Overlooking the direction that should be taken, they had nothing to say about how a housing policy could be used to help cities compete with their suburbs and not much that is useful about how urban residents who face a bleak future in the city might be helped to relocate outside it for a better opportunity. The fact that all missed the desirable direction for a national housing policy suggests that their common oversight, rather than being a mere coincidence, is rooted in an unduly pessimistic vision of American society.

9. WHAT VISION OF AMERICA SHOULD BE OUR GUIDE?

The Dimming of an Earlier Vision

A decent home and a suitable living environment for every American family a quarter of a century hence is not an impossible goal. "As soon as feasible" was the elastic but urgent deadline set in the Housing Act of 1949. In light of the major housing gains in the quarter of a century since the goal was proclaimed it is believable that we are now about half way there. But the prospect depends upon a very large improvement in the economic well-being of those amongst us who live in poverty or close to it. That number is still large and it includes many who do not receive welfare assistance.

Theoretically, enough of a subsidy could be provided to make a decent home available to all who lack one. We probably have the resources. Practically, a subsidy of such magnitude is unlikely. In four decades of a national housing policy, so large a subsidy has never had a chance. Something of a utopian outlook is required if one is to believe that indefinitely continuing subsidies comprise the main road to the goal of decent housing for all. The notion of a large class of Americans permanently dependent upon public assistance runs contrary to our national experience and to common sense. Of those who have acquired decent housing in the past quarter of a century, far more did so by escaping from poverty rather than by gaining access to subsidized housing.

During the Depression, even when a quarter of the labor force was unemployed, a permanently large welfare class was never anticipated. World War II and its early aftermath were years of intense uncertainty, of a kind that is difficult for a newer generation to understand, but they were also years of a bold vision of America's place in the world and of big goals in our domestic life. It is important to remember that the Housing Act of 1949 followed two other legislative landmarks and was consistent with the boldness expressed in them.

One was the Employment Act of 1946 which committed the federal government to pursue economic policies designed to foster the maximum level of self-reliance, namely, full employment (even though the specific phrase was not in the Act). The other was the Marshall Plan, which was designed to give temporary and diminishing subsidies to European nations ready to participate in their mutual recovery. Americans expecting to undertake these ambitious tasks were prepared also to proclaim a goal of universal decent housing.

The goal seemed possible because the nation was confident that the economy could be fashioned to enable most persons of working age to stand on their own feet. Self-reliance in an urban society can never be as easily achieved as in a frontier or an agricultural society. Its essence is work at a living wage, and for this individuals need work opportunities plus the mutual protection they obtain through trade unions and the legal protection of a minimum wage.

It is a paradox of our times that although the nation has recently experienced the longest sustained period of prosperity in our history, during which millions advanced to an economic well-being significantly above the poverty level, confidence in the potential of self-reliance for those who remain in poverty has surely never been lower. It is an astonishing contrast to the vision of a generation ago which gave rise to the Employment Act of 1946, the Marshall Plan and the Housing Act of 1949.

The reasons for the dimming of a vision will doubtless intrigue future historians for a long time to come. It is foolish to suppose that a single cause could be responsible, but without doubt a major force has been the unforeseen and wrenching effect of the tandem migrations on cities. The consequences were too sudden and too contradictory in their apparent meaning.

In any event, whatever the reasons the earlier vision lost its power, any public policy must fit some vision of American society. I shall attempt here to describe a worthy and believable one.

The Prevailing Pessimism about Self-Reliance for the Poor

A worthy goal of the American nation concerning those who require public assistance should be twofold: Those who unavoidably need it should receive it generously enough to be able to live in security and comfort, and at the same time the number who need assistance should be drastically reduced by significantly enlarging the opportunities for self-reliance.

This is not the goal motivating the plans for welfare reform under consideration by the U. S. Department of Health, Education and Welfare (HEW), the agency responsible for federal support of public assistance. The best available statement of plans under consideration is contained in *Toward an Effective Income Support System: Problems, Prospects and Choices,* published in 1974 by the Institute for Research on Poverty, affiliated with the University of Wisconsin. The greater part of the document consists of a comprehensive report prepared by senior staff officers of HEW and by consultants to the agency. It also contains an introduction by HEW's Assistant Secretary for Planning and Evaluation attesting to the high status of the report within the Department and a commentary by Irwin Garfinkel of the Institute staff.

The merits of the study are particularly evident when it is viewed alongside HUD's *Housing in the Seventies.* In contrast to the one-sided nature of the latter, the HEW report is a reasoned analysis of choices. It is not bedtime reading, however. The authors show a fondness for dressing simple ideas in crinoline skirts—*afford enough,* for example, is presented as *attain to a minimum adequate level of command over goods and services.* The text is also studded with technical terms which require an accompanying glossary. Nonetheless, a patient layman may obtain from this report a clear and balanced account of the variety of present welfare programs, the many proposed reforms and a weighing of the arguments for and against each.

As classified by legislative authority and administrative responsibility, the present welfare system has five principal parts: Aid to Families With Dependent Children (AFDC), food stamps, Medicaid, housing programs, and Supplementary Security Income. The last, which went into effect at the beginning of 1974, is a replacement of former state-administered aid to the aged, blind and disabled. It is a departure from other welfare programs in that it is administered directly by the federal government, although some states provide supplementary benefits.

A spirited debate about the programs has developed in the past decade or so. The debate is sharp within the Congress, within executive branch agencies, and among welfare experts, and it pertains to the extent to which the programs reach people in need, the adequacy of the benefits, inequities, inefficiencies, program costs, and work incentives as a means of reducing the number of beneficiaries. Everyone agrees that major reforms are needed. But what kind of reforms? The HEW report can describe choices but not a prospective consensus.

Broadly, two schools of thought have emerged which Garfinkel summarized as strategies of "incrementalism" and "basic overhaul." The advocates of step-by-step progress, or incrementalism, point to major gains in the past decade: the introduction of Medicare as a supplement to Social Security and the companion introduction of Medicaid, expansion of the food stamp program, and liberalized AFDC benefits. They emphasize political feasibility as a guide. The advocates of a radical overhaul point out that some poor families are not aided and that there are inequities and inconsistencies in the present system. They emphasize efficiency in administration as a central purpose of reform.

This latter group do not agree among themselves on what they would substitute for the present five categories of welfare assistance. There are, however, common features among the alternatives that would depart the furthest from present practice. They are that (1) a single consolidated system would replace present programs, except possibly with respect to some emergency needs, such as unusually high medical costs; (2) all assistance would be given in cash, replacing such in-kind aid as food stamps and housing subsidies; (3) the assistance would be universal below some specific income level, whether or not beneficiaries accepted available work. Between plans which incorporate these features and existing programs, numerous other changes in welfare objectives and practices have been proposed.

There are two principal variants of a single, universal, all-cash welfare system. One is commonly known as a negative income tax. It would be coupled to the conventional or "positive" income tax. Everyone of taxable age would file an income tax statement. Persons whose income after exemptions was above a specified level would pay a tax at graduated rates. Those whose adjusted income fell below such level would receive a payment from the government. It, too, would be at graduated rates. The smaller the income, the higher the payment, a proposal designed to bring every person or every family to a guaranteed minimum income.

The other variant would be an income allowance by the federal government to every person or every family according to its size. The proposed allowance has sometimes been called a "demogrant," sometimes a refundable tax credit. In principle, this might be a cash payment made to everybody, but most advocates of the plan propose that the allowance should be in the form of a tax credit. Cash would actually be paid only to persons whose income fell below a specific level after the tax had been computed. Depending upon revisions in the present income tax deductions and rates, the effect of a universal allowance could be the same as that of a negative income tax. The difference between them is technical rather than substantive.

The idea of a negative income tax or a universal income allowance exerts an appeal for a variety of reasons. The universal feature would assure full coverage of the working poor, many of whom do not benefit from AFDC or subsidized housing. Consolidation of all aid into one system would, in theory, reduce administrative costs. Even HUD's proposal for a housing allowance as a substitute for other housing subsidies would be scrapped in favor of a single cash payment. Food stamps, too, would be "cashed out," in the jargon of the profession, and submerged in the consolidated payment. The justification? Efficiency.

Going beyond greater efficiency in its intellectual appeal to many advocates of a negative income tax or universal allowance is the very simplicity of the concept. In the words of the HEW report, "Under a unified tax-and-transfer system, there would be no 'welfare population' that could be delineated and stigmatized." There would be merely a standard tax accounting with payments due or receivable. Again, according to the HEW report: "In a conceptual sense, the welfare principle might be the converse of the ability-to-pay principle—that is, people should receive transfer payments according to their ability-to-receive, their need."

One can hear the screech of chalk on a blackboard as a diagram is sketched. On one side is written *ability-to-pay* and beneath it an arrow points downward to *positive income tax.* On the opposite side is *ability-to-receive* and beneath it *negative income tax.* As neatly balanced as the scales of justice, the schematic idea intrigues people who seek elegance in solutions. Positive, negative, ability-to-pay, ability-to-receive: The idea can be put to rhythm and has the intellectual depth of slogan-think.

Practical problems arise as soon as an attempt is made to join the principle of universality with adequate payments to persons in need. If a universal payment is low enough so that able-bodied people of working age cannot substitute leisure for work, it will be too low to meet the needs of the blind, the elderly or those who for other reasons are unable to work. If the payment is high enough to meet *their* needs, the incentive to work by those who can do so would be diminished.

Advocates of a negative income tax or a universal allowance protest against "categorization," i.e., distinctions among persons eligible for public assistance, claiming that the categories create inequities. Inequities do exist. But treating everybody alike would create still greater inequities. Those who need help are not interchangeable units in an automated system but real people with widely varying needs and widely varying opportunities for self-help. Whatever reforms may be made in the welfare system, the preservation of distinctions is the essence of equity.

The Crippling Premise of a Permanently Large Welfare Class

What is truly dismaying about the plans for welfare reform under consideration within the executive branch of the government is not that some are superficial but that all—at least all reported by HEW as the responsible agency—assume that a large segment of the population must depend upon welfare indefinitely.

Nowhere in the HEW report is there a recognition that a resettlement of some city residents for better access to job opportunities would reduce their need for welfare. Nor is consideration given to an increase in the legal minimum wage in place of welfare for the working poor. The benefits which full employment would bring to unemployed workers, their families, and society as a whole are ignored. These omissions typify a great void.

It may be said in defense of the researchers, planners, and consultants who prepared the report that an examination of ways to reduce the number of people who need welfare was not their given responsibility and may not be within their competence; that, rather, they are technocrats whose job is to devise the best techniques for delivery of welfare assistance. It is a reasonable defense for them. It is not a defense for the Nixon administration that defined their task.

The failure of the HEW high command to couple welfare reform with increased opportunities for self-reliance is even more curious in light of the recommendation of a special task force which preceded the welfare reform study. This task force was appointed by Elliot L. Richardson when he was HEW Secretary and its report, published as a book under the title of *Work in America,* carries his foreword. The task force obviously took its broad-ranging assignment seriously. It commissioned 39 special papers for its use and, according to the published bibliography, drew also upon 648 books and articles as source material. With respect to work and welfare it said:

The key to reducing familial dependency on the government lies in the opportunity for the central provider to work full-time at a living wage. The provision of this opportunity should be the first goal of public policy.

The task force was content to leave its recommendation in this generalized form, and HEW, as we have seen, has not pursued it. Let us, then, try to do what HEW has not done: To examine specific steps that could be taken to reduce the need for welfare.

Irwin Garfinkel, in his gently critical commentary on the HEW welfare reform survey, provides a good point of departure. He wrote:

> There is a general consensus in society that able-bodied, non-aged males are expected to work. There is an equally broad consensus that the blind, aged and disabled are not expected to work. No such consensus exists on either side of the issue for able-bodied female heads of households.

I, myself, would include female heads of households while they are rearing children in the category of people who should not be expected to work. Concerning those from whom work is expected, society has two obligations. One is to allow them the chance to work. The other is to protect their right to a living wage.

Let us consider the problem of the working poor first because it is easier to handle than the problem of the unemployed. Advocates of a negative income tax or a universal allowance point to the automatic coverage of the working poor as a major virtue of their plans. But since these plans would, to an unknown degree, encourage some people not to work (only the most naive can believe otherwise, writes Garfinkel), other plans have been proposed which call for the government to make up the difference between the wage paid by an employer and a wage that is considered to be adequate. Some plans, such as the wage rate subsidy and the earnings subsidy, would pay the differential to employees. Another proposed plan would directly subsidize low-wage employers.

A simpler method is available: Raise the legal minimum wage to a point that a fully employed worker has no need for public alms. Some increase could be expected in the price of products which before had been made with underpaid labor. It would be better than a tax increase to serve the same end. An increase in the price of such products could make them more vulnerable to competition from imports made with underpaid labor. Then some trade protection is in order for the domestic product that meets fair labor standards. Benefits to consumers from cheap imports are fictitious if they are achieved by an increase in the number of workers' families who must rely upon welfare.

No one can say so with certainty, but an adequate minimum wage might quite possibly be the biggest step that could be taken to reduce the cost of Aid to Families With Dependent Children, the costliest of all

welfare programs. Such aid cannot be given if the family includes a father
who works more than 100 hours a month (a provision to hold down the
costs of an expensive program). If the father works one hour more, no
matter how low the pay, all welfare payments for the children must be
stopped.

So, by one of our stranger customs, some fathers must technically
abandon their children in order to protect them. As is well known, many
low-paid fathers either never wed or they quit living at home so that their
children may be eligible for welfare.

Suppose, however, that such fathers could earn enough to support a
family without public assistance. While some will be bums under any
circumstances, it is reasonable to believe that many of them, if they
earned enough, would reestablish a united family. Or marry the mother
of their children if they had not done so.

There are two basic ways to help the working poor. One alternative
places emphasis upon self-reliance under government protection against
wage exploitation. The other offers a government dole as a substitute for
self-reliance. *Dole* is an unfashionable word excluded from
contemporary speech by a topsy-turvy Victorian code which exalts short
and explicit words for functions of the body but veils the works of the
mind in delicate euphemisms or scholastic jargon. Thus, Prof. Milton
Friedman, a conservative, has given the dole that he favors the genteel
name of a negative income tax. Senator George McGovern, a liberal, has
proposed a universal income allowance or "demogrant." As proponents of
a dole as a substitute for self-reliance, they differ from each other like
peas from opposite ends of the same pod.

A passage from *English Social History* by the British historian, G. M.
Trevelyan, has a modern timeliness:

> The danger of sheer starvation with which the rural poor were
> faced in many districts owing to war prices and low wages, was
> averted by a remedy that brought much evil in its train. In May,
> 1795, the magistrates of Berkshire were summoned to meet at
> Speenhamland, a northern suburb of Newbury, for the expressed
> purpose of fixing and enforcing a minimum wage for the county in
> relation to the price of bread. . . . If it had been adopted for
> Berkshire and for all England, it might have diverted our modern
> social history into happier channels. . . . Unfortunately, the J. P.s
> who had come to Speenhamland for this good purpose were there
> persuaded not to enforce the raising of wages but to supplement
> wages out of the parish rates. . . .
>   This payment of rates in aid of wages relieved the large employing
> farmer from the necessity of giving a living wage to his workpeople,

and most unjustly forced the small independent parishioner to help
the big man, while at the same time it compelled the labourer to
become a pauper even when he was in full work. The moral effect
was devastating for all concerned. The large farmers were confirmed
in their selfish refusal to raise wages, the independent classes
staggered under the burden of the poor rate, while idleness and
crime increased among the pauperized labourers.

For parish rates we would say local taxes. J. P. s (an abbreviation for
Justices of the Peace) then had local legislative authority. The sequel,
when it came nearly forty years later, was described by Trevelyan in
these words:

> And on the labouring poor, in field and factory, fell the heavy
> weight of the New Poor Law of 1834, when outdoor relief was
> abolished . . . and the "workhouse test" was imposed on applicants
> for public alms. . . . It was a harsh remedy for a terrible disease: the
> Speenhamland policy of granting the poor-rate in aid of wages had
> pauperized even the employed workman and kept wages down;
> moreover it was now ruining the ratepayers. An operation was
> necessary to save society, but the knife was applied without
> anaesthetics.

The English experience might well be pondered by all who would
promote a dole, under whatever gilded name, in lieu of a living wage and
steady work. During a transitional period which will continue for some
years before work can be assured to all who want it, a large volume of
public assistance will continue to be needed. Major improvements
should be made in its delivery to ensure adequacy, reasonable equity,
and efficiency. Nonetheless, it will be better to put up with substantial
flaws in a system which is being reduced to a feasible minimum than to
accept a permanent dole in the belief that it is a reform.

The Goal of Full Employment

Assuring people who wish to work an opportunity to do so is a
more complex matter than establishing a living wage. There are several
kinds of unemployment which together comprise total unemployment at
any given time, and a remedy for one may have no effect on another. We
will have a better understanding of what is needed to overcome the kinds
of unemployment that are serious obstacles to the recovery of cities if we
note the nature of the principal kinds.

There is, first of all, a certain irreducible minimum of unemployment. *Full* employment, in its common definition, does not mean that everybody in the labor force is working at the same time. No matter how vigorous the national economy may be, some employers will experience a decline in sales because of a change in public taste, a shortage of materials, a failure to keep abreast of competitors or some other reason, and as a result some workers will be laid off. Or some workers will give up the job they have to seek a better one. Economists call this condition *frictional* unemployment. It could even be called *lubricating* unemployment because it serves the function of maintaining a necessary flexibility in the national economy. The irreducible minimum in normal circumstances is probably somewhere in the range of one and a half to two percent of the regular labor force, and as long as workers who are involuntarily unemployed are protected by unemployment insurance and have a good prospect of alternative work, this level of temporary unemployment is compatible with the national welfare.

On the other hand, *structural* unemployment is the most damaging of the several kinds to the income and morale of those who experience it, because it is the most enduring and the most frustrating. A classic instance of structural unemployment is that of people who live in inner cities but cannot find work within their travel range because many manufacturing plants have left. This variety is geographic in nature. Another variety, less well understood, is demographic and is represented by the many young people who, because of a major imbalance in age groups, comprise a surplus of beginners in the labor force and are therefore outside the normal structure of work in the national economy. Young people in inner cities who do not have the educational qualifications for white-collar work are vulnerable to both. In the long term, structural unemployment in both of these varieties does more damage to cities than any other kind short of the unemployment that a major depression would cause.

The kind of unemployment which makes the front pages and the evening news broadcasts is the fluctuating kind that historically has been called *cyclical.* In view of the dominant influence which government policy now has, for good or ill, on the production levels of the national economy, *managerial* unemployment would be a more appropriate name. The magnitude of this fluctuation in employment now depends primarily upon how well or how poorly the federal government manages tax revenues, government spending and the supply of money. The behavior of investors, which governed the old-style business cycle, has become subordinate to the managerial actions of the federal government.

Broadly, there are two schools of thought among economists about what kind of actions the government should take to sustain the national economy at a high level of production without incurring an intolerable degree of price inflation. One school, for which Professor Walter Heller, former chairman of the Council of Economic Advisers under Presidents Kennedy and Johnson, is the most prominent spokesman, places primary emphasis upon fiscal actions by the federal government. When economic activity lags, this school normally favors an increase in government spending and possibly tax cuts to encourage consumer spending or new investments by industry in productive facilities. Contrarily, if the economy becomes overheated, tax increases and a cutback in some types of government spending are favored. Advocates of fiscal actions to regulate the economy point out that such measures can be used selectively to stimulate particular sectors of the economy, such as housing, if its level of output is low.

The rival school, for which Professor Milton Friedman is the theorist and principal advocate, relies upon changes in the money supply (by the Federal Reserve Board) to stimulate or curtail economic activity. The monetarist school favors a stable rate of increase in the supply of money to keep pace with population growth and a consistent per capita increase in goods and services, and holds that if the rate of increase is wisely selected the economy will be maintained on an even keel by the normal play of supply and demand without need for special stimulants or restraints.

Because the monetarist school favors a hands-off role with respect to specific stimulants or restraints, it is frequently but mistakenly identified in the public mind with the classical theory of laissez faire. Actually, this school is as firmly committed as the fiscal, or Keynesian, school to a managerial role by the federal government in establishing the general level of production and employment in the national economy. The difference between them is a matter of method—or, more precisely, a major difference in emphasis, since government economic policy is always a mix of fiscal and monetary measures.

Both schools of economic thought rely unduly on macroeconomic policy—that is, broad, sweeping measures which affect the general level of economic activity but do not reduce the hard core of structural unemployment that remains in cities even when the economy is operating at a peak level. The monetarist school offers nothing to overcome the structural unemployment so burdensome to cities, but in practice the Keynesians have also been largely unresponsive to the special problems posed by the demographic and geographic varieties of structural unemployment. The solutions which are appropriate to these varieties lie outside the scope of macroeconomic policy.

Economists of both schools tend to define full employment as the highest level that can be achieved with the policies which they advocate—and these are policies which are not effectual in overcoming the high level of unemployment in inner cities. Thus, too complacently, a four-percent rate of unemployment has been equated in recent years with full employment. It is a rate which would have been thought excessive when the Employment Act of 1946 was adopted. In 1953, before the condition of a lopsided proportion of beginners in the labor force had developed and before the departure of factories from cities had become widespread, the unemployment rate was 2.9% and was not regarded at the time as an exceptional achievement. (Under war conditions, the rate was 1.0% in 1944.)

Actions which need to be taken to overcome structural unemployment in cities have already been described, and in this place need only to be briefly restated. As we observed in Chapter 5, if the proportion of workers under age twenty-five in the total labor force had been the same in 1974 as it was in 1950 and if other conditions had remained unchanged, there would have been a shortage in 1974 of 1.2 million workers instead of 5.6 million unemployed. The surplus of beginners, however, will come to an end in about a decade and a half; in the meantime young people who cannot now be absorbed in private employment should receive transitional work in useful public service through the proposed youth opportunity corps. The second measure to be taken is to enable many inner city residents to resettle outside large cities in places where jobs may be found that they can fill.

The measures to overcome managerial unemployment—that is, the fluctuating unemployment which results from mistakes made by the federal government in fiscal and monetary policies—are not within the scope of this book. A few observations about their general nature, however, are germane to the recovery of cities.

Recovery is probably not practical except in the framework of an expansive economy. Certainly it would be slowed by a high level of unemployment that continued very long. It would be slowed also or badly disrupted by a high rate of inflation of long duration. In short, it will be necessary to reduce both unemployment and inflation to low levels if the basic problems of cities are to be overcome.

The architects of government policies aimed at combatting the high rates of unemployment and inflation of the mid-seventies have been strongly influenced by a doctrine based on a phenomenon professionally called "the Phillips Curve." The curve depicts an apparent interaction between unemployment and inflation that may be observed when varying rates of the two are plotted as points on graph paper. The British economist, A. W. Phillips, found, in studies he made of the corresponding rates of unemployment and inflation at different times and in several countries, that one rose as the other fell. When unemployment was low, the rate of inflation increased in increments which were larger than any continuing reductions in the unemployment rate, and the relationship between the two was thus expressed in the form of a curve when plotted.

The Phillips Curve is the father of the Trade-Off Principle. We are bound, so we are told, to have some inflation and some unemployment. The problem is to decide upon a suitable mix of the two—a trade of so much of one for so much of the other. To hold inflation in rein, unemployment must grow. Put another way, in order that a society which cherishes self-reliance in principle may hold an erosion in the value of the dollar to a modest rate, several million able-bodied citizens must be denied the opportunity to be self-reliant. When they have exhausted their unemployment insurance, they will be given a dole. Unemployment thus created as an instrument of public policy deserves to be described as managerial unemployment. The earlier vision of America has sorely dimmed when some of the nation's most respected economists defend a planned denial of self-reliance with the confidence with which some of their illustrious forebears in the dismal profession once held child labor right and necessary.

Leon H. Keyserling, who was chairman of the White House Council of Economic Advisers in the latter years of the Truman administration, has been a persistent critic of both the Keynesian and monetarist schools. The policies of both, he says, have resulted in unnecessary unemployment and inflation. Often he was a lonely critic, but after more than twenty years the performance of the economy when he was Truman's principal economic adviser is being rediscovered, and his views are receiving wider attention. Although 1953 was the first year of the Eisenhower presidency, the performance of the economy reflected policies that Keyserling had promoted since 1947 when he was appointed to the first Council of Economic Advisers. The 2.9% unemployment rate that year was matched by an inflation rate of a mere 0.8%, measured by the consumer price index. In 1947 it had been 7.8%.

In *Full Employment Without Inflation,* published in 1975, Keyserling contends that policies to curtail production have been a major contributor to double-digit inflation. His argument is that in industries where dominant companies can "administer" prices—in contrast to lesser industries in which prices are still governed by competition—prices have been raised excessively to compensate for lower output; that high interest rates are themselves a major cause of inflation; that lower production, by reducing tax revenues, results in inflationary budget deficits; and that productivity and production rise or fall together (as shown consistently in Department of Labor data), instead of inversely.

In support of his claim that full employment is the best antidote to inflation, Keyserling has made a comparison of economic performance in

the Truman and later administrations. The accompanying table is
adapted from data published in *Full Employment Without Inflation,*
which in turn was derived from conventional government reports.

U.S. ECONOMIC PERFORMANCE IN FOUR PERIODS, 1947-1974

	1947-1953 (Truman)	1953-1961 (Eisenhower)	1961-1969 (Kennedy-Johnson)	1969-1974 (Nixon-Ford)
	%	%	%	%
Unemployment				
First year	3.9	2.9	6.7	3.5
Last year	2.9	6.7	3.5	5.6
Inflation				
First year	7.8	0.8	1.2	5.4
Last year	0.8	1.2	5.4	12.2
Economic growth rate (annual average in real terms)	4.9	2.4	4.8	2.5
	$ billion	$ billion	$ billion	$ billion
Budget surplus or deficit (annual average)	+2.4	−2.3	−6.4	−10.7

Note: In the above table the last year of one administration is shown as identical with the first
    year of the next in order to reflect the momentum of economic policies that a new admin-
    istration inherits. In 1975 the unemployment rate was 8.5%, inflation 8.6%, and economic
    growth 2.6%. The federal deficit was $75.1 billion, equal to $35.0 billion in 1953 dollars.

Table 21

Keyserling's comparison is a formidable challenge to defenders of the
trade-off policy. Even if it is conceded that in some circumstances or to
some degree unemployment and inflation ride a seesaw, defenders of the
trade-off theory are hard put to explain why the fulcrum of the seesaw
itself lifts both unemployment and inflation to the excessive rates
prevailing in 1975.

The Preservation of Liberty in an Urban Society

The latter half of the eighteenth century was a time when political
philosophy was often expressed with both clarity and eloquence. One of
the maxims that is our heritage from that age was voiced by John Philpot
Curran, member of the Irish Parliament and advocate of independence
from England. "Eternal vigilance is the price of liberty," are the

words by which he is remembered and they are as timely today as they ever were.

In our efforts to overcome baffling problems that arise from the complexity of an urban society we have placed a top-heavy concentration of authority in the federal government which with benign intent has become a creeping encroachment upon individual liberty. We have reached a point where the defense of liberty requires a selective pruning of the role of the federal government.

There should be no misunderstanding: In no sense is it intended that the pruning should weaken the responsibility which the federal government has assumed in the past four decades to promote the well-being of the American people. There should continue to be federal support for full employment, a decent home and a suitable living environment for every family, comprehensive social security for the elderly and the disabled, adequate health care, collective bargaining, and a rooting out of the handicaps which have been placed upon blacks and other minorities. Had these aims been more vigorously supported many of the bungling fix-it remedies attempted in recent years would have been avoided.

For these needs to be served it is not necessary that local governments be enfeebled wards of the federal government. Although there has been a shift of some federal aid from categorical grants to block grants and revenue sharing, the federal government retains immense powers to intervene arbitrarily, even impulsively, in affairs which could be determined locally with probably as much wisdom as would come from afar. In community affairs the powers of the federal government have grown well beyond the needs of any reasonable definition of sufficiency. It is this excess growth which should be pruned away.

Excessive authority presents a constant temptation to encroach upon individual liberties, not with malign intent, but in the interest of "the higher good." If local communities are wrong-headed, should not the federal government set them aright?

"I do not know the method of drawing an indictment against an whole people," exclaimed Edmund Burke in his unheeded plea to Parliament that the British Crown not press the actions that brought the American Colonies into rebellion. There are Americans today—not on a far-out fringe but respected enough to be invited to counsel the House of Representatives Subcommittee on Housing—who are prepared to indict and punish all residents of a local community until a majority abandon their wrong-headedness. Such punishments, for example, as a curtailment of mail delivery, which the Dean of the School of Planning at the University of California at Berkeley has suggested as a means of persuading laggard communities to remake themselves into the racial and income mix which would conform to a federally decreed target.

In the summer of 1973, twenty-three scholars and professional consultants gathered at the invitation of HUD for the Study Conference on Urban Research Strategies. As the conference report noted, "the annual budget for research in HUD has grown from $10 million in 1968 to $70 million in 1973." If each adult and child in the United States had contributed equally to HUD's research budget, the contribution that year would have been 33 cents per person. With a budget that large, the Assistant Secretary for Policy Development and Research sought outside counsel on how it should be spent.

The specific research recommendations need not concern us here. Rather, it is the concept of HUD's role and its bearing on local government and individual freedom that merit our attention. The opening sentences in a section on *Housing and Labor Markets* were these (italics have been added):

> HUD programs and policies are best conceived as efforts *to modify the actions of lower levels of government and private decision makers,* primarily households and firms, to achieve more desirable social outcomes. *Effective intervention* requires an understanding of both the factors that determine individual actions and of the way individual actions aggregate to produce collective outcomes.

Some intriguing assumptions underlie this bland language. HUD is assumed to be capable of determining "social outcomes" which will be "more desirable" than will be found in the intent of "lower levels of government and private decision makers." Knowing what is best, HUD should therefore intervene "to modify" their actions.

The "more desirable social outcomes" requiring HUD's intervention were not discussed because they were not yet known. They would be the product of research yet to be conducted. But not one of the assembled scholars appended a footnote of doubt. Was it not self-evident that the research they proposed would yield goals worthy of a HUD intervention to modify whatever might be conceived by persons of lesser rank?

No purpose is righteous enough to justify the abuses of power which reside in these good intentions. The power which federal agencies now have in relation to local governments—a power which invites the proposals we have noted—is dangerously excessive. A separation in federal payments to local governments between true subsidies and a return of revenues of local origin, so that the latter may be automatic, is justified by several reasons, but none is more compelling than the protection of individual liberty and a restoration of effective self-government at the local level.

A vision of America as a dole-oriented society which must be manipulated and coerced by a regime of technocrats is unworthy of our heritage and our potential. We have viewed ourselves better in the past and will surely do so again.

10. *MAKING THE TURN*

A Summing Up

Once more we define what we mean by the recovery of cities: a regained ability to compete with their suburbs as a place of residence and financial independence. The nature of what is required to achieve these things can be known. Coming to understand it has been the purpose of the preceding chapters, and now a brief summing up is in order. For large cities, at least, there is a need for four complementary policies, which together should make it possible to achieve full recovery in approximately two decades.

The first policy is:

> *Decayed and obsolete inner city districts should be transformed into neighborhoods attractive enough to compete with suburbs, especially for people who work in the central business district and other nearby places.*

We face a situation which is new in our national history. As long as there have been American cities there have been the tandem migrations of urban-start by the poor and of move-up by those leaving poverty, but now the urban-start migration has dwindled, probably never to resume strongly, and the grim inner cities are emptying. Mostly, this migration was composed of people who arrived in cities terribly poor. They found cheap housing in the oldest districts, and not far away they found work which enabled most of them or their children or their grandchildren to escape from poverty, and as they prospered they left the housing which only the poor would live in and moved to newer and better housing continually added at the advancing edge of cities and their suburbs.

For more than a century housing in American cities was overcrowded. The condition developed during the time when the powerful stream of immigrants exceeded the supply of new housing, and it continued during the Depression and World War II. Then rising incomes and a revolution in home financing gradually increased the supply of housing per capita despite the suddenly swollen flood of new arrivals from the countryside. As long as housing for the poor remained in acute short supply, it was necessary to preserve inner city residential districts primarily for people of low income.

That policy of every city, accepted as implicitly as if it were a natural law, is obsolete. The new situation—dramatized by widespread abandonment of inner city housing and a sharply accelerated loss of population by cities since the 1970 census count—offers cities a momentous opportunity to rebuild on land of dwindling use close to land of intensely concentrated employment. Reconstruction of inner cities as homes for people who work nearby is wholly logical, but only now is it becoming practical.

The second policy is:

Adequate opportunities for self-reliance should be created by means of an expansive national economy and by a specific effort to sustain and expedite the historic move-up migration of the city's poor away from the inner city. In particular, they should be assisted to obtain suitable housing and nearby work opportunities outside large cities.

Inner cities are emptying but not completely. Whereas they once offered opportunities for self-reliance, however harshly, residence in them today handicaps many of the unskilled in finding work. Those who remain find the historic move-up more difficult to make because manufacturing is moving from most large cities at a rate strong enough to cause a shrinkage in nearby blue-collar jobs.

A concentration of unemployment in inner cities has been gravely aggravated by an oversupply of beginners in the labor force. In time this will be corrected by the falling birth rate, but until then young people who are surplus to opportunities which can be offered in the private sector should be employed in useful public service, trained for self-reliance and prepared for resettlement outside of cities.

The third policy is:

The federal government should adopt a neutral stance toward
decentralization of functions in the metropolis, thereby ending its
tilt toward an increase in costly congestion at the hub.

Decentralization of trade and employment in the wake of dispersed
residence is not only a universal phenomenon but is a desirable one
because it tends to shorten journeys to work, allows an increase in urban
space per capita and at the same time moderates the cost of urban land.
Decentralization is not necessarily adverse to the recovery of cities, but it
can be if it is blindly resisted.

The fourth policy is:

Federal aid to cities should be made conditional upon effective
action by them to overcome their need for aid as early as may be
practical.

The present pattern of federal aid carries no requirement or incentive
to cause cities to become independent of outside aid. The pattern reflects
an implicit assumption that cities must be subsidized permanently.
Financial independence is not even a declared goal in any of the federal
laws which govern aid to cities, and at the present time it is not possible to
distinguish between subsidies and the return of revenues of local origin.

Big and Small Metropolises

In generalizing about cities, one inevitably slights their
differences. Any city differs from any other in details that are literally
countless. Given a truly great diversity—including, among other things,
the matter of size—is it realistic to propose policies which could apply to
all?

Let us begin by trying to establish a pattern of order among the 243
urban concentrations which are listed as Standard Metropolitan
Statistical Areas in the Census Bureau publication titled *1970 Census of*
Population and Housing: General Demographic Trends for
Metropolitan Areas, 1960 to 1970.

The definition of a metropolitan area is necessarily arbitrary.
According to the Census Bureau, such an area is "a county or group of
contiguous counties which contains at least one city of 50,000 inhabitants,
or 'twin cities' with a combined population of at least 50,000." But some
metropolitan areas, thus defined, are contiguous with others: those, for
example, of New York City, Newark, Jersey City and the New Jersey area
known as Paterson-Clifton-Passaic. Recognizing that all are within the

"metropolitan complex" of New York City, the Census Bureau has grouped them, plus two other New Jersey counties, into what it calls a "Standard Consolidated Area." The Bureau makes a similar consolidated area of Chicago and Gary-Hammond, and in New England it groups some SMSAs into "State Economic Areas"—Lowell and Lawrence-Haverill, for example, with Boston. The Bureau's classifiers deserve sympathy.

For the purposes of this book, I have made some changes in the Bureau's classifications. The Vernon study defined the New York City metropolitan area as consisting of 12 counties in New York, nine in New Jersey and one in Connecticut, which is larger than the Census Bureau grouping. I have done likewise. I have followed the usual unofficial practice of putting five counties (big ones) in the Los Angeles area and I have used the Bureau's optional combinations in New England and its grouping of Gary and Hammond with Chicago. By these consolidations, the number of metropolitan areas has been reduced to 224. After various trial-and-error classifications by size, I have found the four classifications shown in Table 22 to be the most useful for analyses of population growth and employment.

U.S. METROPOLITAN POPULATION BY SIZE OF METROPOLISES, 1970

Category	No. of Metro- polises	Population in 1970 (000)	Average growth rate 1960-70 %	Share of U.S. total population %
Over 2,000,000	12	62,626	14.4	30.8
750,000–2,000,000	28	31,888	24.1	15.7
250,000–750,000	79	31,986	13.8	15.7
Under 250,000	105	15,386	12.2	7.6
Total metropolitan	224	141,886	16.8	69.8
Non-metropolitan		61,349	6.1	30.2
U.S. total		203,235	13.3	100.0

Table 22

Because of the differences in definitions, the metropolitan population shown above is about 1.7 million greater than in the official classification. Both include some rural population because of the county unit of measurement and both are less than the total urban population (149.3 million), which includes residents of cities and towns as small as 2,500.

Metropolises range in size like suns in the universe. The unofficial metropolitan region of New York City held 17.8 million people in 1970, equal to the number in the Los Angeles and Chicago regions together or—harder to grasp—equal to all residents of the 105 metropolises with a population below 250,000, plus the 2.4 million in the St. Louis area. The city of New York alone holds more people than the combined number in 19 member countries of the United Nations, casting nearly one-seventh of its votes.

In the 12 biggest metropolises in 1970, each central city was surpassed in population by its suburbs. Taking these metropolises together, only 41% lived in central cities. On the other hand, among the 105 metropolises with fewer than 250,000 people, 54% lived in cities, and in two-thirds of the cases the central city held more people than its suburbs. Partly, this was because many of the smaller cities, especially in the South and West, are still able to annex some of their suburbs. Including three city-county mergers, annexation took place in more than half of the nation's metropolises during the sixties, but none in the largest.

ANNEXATIONS BY CENTRAL CITIES, 1960-1970

Size of metropolis	Number of metropolises	Number where annexations occurred
2,000,000 or more	12	0
750,000-2,000,000	28	17
250,000-750,000	79	37
Under 250,000	105	74
Total	224	128

Table 23

There is a common pattern among metropolises irrespective of size: The older districts—broadly, the inner cities—lose population to outer and newer areas. An inspection of published population data for all metropolises indicates that without the annexations which occurred, most of the affected cities either would have lost population or lost more heavily than they did. When annexations are taken into account, the supposed "flight" from cities to suburbs appears to have been no less in very small metropolises than in big ones, even in cases where the proportion of blacks is one or two percent.

Given the common pattern of an outward movement of population from poor housing in deteriorating old districts, it is tempting to say that the proposed recovery policies apply to all metropolises irrespective of size, but prudence suggests that a substantial distinction in this respect must be made between large and small metropolises. In small cities, particularly those which are heavily industrial in character such as Kenosha, employment is more dispersed than in large cities and the distance between home and workplace is not a factor of major importance. The policies of recovery do have a relevance to small cities, as we shall see when we examine how they may be applied, but there is less need for them.

I feel no hesitancy, however, in saying that the proposed policies are clearly needed in the case of the nine largest cities in our group of ten. Some are in much greater need than others and it may be expected that their recovery will take longer. Considering both burdens and resources, the recovery of New York City, Baltimore, St. Paul, and Fort Worth should be distinctly less difficult to achieve than the recovery of St. Louis, Detroit, and Minneapolis, but more difficult than that of Dallas and Los Angeles. Thus, among cities which in 1970 had a population range of about 300,000 to nearly 8,000,000 size is less important than other factors affecting recovery needs and prospects. A crude measure of the difficulty a city will have in recovering may be found in the relative magnitude of its population losses. We must look closely at their cumulative effects.

The inner city population losses that we have seen may be expected to become much larger. More whole cities will lose population. Thus far natural increase—the excess of births over deaths—has offset net losses from migration. But with the birth rate continuing to fall and the move to suburbs having already been made by many families of childbearing age, city population losses from *two* causes are a strong prospect: fewer births than deaths and fewer arrivals than departures. This did happen in Atlantic City in the sixties and was almost the case in a dozen other cities, including six in Pennsylvania: Pittsburgh, Altoona, Johnstown, Reading, Scranton, and Wilkes-Barre. As a guess, at least fifty metropolitan cities, including St. Louis, Detroit and Minneapolis, will lose population from natural decrease as well as from net migration in the eighties or nineties unless they transform failing residential districts into thriving new ones.

It is only when we make a breakdown between net migration and natural increase that we recognize the extent to which not only cities but many metropolises have been losing population from net migration. We should bear in mind four major facts concerning population changes revealed by the 1970 census.

One, population growth from natural increase fell from a high rate in the early sixties to a modest one by the end of the decade, but for the decade as a whole such growth was large—much larger than it seems likely to be in the seventies.

Two, in every one of the 224 metropolises (when account is taken of annexations) city population either fell or grew more slowly than the population of suburbs.

Three, there was a very big shift of population from some metropolises to others—so much so that two-fifths of all metropolises lost population from net migration and one tenth actually lost population even with the benefit of natural increase. In general, there was a shift from the Northeast to the Southwest and the Pacific Coast, but this overlooks changes within the regions. Thirteen small metropolises in Texas and two in California lost from net migration. The big gainers from net migration were concentrated mainly in the 750,000 to 2,000,000 category.

METROPOLISES WHICH LOST POPULATION FROM NET MIGRATION 1960-1970

Category	Number of metropolises	Number which lost from net migration	Number which actually lost population
Over 2,000,000	12	4	1
750,000-2,000,000	28	4	0
250,000-750,000	79	27	4
Under 250,000	105	56	17
Total	224	91	22

Table 24

The *fourth* important population change bears the most strongly on the recovery of cities. The greatest loss occurred in inner cities, especially from net migration. We cannot measure the change with the precision that is possible for the others, because the Census Bureau does not designate inner cities as such. But when the inner census tracts are examined, the population losses in unofficial inner cities are found to run as high as a third, as in St. Louis and Detroit. It is a reasonable speculation that inner city population losses were everywhere greater than in the whole city.

Creating Inner Cities Where People Wish to Live

As inner cities continue to empty, housing will be abandoned on a huge scale. A large part of the abandonment should be welcomed. Much inner city housing was of poor quality when built. With aging and neglect it has become unfit and should be removed. Unfortunately, some nearby housing which could be satisfactorily rehabilitated may also be lost as whole neighborhoods come to resemble ghost towns. Reconstruction of these districts could enable cities to regain the lead in the long losing competition with their suburbs.

What is new is not the idea but the magnitude of the opportunity. Some new housing for middle- and high-income residents near downtown may be found in almost any city. Some of luxury quality has been built in recent years. The great Watergate complex in Washington, near where the gas works once stood, is close enough to the White House that high officials who work there and live in the Watergate can walk to work if they choose. The ambitious Renaissance project in Detroit abuts downtown. When the Gateway Center apartments were built in downtown Minneapolis, the census tract in which they are located jumped from one of the lowest median income to the second highest in the city. In St. Paul there is Kellogg Square; in Los Angeles, Bunker Hill; in St. Louis, Mansion House; in Baltimore, Inner Harbor. In Kenosha, new apartments, although not of luxury quality, have been built between downtown and the high-cost Allendale district along the south lakeshore. And for many years luxury residential districts have lined the east and west sides of New York's Central Park. These, however, are small in relation to the new construction that is needed, and they are generally not well suited for families with growing children.

From one major reconstruction that is planned and two that are under way we may make some early assessments of possibilities and of mistakes to be avoided. A tentative design of a new "town-in-town" has been prepared by the St. Louis Plan Commission and a private developer is being sought. The first actual "town-in-town" is Cedar-Riverside in Minneapolis, and the first of its ten planned development stages has been completed by local private developers. The other under construction is Roosevelt Island in New York City. The location was known as Welfare Island when it housed city prisons, juvenile reform schools, asylums, and hospitals for the isolation of tuberculosis and smallpox patients. The developer is the New York State Urban Development Corporation, and both the project and the developer are in deep financial trouble.

The St. Louis project, if it materializes, will be the largest. It would occupy approximately two square miles, adjoining the central business district on the east and St. Louis University and its big medical-hospital complex on the west. The area was developed between 1850 and 1870 and many original residences survive. As recently as 1960 the area contained 28,000 residents but by the end of 1974 the number was about 12,000.

The tentative design projects a population of 50,000 in 18,500 housing units. The housing would be a mix of high-rise apartments, townhouses

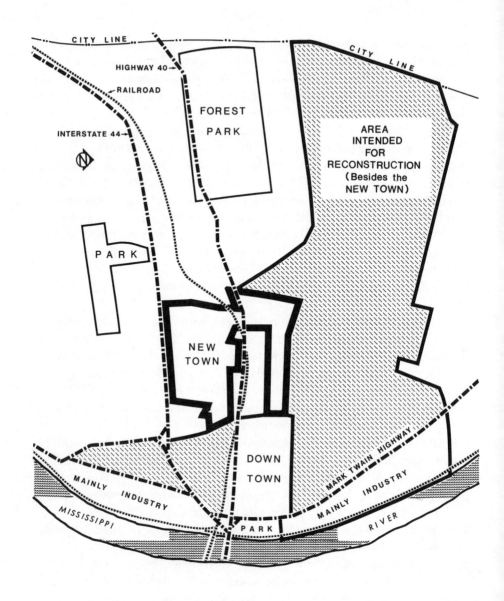

Figure 14. *Central Sector of St. Louis, Showing Proposed New Town-in-Town and Other Intended Inner City Reconstruction*

on terraced hillsides, and suburban-style single-family homes in cul-de-sacs bordering an artificial lake. A small number of old houses would be preserved. About 15% of the housing would be for low-income residents, with the remainder ranging from moderate- to high-income.

The area is divided by a valley which contains a fading industrial district with excess railway trackage. A major highway also intersects the area. The planners hope to retain some industry and to convert other parts of the old industrial district to residential use. They have not found a solution in the valley that is really satisfactory.

The proposed "town-in-town" is viewed by the City Plan Commission as the first stage of the reconstruction of a much bigger blighted area that reaches from the Mississippi River on the east to suburbs on the west. It is highly unlikely that the larger area can be populated at a density near that contemplated for the "town-in-town." Prediction of any city's population after redevelopment of the inner city would be risky, but a smaller population than in the past may often be the case.

Originally, Cedar-Riverside was planned for a density more than double that intended in St. Louis, but the developers now expect to reduce the goal. The housing and commercial centers will occupy 99 acres in a 340-acre triangle that contains the West Bank campus of the University of Minnesota, the campus of Augsburg College and two hospitals. The triangle is bounded by two highways and the Mississippi River. Downtown is a mile from the nearest apartment cluster.

In 1910 about 20,000 people—families of Scandinavian and Bohemian lumbermill and river boat workers—lived in the area's cheap single-family and duplex houses. By 1970 the population was down to 4,000. Some of the original houses had been razed to make way for college and hospital buildings. Cedar-Riverside's developers expect 25,000 people to be housed eventually in structures that will range from riverview townhouses to 40-story apartment buildings. To retain some of the character of the earlier period, Dania Hall is being refurbished as a community center, and some other historic buildings are being preserved.

Cedar-Riverside had a remarkably modest beginning. In 1962 Gloria M. Segal and her husband, a pathologist, were looking for a tax-shelter investment. Keith Heller, a young assistant to the dean of the university's school of business, advised them to invest in real estate. At first, they planned a small three-story apartment building. The idea grew. They began buying more old houses, brought in other investors, and created Cedar-Riverside Associates, Inc., with Heller as president and Mrs. Segal as vice-president. Donald A. Jacobson, the city's assistant coordinator and a professional engineer and planner, was enlisted as vice-president for planning and development. In 1971 they obtained a commitment from HUD for a $24 million new community loan guarantee which enabled them to obtain long-term loans at prime market rates. About half of the first 1,299 units carry HUD interest-rate subsidies. Rents in 1975 ranged from $50 to $550 per month. The project has survived thus far on a narrow financial base.

Roosevelt Island, the site of New York City's "town-in-town," is a two-mile sliver in the East River and is 800 feet at its widest. There are 147 acres, or less than a quarter of a square mile, on which the developer has planned 5,000 dwelling units. Rents are expected to range from $1,000 a month for a 4-bedroom apartment with a good view to as low as $80 (subsidized) for a studio apartment. Tenants of the high-cost apartments may behold the serried skyscrapers of midtown Manhattan. People who live less expensively on the east side may contemplate the Ravenswood power plant and the riverfront factories of Queens.

About 2,100 apartments are being built in the first stage at a cost of $180 million. The next stage has been halted. The rationale for the state-owned Urban Development Corporation was that it would show how to provide urban development that the state's cities could not or would not provide. It was empowered to override local governments. Lately, the trumpets that hailed it have been muted. Despite its broad powers, it has not produced new ideas, and the developments it undertook were improvidently managed. When it became evident in early 1975 that the agency would default in the payment of interest on its bonds, the state government agreed to pay instead. A new chief officer and board of directors were installed by the new governor, Hugh L. Carey, and the agency was told to finish construction under way, but not to start anything new.

Whether or not the island is a good location for a housing development is disputed by New Yorkers. The single bridge (other than the 59th Street Bridge which crosses the island at a level too high to serve it) leads only to Queens. A Swiss-designed aerial tramway will carry commuters to Manhattan. New York City is large enough to absorb the development readily, but it appears that a large continuing subsidy will be required.

The potential New Springtime of Cities should not be judged by these early swallows. None of the three developments was specifically planned to serve the recovery of cities, although each could fit suitably into a recovery plan. Cedar-Riverside is well situated in relation to its market and its size is probably not too large, but the market is a special one. Heavily oriented as the project is toward singles and childless couples (the projected ratio of dwelling units to occupants is an abnormally high 417 per 1,000), Cedar-Riverside seems better suited to compete with the city's own Calhoun-Isles (the "Mary Tyler Moore district") than with most suburbs.

Even so, it is probably in the city's best interest that it does compete with Calhoun-Isles, which was built to house families with children and does not now adequately serve that purpose. Had Cedar-Riverside existed earlier, Calhoun-Isles would no doubt have retained its original character. With that character restored, it should be able to compete with suburbs quite well.

As the chief development officer of the first and thus far the largest "town-in-town," Jacobson is entitled to speak with particular authority concerning the conditions essential to the success of such ventures. It is indispensable, he maintains, that they have a scale large enough to overcome the negative influences of the blighted setting in which they begin. We encounter again the principle of critical mass. It is surely of fundamental importance in reversing the decay of inner cities. If the redeveloped area is large enough, it can succeed and also trigger the start of others that eventually will result in a comprehensive rebuilding of the obsolete districts.

Although Cedar-Riverside offers the brightest prospect of reversing the city's disastrous loss of population, it has been delayed in its construction program by the actions of some environmental groups. Environmentalists in Minneapolis have a record of meritorious achievement; as we have seen, long before their present name had come into use, an earlier generation of conservationists prevented lakes in the Calhoun-Isles district from being drained for building sites. But today's environmentalists include a minority of hard-liners whose good intentions lead to extreme positions; some, although committed in principle to recycling waste materials, have sought to ban city scrapyards needed for the collection of scrap. A few years ago when student demonstrations were in vogue, some students discovered a romantic virtue in dilapidated houses and demonstrated against Cedar-Riverside for removing them. Since then some environmentalists have persistently sought to invoke national and state environmental protection laws to restrain the Cedar-Riverside development.

Cedar-Riverside, Roosevelt Island, and the St. Louis plan that lacks a developer are steps in the right direction, but each illustrates difficulties that cities must contend with if a sound idea is to be put into practice.

The purpose of the proposed reconstruction is to restore cities to competitiveness as a place of residence, and it should constantly have the center of the stage. Other purposes should stand on their own merits. However, there are parallel purposes which must be achieved if the neighborhoods are to be competitive. Probably none is more important than that the city's schools should be of as high quality as suburban schools. Obviously, no preference can or should be given to the schools that would be attended by the children of families residing in the new developments. Although the goal admittedly will be difficult to achieve, the effort should be made to make every city school competitive in quality with the best suburban schools. For this purpose a larger federal subsidy for city schools would be justified.

A subsidy for housing in the new developments would not be justified. The new residents will have a comfortable income and should pay their own way. They will have the advantage of living near their work and will save what could be a significant amount of money on commuting as the relative cost of transportation rises in the future.

One form of federal assistance to the reconstruction, however, would be justified. If the costs of site clearance were to be borne by developers, the housing could be priced out of the market. Since the new housing will increase city tax revenues, it would be justifiable for cities to assume the costs of site clearance, with the costs eventually to be recovered from taxes. The federal government should be prepared to provide insurance against default for city bonds issued for site clearance. Adequately financed by premiums, it would not be a subsidy.

The most important tax for this purpose—to be applied not only to site clearance but also to the provision of public amenities in the new neighborhoods—should be one created to recapture windfall profits resulting from a rise in land values attributable to the redevelopment. To the extent that other taxes may also be needed they should be, first, a special tax on property in the redeveloped district and only then a recourse to general taxes.

As thus visualized, the redevelopment of obsolescent city districts into neighborhoods that compete with suburbs can be self-sustaining projects that will not require a subsidy. Once this principle is accepted, it is easy to see that major changes should be made in the traditional housing policy. However, unlike the shrunken role sought by HUD, there should be a continuance of the three intertwined purposes of traditional policy—an increase and improvement in housing supply, slum clearance, and housing subsidies for the needy—but they should be rearranged in a new combination. The new combination would have these characteristics:

1. Slum clearance would be undertaken on a far larger scale than in the past—large enough to result in the removal of all unfit housing and other obsolete structures in two decades or so.

2. Slum clearance would also be divorced from the use of subsidies to construct new housing on the cleared sites. Instead, the new construction would be consistent with two basic principles: (a) Land now occupied by slums is potentially the most valuable residential real estate in the metropolis; (b) new residential construction in the city should reduce the need for transportation. If the new housing is designed and priced to

reflect these principles, a subsidy will not be needed, provided that arrangements are made to meet the abnormal costs of site clearance.

3. Reconstruction of obsolescent districts will unavoidably require a resettlement of people who still remain in housing to be replaced. Their relocation in decent housing will in frequent cases require a subsidy of some kind, even if they do not receive one now. The method of subsidy should be flexible, but in cases of this kind there is obvious merit in a cash allowance which would give those who are obliged to move the maximum freedom in choosing a new location.

4. The cash allowance method of subsidy is also suitable for use on a broader scale. (The proper objection to HUD's proposal is the attempt to make this method the only one.) In cities where there has been a heavy loss of population (as in St. Louis, Detroit and Minneapolis), a cash allowance may frequently be the most practical method to take advantage of city housing that is now underutilized.

5. In the new perspective a large role for subsidies in new construction is not foreseen, although a huge amount of new construction will be required in the redevelopment of inner cities and in the further growth of suburbs (because of population growth, suburbs will still expand even as rebuilt cities draw away many commuters). Eventually, most housing subsidies will become unnecessary in an economy characterized by full employment and low commercial interest rates consistent with little or no inflation. But for the foreseeable future some subsidized new construction will still be needed to provide more decent housing for the elderly and in locations where housing shortages persist.

Helping the Poor to Leave Cities

The purpose of a resettlement of inner city residents who cannot achieve self-reliance where they live now is to help them achieve it in a new location. Their race or surname and the race or surnames of their new neighbors are utterly irrelevant, and should find no place in a resettlement program.

The proportion of inner city residents who will fare better by relocating may be expected to vary widely from one city to another. Despite the deficiencies of city schools, many children from poor families qualify for white-collar jobs available in the city and obtain them. Although the number of blue-collar jobs shrinks in most cities, there are nonetheless openings from attrition which can still be filled by inner city residents. Others, especially those who do not acquire the education needed for white-collar jobs, should be assisted in leaving the city. One of the

COMPARATIVE GROWTH OF POPULATION AND MANUFACTURING JOBS, 40 LARGEST METROPOLISES AND THE REST OF THE NATION 1960-1970

	Increase in population %	Increase in manufacturing jobs %	Increase or decrease in manufacturing jobs per capita %
12 largest metropolises (2,000,000 or more)	14.4	4.4	−8.7
28 next largest metropolises (750,000-2,000,000)	24.1	26.0	1.6
Rest of the nation	9.9	20.0	9.2

Computations by the author from data of the Census Bureau and the Bureau of Labor Statistics

Table 25

12 LARGEST METROPOLISES: CHANGES IN POPULATION AND MANUFACTURING JOBS PER CAPITA, 1960-1970

Metropolis	Population in 1970 (000)	Change in population 1960-70 %	Change in manufacturing jobs per capita 1960-70 %
1 New York City	17,778	10.8	−13.4
2 Los Angeles	9,972	28.6	2.8
3 Chicago	7,612	12.0	− 1.1
4 Philadelphia	4,818	10.9	−10.6
5 Detroit	4,200	11.6	− 3.1
6. Boston	3,375	8.6	−15.4
7 San Francisco-Oakland	3,110	17.4	−12.1
8 Washington, D.C.	2,861	38.6	− 9.7
9 Pittsburgh	2,401	− 0.2	− 4.3
10 St. Louis	2,363	12.3	− 7.1
11 Baltimore	2,071	14.8	−14.3
12 Cleveland	2,064	8.1	− 3.1

Computation of manufacturing jobs per capita by the author from data of the Census Bureau and the Bureau of Labor Statistics

Table 26

reasons the Jobs Corps and many manpower training programs were disappointing is that those trained in them could not find work within travel range of their homes.

A resettlement program should not be restricted to any particular classification of work, but manufacturing is the most important because factory jobs are more numerous. As we have seen, there is no reason to believe that the departure of factories from cities can be arrested in the near future. An effective resettlement program, in fact, cannot be contained within metropolises, since there is a strong declining trend of manufacturing jobs on a per capita basis in the largest metropolises while they increase in smaller population centers. The strength of the trend is dramatically evident in the two accompanying tables.

The decline of manufacturing jobs per capita in the largest metropolises is so nearly universal that it seems unlikely that it is a short-term phenomenon. It must be supposed that many residents of the central cities of these areas—New York City, Boston, and San Francisco-Oakland, for example—will need to resettle in smaller and perhaps distant communities if they are to find steady work.

A resettlement program will encounter many difficulties. It can be carried out on a significant scale only in an expansive national economy which generates a high level of jobs. Even then it will require a long period of time to complete. Careful preparation will be indispensable. These considerations suggest that a resettlement program should be based in large degree (although not exclusively) on the proposed youth opportunity corps. Historically, most resettlements have been made by the adventuresome young who have not yet established roots of their own in a community. It would be desirable to recruit young people into the corps as soon as they leave school. There they would not only be engaged in transitional employment of a public service nature, but would receive vocational training to fit them for a regular job later. They should also receive citizenship training which they may have missed at home or at school and which would prepare them for resettlement.

The public agency which would have responsibility for recruiting and training members of the youth corps should also have responsibility for seeking to place in private employment all those who by aptitude, training, and conduct qualify for the agency's certification. Within the framework of a high level of employment in the national economy, it should become a normal event for all those certified to find regular employment somewhere after completing their service.

The youth corps could be operated by city or state governments or by the federal government; most desirable would be for the federal government to provide the funds as part of a recovery program, with operating responsibility decentralized to cities. Such arrangement would place the operating responsibility with the unit of government that has the most to gain from good performance. In finding jobs for certifiable youth corps members, the city government would be expected, pursuant to its aid agreement with the federal government, to search out possibilities within the city itself, within the metropolitan area, and outside the metropolis as necessary.

With a high national level of employment it may be expected that a job scarcity will develop in some communities while people remain unemployed in large cities. In such circumstances it may be practical for a city to provide resettlement assistance during a transitional period to help qualified residents of the city to relocate. If the assistance enables them to become self-reliant, part or all of it should be reimbursed by the federal government as a contribution to the city's recovery.

In the metropolises that were studied, housing priced for blue-collar workers was generally not available in adequate supply near new industrial districts in the metropolitan outskirts. This condition probably prevails in many other large metropolises. Where it does, cities should be enabled to sponsor the construction of nearby new housing to be made available to qualified city residents who wish to leave the city to become self-reliant. Federal housing subsidies that may be required in such circumstances should be transitional in nature.

The job placement function of the proposed youth corps should not be viewed as serving only large cities. Some small cities are losing jobs and will probably continue to do so. The youth corps should bring the youth of these communities the same benefits as intended in the big cities. Although it seems desirable to give city governments the operating responsibility in big cities, states should probably have it in smaller communities.

Decentralization: A Case for Federal Neutrality

It is understandable that city governments resist the decentralization of traditional city functions. When the city loses population, retail trade, and employment to suburbs, its tax base is narrowed. Expansion of the central business district as a source of new tax revenues seems to be the best way to compensate for the losses. Hence, planning departments are instructed to prepare ambitious schemes to bring more commuters to the hub on work days.

Nearly every large city has some plan for a major expansion of its central business district, such as the proposed Central City in Los Angeles, MetroCenter in Baltimore or Metro '85 in Minneapolis. Under present conditions, cities have a vested interest in congestion. More congestion, however, is a false remedy for a city's decline. The true needs of a city are to turn a host of commuters into residents and to be freed of its burden of poverty—the aims of the first two recovery policies. If these are pursued, cities can afford to take a relaxed view of decentralization.

As we saw in the chapter on "The Evolving Metropolis," rising incomes and the technologies that underlie modern urban settlements are both decentralizing forces, and so strong and universal are their effects that we should assume we are still in an early stage of the decentralization trend. The powerful decentralization process is not the result of a plan, which may be a reason why it is viewed unfavorably, not only by urban traditionalists, but also by people who have come to believe—even if they never quite say so—that nothing good about human settlements ever happens except in conformance to official plans. Anything else is supposed to be the product of "blind forces" leading to "chaos."

The "blind forces" doctrine underestimates the rationality in individual choices of housing which together produce a fairly sensible collective result. Even if a family moves every year, the housing choice is one of the more important family decisions that is made that year and consequently is the product of a rational analysis and a weighing of alternatives. The outward relocation of factories, department stores and business offices is usually the product of research, some of it quite sophisticated. It is a gross error to suppose that simply because decentralization is not centrally planned and directed it is in the grip of blind forces. On the contrary, it is the result of a multitude of rational individual decisions which are well enough considered to be remarkably similar in their outcome.

A recognition that the behavior of the market is a reasonably sensitive barometer of what people want and is therefore an essential instrument of a democracy is in no sense a rejection of planning. It simply means that planning should be an ally and not the foe or master of the market.

We may find confirmation in the experience of the planned new cities, Columbia and Reston, which have achieved a generally satisfactory marriage between planning and market demand. Their developers plan the basic uses of land, and have done quite well in establishing a good balance between residential, commercial and industrial districts, recreation areas and roads. At the same time, the developers have let market demand determine the housing that is built.

Neither cities nor other communities can be expected to be neutral about decentralization of residence, trade, and employment. Cities may continue to promote congestion although it is against their long-term interests. Some suburbs will seek to slow further residential development almost to a no-growth result. They may zone out most kinds of industry. But nearly all will welcome new office work centers. In short, local governments will respond to local interests.

More must be asked of the federal government, which is expected to serve the broadest domestic interest. It should not subsidize urban renewal in central business districts, or transportation which will increase the number of commuters. Decentralization is a desirable trend which does not need the assistance of the federal government, and should be free from its interference.

11. IS RECOVERY
REALLY POSSIBLE?

A Testing of Ourselves

If American cities do not recover, it will not be because the physical effort is too much for us. Relatively, the task calls for less material effort than was shown by any one of a dozen devastated cities of Europe in their rebound from the war. Or by the rebuilding of Hiroshima. At home we have the example of the postwar surge in housing construction; in 1970 every third home had been built in the preceding twenty years.

The nature of the political adaptation should not be beyond us. A new expansion of governmental powers is not needed; there would, instead, be a reduction. The enabling laws which would be required are few and almost prosaic compared to the legislation that was the underpinning of the New Deal. The idea is no bolder than the Marshall Plan.

If we muff the beckoning chance to restore our cities to health, it will be because of ourselves—something in our present view of things or in our spirit that sets us widely apart from the generations of Americans who came before us. I do not believe that we are that different, but nonetheless we ought to look behind some indications that we may be.

The confident vision of America we had thirty years ago has undeniably become dimmer and without another to take its place we are uncertain about goals. If, in Dr. Sternlieb's words, the reality has outrun the "scholarly apparatus," it has outrun the rest of us as well, but it is not because the world around us has become too complex for us to understand. Rather, we are held back by mood and habit.

The mood permeates our speech, which has grown shrill and extravagant. Words of the greatest intensity are preferred to those of moderation, and our speech, like our currency, has been depreciated. George Orwell's foreboding that a loss of integrity in language would cripple the politics of a democracy finds a melancholy confirmation in our habits of speech about our urban problems. Even so basic a need as recognition of the facts has been made difficult by language litterbugs who clutter the public discourse with inflamed metaphors and clichés of slovenly thought. Sober journalists and scholars are not immune to the contagious habit.

Like the dimming of a vision, a loss of historical perspective characterizes our peevish mood. Leaders of the American Historical Association, deploring a decline in the teaching of history, have coined the graceless word, *presentism,* as a name for the trend, illustrating in their own insensitivity to the teaching and use of English the validity of their distress about the fragmentation of learning. Whatever name may be given to the trend, a lost sense of the past diminishes our always puny capacity to conceive the future.

Of central importance in our prevailing mood is an unresolved confusion about the potential of self-reliance in an urban society. The confusion has grown worse as we have become more urban. It has produced, as we have seen, a strange convergence of some conservatives and some liberals in support of proposals which undervalue self-reliance—a government dole, for example, in preference to an adequate minimum wage. Others are untroubled by policies which deliberately deny self-reliance to some workers as a way to control inflation. Perhaps the greatest damage to the practice of self-reliance arises from the casualness with which we now reach for a subsidy to close a gap between costs and income. A clear understanding of subsidies (and of payments which are *not* subsidies) is fundamental to the recovery of cities.

The Tendency of Subsidies to Become Permanent

The Joint Economic Committee of the Congress, worried by the trend toward even more subsidies, has had its staff make estimates of the mounting costs to taxpayers. A recent staff study, estimated that private sector subsidies rose by 50% between the fiscal years 1970 and 1975. While some of the reasoning is in error—the study, for example, accepts uncritically the fallacy of a homeowners' subsidy—correction of the error does not change the finding that an enormous jump occurred in just five years.

People who carry the tattered banners of conservative and liberal usually disagree about the subsidies that they want, but both groups have contributed heavily to the spread of the practice. Commonly, the political concern about subsidies is simply the question of who will benefit. Affluent suburban commuters may grow indignant about a subsidy to ranchers which raises the price of beef but feel no embarrassment in telling their congressman that an operating subsidy for mass transit is one of the most important issues before the nation.

There is an essential place for subsidies in our economy. Cities will need help for another twenty years or so and there are other subsidies—the delivery of mail comes to mind—which are not hard to justify. The many kinds of subsidies and the conditions under which they may be justified are complex questions which are largely outside our specific interest, but so far as cities are concerned a simple statement suffices. The purpose of the subsidy should be to cure a condition and not to perpetuate it. Yet, once a subsidy is established, there is a danger that it may become unshakeably permanent.

I believe I can make my point with an anecdote. When I was head of the Marshall Plan mission to Greece a quarter of a century ago, a Greek organization asked me to support its plea to the Greek Government for a cost-of-living adjustment in pensions received by its members. The organization called itself the Society of Descendants of the Former Water Carriers of Piraeus and so intriguing was its name that I inquired about its history, which was this. Until about the turn of the century households in Piraeus, the port of Athens, were supplied with water by men who delivered it from door to door in buckets. Then a modern water system was installed and the water carriers became technologically unemployed. With commendable humaneness, the government gave them termination pay in weekly installments.

Jobs, however, were scarce, and after several renewals the termination pay was formally converted into lifetime pensions. But then a problem of justice arose which might have been the inspiration for Professor John Rawls and others who hold that justice requires, not equality of opportunity, but equality of results. The ages and health of the former water carriers varied and some died sooner than others. The heirs of some complained that families of the deceased, already at a disadvantage, were deprived of pensions paid to the fortunate living. The Greek Parliament's member from Piraeus quickly grasped the unfairness of the situation and persuaded his colleagues to amend the special pension law to provide that rights to the pension would be inherited for his own lifetime by the beneficiary's eldest son, who by custom was expected to help other members of the family. With frequent adjustments for inflation, this was the status a half century later of pensions that began modestly as termination pay.

Mayors of large American cities, upon taking the oath of office, automatically become honorary members of the Society of Descendants of the Former Water Carriers of Piraeus. They would be derelict of duty if they did not use their membership card to press for improvements in the permanent pension that without deliberate intent we have established for our cities.

Yet, even within a tolerance for an excessive reliance on subsidies, I believe most people will recoil from the idea of a *permanent* subsidy for cities. A prudent assessment must begin with the obvious fact that their political influence is falling as their share of the national population shrinks. Added to this is the fact that they are losing the sympathy of friends upon whom they are increasingly dependent.

The New York City financial crisis had uncommon aspects: It was universally agreed, for example, that in the past the city had been improvident in its borrowing, and there was no doubt a basis for the belief of many New Yorkers that elsewhere in the nation many people were not upset to see the nation's biggest city receive a come-uppance. But other cities, even without a financial crisis, are also likely to encounter growing impatience with their need for help. Contributing to that impatience is the continued plea for more money without a corresponding assurance that the need for help is temporary. It will be good politics for mayors to generate confidence in the recovery of cities; bad politics to act as if the idea were imposed upon them. A part of a mayor's job is to lead parades.

I have dwelt upon the prevailing national mood as an obstacle to the recovery of cities because by its nature it could cause failure or even prevent the idea from being tried. No aspect of the mood is more puzzling than how far we have moved from the confident vision of America that we had a generation ago. Of another faltering, Burckhardt has written:

"The movements of the human spirit, its sudden flashes, its expansions and its pauses, must for ever remain a mystery to our eyes, since we can know this or that of the forces at work in it, but never all of them together." (*The Civilization of the Renaissance in Italy*).

A *pause* of the American spirit—this, at least; how long it may last and how damaging to our will it may prove to be, we cannot yet know. But if we cannot know all the forces which sway the spirit, we can nonetheless believe that a turn toward recovery by our failing cities would again quicken the spirit. Even the prospect of recovery, if the way seems clear, can itself help to crystalize the will.

So let us turn to problems of a more technical nature.

Ending the Federal Guardianship

Because the proposal made in this book about federal payments to cities is a drastic departure from present practice, let us go over it once more in order to avoid any possible confusion. Federal grants to cities are now of three kinds: categorical grants, block grants (a consolidation of some former categorical grants), and revenue sharing. A categorical grant may be used only for a specified purpose. A block grant allows for discretionary use among several purposes, while no restriction is placed on the use of funds from revenue sharing. Obviously, the latter is popular with local governments. "The best thing since ice cream," Mayor Moon Landrieu of New Orleans has said of it.

I propose a distinction of an entirely different kind. I start with the fact that a large part (though not necessarily all) of the money which a local government receives from the federal government has merely made a round trip. Only a short time earlier it was paid to the federal government as income taxes by people who live in the community to which it is returned.

This has been going on for over forty years and all that time we have thought that the earth was flat, so to speak. The flat-earth view holds that money which the federal government takes from a local community and returns to it is *federal* money. But let us think of the earth as round. The round-earth view holds that money collected from and returned to the same community is actually *local* revenue which has been fitted into the federal individual income tax as a convenient way of collecting it.

The fit is a poor one since the amount that comes back is irregular, uncertain and subject to negotiation with a half dozen federal agencies. Nonetheless, in the round-earth view, it is still local money. To obtain a good fit, eliminating the losses and frustrations which now occur in the local revenue's homeward journey, I propose that the federal government remit to each local community a uniform percentage of the federal individual income tax paid by its residents, to be shared among overlapping local governments as each state government may decide (and subject to an upper limit to be described later).

In adjusting our perception to a round-earth view, it helps, as was said earlier, to think of the returned revenues of local origin as an implicit local income tax. As a future policy formalized in legislation, a better name will be the Universal Local Income Tax. Think of it not as an additional tax, which it is not, but as a spin-off that, as a convenience to taxpayers, rides piggyback on the income tax which the federal government collects for national purposes. In practice, the individual income tax would have two parts—one for local, one for national purposes—and both would be collected together.

This tax spun off for exclusively local use would be set at a level that would be all the "federal payment" most local governments would need. But several hundred, including (by my estimate) all large cities, must have outside help and would therefore receive, in addition, a subsidy based on each city's need (which would diminish and disappear as the city recovers).

This is the substitute that I propose for the present system of federal grants. It would bring a revolution in federal-local relationships. Financial independence would be restored promptly to all local governments that could meet their costs from conventional revenues plus the Universal Local Income Tax. For those that must also have a subsidy, the restoration would take place progressively.

Local governments should like the idea because the remitted local income tax would be larger than revenue sharing and would have the same unrestricted use. It should appeal to people who are attracted to the graduated income tax and would like all states to have one because of its progressive nature. Indeed, one can foresee proposals being offered to make the federally collected local income tax higher, in order to replace regressive sales taxes and possibly to reduce the burden of the property tax on residences.

However, some who may favor the idea of a local income tax in principle will balk at it if local governments are free to use the revenues in accordance with the apparent wishes of their electorate. They hold that local governments will not do the right things unless important parts of their budgets are under the control of federal agencies, which exercise that control by making or not making categorical grants and by agency guidelines that govern the use of a grant.

There are clearly many people who believe that without a powerful and pervasive federal guardianship, local governments may fail to perform certain functions which in themselves may or may not be wise ones. Can they be depended upon to keep the air clean, enforce suitable health standards, provide manpower training for unemployed youth, build a subway, combat crime, or house the poor? These individuals feel intensely about one or more such purposes and are prepared to sacrifice a great deal of home rule to achieve them.

Their concerns deserve to be treated with respect and sympathy. We can do so by first considering if the low esteem for local government implicit in their thinking is justified, and then by looking at the comparative merits of home rule and the federal guardianship in particular cases.

The case for freeing local governments from financial dependency does not rest upon a supposed return to a Golden Age. Local government has never had one. Towns and small cities in which a personal relationship between voters and officials is possible generally have the kind of local government that is acceptable to a majority of the citizens who vote. In many communities the number who could vote was restricted until recently by a shameful denial of voting rights to blacks, but that practice has been largely overcome. A big increase in the number of black local officials is evidence of the change.

The historical record of local government in big cities is generally not a cause for national pride, although there are exceptions. Among them, the record of honest and efficient administration, initiative, fiscal responsibility, and genuine rapport between city hall and neighborhoods which prevailed in Milwaukee during the twenty years that Dan Hoan was mayor probably has not been excelled anywhere. But for a long period misrule and scandal were as common as good administration, and in the early years of this century there was some merit in the reluctance of state legislatures to grant cities the larger degree of home rule that reformers sought. (There was also much corruption in many state legislatures.)

If there was never a Golden Age, there has been, however, a great improvement in the quality of big city government in recent decades. Instances of corruption are not unknown, but on this nasty issue the statistical record of contemporary mayors compares favorably with that of governors, congressmen, and judges. Nor is honesty the main measure of improvement. Professionalism in administration has blossomed in the years the condition of cities has worsened (there is no evident relationship between one event and the other). Moreover, in at least the ten cities which were studied for this book, a real sensitivity for the concerns of all citizens is unmistakably evident at city halls. On the record of the last several decades most local governments may be expected to use their recovered powers honestly, fairly, and competently. This deserves to be said despite some financial mismanagement (which is not confined to local governments).

In weighing the merits of the guardianship it should be recognized that the federal government has played a valuable role in spurring local governments to a broader view of their responsibilities. Categorical grants, on their plus side, have been useful in pinpointing some neglected areas of public service. But with these things having been largely accomplished, it is time to ask: How much of the guardianship is still needed?

The purposes that the guardianship is expected to serve are a miscellaneous lot. There is one set, including such goals as clean air and reduction of crime, which, although they do not affect all citizens equally, are nonetheless broadly based. Because they are purposes of general concern, they should be financed by conventional revenues and the Universal Local Income Tax.

Financial assistance to mass transit, if local electorates wish it to be subsidized at all, should be switched from categorical grants to the Universal Local Income Tax. The magnitude of sums involved is a special reason to bring decisions under home rule. Under the Mass Transportation Act of 1974, the federal government may pay 80% of the new capital costs of mass transit and 50% of the operating costs. If the same amount of money represented by these potential grants were available to a local government without being earmarked (that is, as a part of the Universal Local Income Tax), more important uses for it might be found. This is precisely why decisions on its use should rest exclusively with officials directly responsible to local voters. When such large sums must either be used for an earmarked purpose or lost altogether, local officials may be tempted to spend more on new facilities than is needed and to be lax about operating costs.

The strongest case for a partial supervision of local governments through financial assistance by the federal government exists with respects to the needs of the poor. Welfare, housing, and the preparation of people for self-reliance are the purposes that meet this test. They are also purposes which are intimately related to the recovery of cities. Where the sums they require are relatively modest, local governments should bear the cost with the assistance, of course, of the Universal Local Income Tax. But in those big cities and other communities where the needs of the poor are large enough to require external aid, it would be appropriate to include the financing of these needs, or most of it, within the transitional subsidy.

We come, then, to this principle: Purposes of general interest now financed through categorical or block grants and not specifically germane to the recovery of cities should be financed through the Universal Local Income Tax and through conventional local revenues in such sums as each local government deems fit. The federal guardianship for these purposes would be discontinued in all communities. Costs of government which are caused by poverty, if relatively large, would be financed by subsidies paid to a small proportion of local governments according to their need.

While subsidies continue, a federal control over their amount and use would be maintained.

There is another aspect of categorical grants which thus far has not been considered. In the case of many of them, their potential withholding by the federal government is a means to ensure the protection of rights of minorities. The same protection, however, can be given less awkwardly by agencies of the federal government specifically qualified for the administration of justice.

Standards for Splitting a Tax into Two Parts

Thus far it has been assumed that a universal local income tax is workable. Is it? The problems that will be encountered cover a broad range.

Mechanical practicality is the obvious first test. What is required is a capacity of the Internal Revenue Service to segregate individual income tax payments by designated local political jurisdictions. This is now commonly done by the tax offices of states that collect a local income tax with the state income tax (as in Maryland). There is no major obstacle that would prevent the IRS from remitting to local governments, directly or through state governments, their correct share of the federal income taxes paid by persons residing within their jurisdiction.

Apportionment of such revenues between municipal and county governments will be a problem except in the relatively few instances of cities like Baltimore and St. Louis that have the status of counties. The distribution of governmental functions between municipalities and the counties in which they are located varies so widely that no national formula is practical. The enabling act should therefore provide that the basis for apportionment between municipal and county governments would be determined in each state by that state's government. The states should also have authority to direct some of the revenue to regional special-purpose districts, such as those that may have responsibility for transportation or sewage disposal on a metropolitan basis, but the federal government should not impose a requirement of this kind. The most practical method of distributing revenues from the Universal Local Income Tax may be in two stages: from the IRS to state governments and from the latter to local governments.

The most difficult problem, without doubt, will be that of generating a suitable total volume of the Universal Local Income Tax—not too much, not too little. Since the volume will correspond to an x percent of the federal individual income tax, it will unavoidably be affected by the state of the national economy. But then so are conventional local revenues and the volume of federal grants; an uncertainty about the yield from taxes will not be a new experience. Generally, it should be possible to adjust to the swings through reserves and short-term borrowing.

Arriving at an appropriate x percent will be more difficult, partly because it will be a new experience. If it is high enough to restore financial independence to the great majority of local governments, and thus to limit the provision of subsidies to communities which truly need them, the yield in affluent communities may be large enough to allow reductions in conventional local taxes. In some wealthy suburbs the amount generated by the Universal Local Income Tax could be greater than the cost of local government.

To avoid the oddity of a return to a local government greater than its normal costs, some limit should be established, such as a ratio to conventional revenues. When more data are at hand—data which are beyond the resources of an individual author but not of the House Ways and Means Committee—other refinements can be considered. The main objective, however, should be to get a Model T into operation.

Why should the Universal Local Income Tax be related only to the federal *individual* income tax? Gross injustices would result from any participation by local governments in taxes paid by corporations that operate on a national or regional basis but pay taxes from a particular city in which they have their headquarters. A good reason to ignore excise taxes is that it would be too difficult to determine their origin by locality.

Purists are entitled to make their point that a *universal* local income tax is something of a contradiction in terms and that if local governments wish to benefit from a local income tax, they should levy and collect it themselves. In time this may be the outcome. It is not now a practical choice. At this stage in our history we may usefully take our cue from Edmund Randolph's plea at the gathering in Philadelphia in 1787 which was distinguished for its compromises. Let the role of the federal government, he urged, be "sufficient to the general happiness." Using the federal government as a tax collector for local governments is a reasonable price to pay for restoring home rule and eliminating that part of the federal role which goes beyond sufficiency.

Holding Cities Accountable for Their Recovery

Some degree of federal guardianship for cities that require a subsidy is inevitable while the subsidy lasts. Despite the spread of subsidies in recent years to a much broader range of public services and private activities than we have known before, it is unthinkable that the

Congress will vote aid to cities without requiring some federal supervision of its use. Where subsidies are needed, our course should lie between too much federal control and not enough, and in setting this course our concern should be the purpose of the guardianship.

From time to time someone proposes a "Marshall Plan for cities." The proposal is always highly generalized without any suggestion of how it might operate. The intent seems to be a call for more money for cities, which misses the two valid points in the analogy. Because the recurrent proposal reflects a misunderstanding, I trust that I may be forgiven for drawing upon my experience in the Marshall Plan. Besides directing the operation in Greece, I was at other times assistant administrator for program and resident supervisor of all operations in Europe. In the course of my study of American cities I have come to the firm conclusion that if the money that they receive from the federal government were more wisely spent, they would soon need less of it—which brings us to the valid points in the Marshall Plan analogy.

The purpose of the Marshall Plan was the earliest feasible recovery of the nations that needed our help. Upon recovery aid ended. The second thing in the Marshall Plan experience that is relevant today is the relationship that prevailed between the American government and the governments of the nations that were aided. American aid was contingent upon the development by the European nations of effective recovery programs and upon demonstrable progress, but detailed intervention of the kind that characterizes categorical grants was avoided. For this reason, a large American bureaucracy was also avoided. I estimated once that, apart from persons engaged in technical assistance, one quarter of the agency's working hours were devoted to preparing information for the Congress. I cite this, not to suggest that the information which the Congress requested was excessive, which it was not, but as evidence that we had a lean agency.

In contrast to the Marshall Plan experience, the federal relationship with local governments lacks a central purpose other than permanent aid, severely cramps local initiative, and multiplies employment in the federal supervisory agencies far beyond true need. It is difficult to discover a benefit from the HUD budget for research and policy development that is equal to the construction costs of 2,800 homes at $25,000 each.

Cities should be held accountable for making demonstrable progress toward recovery. To be accountable they need freedom to develop and pursue individualized programs adapted to conditions as diverse as those of New York City and Kenosha or Dallas and St. Louis. The Universal Local Income Tax would free them from federal supervision of local affairs that are not specifically related to recovery, and in the recovery effort itself there should be a large measure of discretion about how to achieve agreed targets.

But with respect to the matter that counts—satisfactory progress toward making the city again competitive with its suburbs as a place of residence and toward relocating able-bodied poor people for better opportunity—the federal government should be a hard taskmaster. It should insist upon difficult targets, and if the local effort is poor, the federal government should be prepared as a last resort to cut the amount of aid until corrective action is taken. Once the federal government has established broad public confidence in its own role, not many local officials will wish to risk a public explanation of why federal aid was cut.

A Sense of Proportion Regained

The writing of this book has been one layman's attempt to understand what brought American cities to their present distress, to visualize what their recovery would be like, and to propose policies of recovery which will be adequate and politically practical.

My search has reaffirmed in a dozen ways my conviction that the quality of mind and spirit that we should bring to the task is, above all else, a sense of proportion. Even in such fundamental matters as understanding the nature of what is wrong and the relationship between critical judgment and constructive action, we are misled by a poor sense of proportion. Our urban situation is serious but not so dire as we have melodramatically portrayed it. Moreover, we have long since passed the point where scolding is an aid to awareness. More flagellations can only bruise the spirit without sharpening the mind.

Because of a poor sense of proportion, the federal guardianship for local governments has gone far beyond authentic need, and the same fault encourages a growth of utopian notions that government is suited to determine how people *ought* to live—even to an elaborate control over their shelter, their means of movement, and the density and blend of population in a given area.

A glimpse into one such vision of the future was provided recently by the magazine, *Saturday Review,* which in celebrating its fiftieth anniversary invited contributors to project the next fifty. Its choice to imagine the coming city was an architect, Moshe Safdie, and what he described approvingly was a giant, gadgety mechanism ornamented with people. Writing from the perspective of an imagined backward look fifty years hence, he described how, with totalitarian thoroughness, "regional monopolies were established in the late 1980s and early 1990s to plan and construct new communities. . . . The entire process of planning, design, manufacturing and construction was controlled by these quasi-public monopolies." To possess such powers they "owned all land space and air rights." In his wishful dream, suburban housing was demolished and "the land was returned to agricultural use or left as open public space. Only in certain areas at some distance from the regional trunk line was land made available for individual home ownership."

Against such hubris it is instructive to set the experience of a small low-income housing project designed for the French Government by a greater architect, Le Corbusier. The project, built at Pessac near Bordeaux in 1926, was an austere arrangement of enclosed cubes painted in vivid colors and alternated with square open spaces of the same size. Four decades later, another architect, Phillipe Boudon, told how occupants of the project reacted to it in a study, *Lived-in Architecture: Le Corbusier's Pessac Revisited.* "After forty years," he wrote, "one would expect the district to look different. But that it should have changed so much appears quite incredible. It seems that everybody has now converted (Le Corbusier's) 'machine to live in' into a 'home.' " Some flat roofs were given a pitch, the vivid colors were replaced, patios were enclosed, and open space under houses standing on stilts was walled in. Boudon saw the project as "a real conflict between what the architect intended and what the occupants wanted."

In his old age, Le Corbusier agreed. "It is always life that is right and the architect who is wrong," he concluded. Even in recanting, he exaggerated. Life is never wholly right, and no change for the better can come without fresh ideas from creative individuals. But in the sense that he intended, that it is wrong for persons to use a position of power to impose their standards upon others, his words are a rebuke to the zealots who in their redesign of human settlements find little room for the will of the people who live in them.

In the long run, the safeguard against zealots is to make living in urban settlements more pleasing and rewarding, and in this quest nothing will serve us quite so well as applying a skeptical sense of proportion to the problems that arise and the solutions that are proposed. We are unlikely to find help in some spectacular new concept, some technological breakthrough, some great truth revealed to a few. We have had enough heady language and we do not need a new crusade. People tire of crusades.

The recovery of cities is possible because the requirements of recovery are rather ordinary. Some day the great decaying patches in inner cities, which people leave as soon as they can afford something better, must be cleared and rebuilt. Rebuild, then, as homes for people who work nearby, and do it now. When factories leave cities, help people who need factory work to follow the departing jobs. The evolutionary trend in metropolises toward decentralization of residence, trade, and employment is not in itself an obstacle to the recovery of cities. The trend means more spaciousness for living, more moderate land costs, and the potential of shorter journeys to work. Stop interfering, and rejoice. Cities must have help, but give it to them in ways that will cause the need for it to fade away.

These are the policies of recovery and if they soon seem prosaic, so much the better.

Bibliography

Because this book has been written for the general reader, footnotes have been omitted in favor of this brief explanation of sources that were used.

All population data were derived from publications of the U. S. Bureau of the Census. The same is true of housing data unless otherwise stated in the text. Most of the other information concerning the ten cities that were studied was derived from reports issued by agencies of the respective city governments and from many interviews.

Employment data shown in Table 5 and Figure 7 were derived (except as noted later) from two separate statistical series of the U. S. Bureau of Labor Statistics and consolidated by me. In one series, sampled employers are the source of data for wage and salary nonagricultural occupations; in the other series, sampled households are the source of data for the labor force, agricultural employment, other self-employment, and unemployment. In my opinion, the consolidation I have made in order to bring all into a comprehensive relationship does not result in significant distortions at the scale of measurement used for the table and figure. BLS data for agricultural manpower, other self-employment and unemployment were not available for the year 1920. Instead, I have used estimates made by Stanley Lebergott in *Manpower and Economic Growth* (McGraw-Hill, 1964).

Building the American City, a report of the National Commission on Urban Problems (U. S. Government Printing Office, 1968), is the source of information on home financing practices before the Federal Housing Administration was created (Chapter 2). Historical information concerning the technologies that have most significantly shaped the growth of large urban settlements was obtained from the Smithsonian Institution and encyclopedias.

The categories of Baltimore neighborhoods shown in Table 16 consist of census tracts as follows: West and Northwest area—1510, 1511, 1512, 1513, 1608, 2716, 2717, 2718.02, 2801.02, 2802, 2803.02, 2804.02; Morgan State University area—902, 2703.01, 2709.01, 2709.02, 2709.03; scattered areas with new housing—401, 2604.02, 2604.03, 2702.03, 2711, 2715.01, 2803.01; Highlandtown and Highlandville—101, 102, 103, 104, 105, 201, 202, 203, 601, 602, 2607, 2608, 2609, 2610, 2611.

The following bibliography lists books and articles noted in the text and some others that were consulted for background information.

Abrams, Charles. *The City Is the Frontier*. Harper and Row, New York, 1965.

Alonso, William. *Location and Land Use*. Harvard University Press. Cambridge, Mass., 1964.

———. "A Theory of the Urban Land Market" in *The City*. Stewart, Murray (ed.), Penguin Books, New York, 1973.

Banfield, Edward C. *The Unheavenly City: The Nature and the Future of the Urban Crisis*. Little, Brown and Company, Boston, 1970.

Barth, Michael C.; Carcagno, George J.; and Palmer, John L. *Toward an Effective Income Support System: Problems, Prospects and Choices*, with a commentary by Irwin Garfinkel. Institute for Research on Poverty, University of Wisconsin, Madison, Wis., 1974.

Belcher, Wyatt Winton. *The Economic Rivalry Between St. Louis and Chicago, 1850-1880*. Columbia University Press, New York, 1947.

Berry, Brian J. L. *Growth Centers in the American Urban System*. (2 volumes). Ballinger Publishers, Philadelphia, 1973.

———. *The Human Consequences of Urbanization*. St. Martins Press, 1973.

——— and Horton, Frank E. *Geographic Perspectives on Urban Systems*. Prentice-Hall, New York, 1970.

Bogue, Donald J. *The Structure of the Metropolitan Community: A Study of Dominance and Subdominance*. School of Graduate Studies, University of Michigan, Ann Arbor, Mich.

Bradford, Mary D. *Memoirs*. Antes Press, Evansville, Wis., 1932. (Reminiscences of Kenosha by a former superintendent of schools).

Burckhardt, Jacob. *The Civilization of the Renaissance in Italy*. Phaidon Press. London, 1945.

Burgess, Ernest W. *The Growth of the City: An Introduction to a Research Project*. Proceedings of the American Sociological Society, Vol. 18, 1923.

Case, Frederick E. *Inner-City Housing and Private Enterprise*. Praeger Publishers, New York, 1972.

Crump, Spencer. *Ride the Big Red Cars: How Trolleys Helped Build Southern California*. Trans-Anglo Books, Los Angeles, 1965.

Doxiadis, Constantinos A. *Emergence and Growth of an Urban Region: The Developing Urban Detroit Area*. (3 volumes). Detroit Edison Company, Detroit, 1970.

————. *Ekistics*. Oxford University Press, New York, 1968.

Falick, Abraham Johnson. *Transport Planning in Los Angeles: A Geo-Economic Analysis*. An unpublished Ph. D. thesis. University of California in Los Angeles. 1970.

Forrester, Jay W. *Urban Dynamics*. M. I. T. Press, Cambridge, Mass., 1969.

Gist, Noel P. and Fava, Sylvia F. *Urban Society*. Thomas Y. Crowell Co., New York, 1964.

Gruen, Victor. *The Heart of Our Cities: The Urban Crisis, Diagnosis and Cure*. Simon and Schuster, New York, 1964.

Harris, Britton. *Quantitative Models of Urban Development: Their Role in Metropolitan Policy Making*. Institute of Environmental Studies. University of Pennsylvania. Philadelphia, 1967.

Hawley, Amos. *The Changing Shape of Metropolitan America: Deconcentration Since 1920*. The Free Press, Glencoe, Ill., 1956.

————. *Urban Society: An Ecological Approach*. The Ronald Press Co., 1971.

Hoyt, Homer. *The Structure and Growth of Residential Neighborhoods in American Cities*. Federal Housing Administration, Washington, D. C., 1939.

————. *Where the Rich and Poor People Live*. Urban Land Institute, Washington, D. C., 1966.

Jacobs, Jane. *The Death and Life of Great American Cities: The Failure of Town Planning*. Random House, New York, 1961.

Johnston, R. J. *Urban Residential Patterns*. Praeger Publishers, New York, 1972.

Keyserling, Leon H. *Full Employment Without Inflation*. Conference on Economic Progress, Washington, D. C., 1975

Kouwenhoven, John A. *The Columbia Historical Portrait of New York*. Doubleday & Co., New York, 1953.

Meyer, John; Kain, John; and Wohl, Martin. *The Urban Transportation Problem*. Harvard University Press, Cambridge, Mass., 1965.

Mills, Edwin S. *Studies in the Structure of the Urban Economy*. Resources for the Future, Washington, D. C., 1969.

Mumford, Lewis. *The City in History*. Harcourt, Brace & Co., New York, 1961.

————. *The Urban Prospect*. Harcourt, Brace & Co., New York, 1968.

Muth, Richard F. *Cities and Housing: The Spatial Pattern of Urban Residential Land Use*. University of Chicago Press, Chicago, 1969.

Owen, Wilfred. *The Accessible City*. The Brookings Institution, Washington, D. C., 1972.

Perloff, Harvey (ed.). *The Quality of the Urban Environment*. Resources for the Future, Washington, D. C., 1969.

———— and Wingo, Lowdon, Jr. *Issues in Urban Economics*. Resources for the Future, Washington, D. C., 1968.

Schnore, Leo F. *The Rural-Urban Variable: An Urbanite's Perspective*. Rural Sociology, June, 1960.

————. *Urban Structure and Suburban Selectivity*. Demography, Vol. 1, No. 1, 1964.

Starr, Roger. *The Urban Choices: the City and Its Critics*. Penguin Books, New York, 1966.

Stein, Clarence S. *Toward New Towns for America*. M. I. T. Press, Cambridge, Mass., 1950.

Stewart, Murray (ed.). *The City*. Penguin Books, New York, 1973.

Thompson, Wilbur R. *A Preface to Urban Economics*. Resources for the Future, Washington, D. C., 1965.

Tocqueville, Alexis de. *Journeys to England and Ireland*. Edited by J. P. Mayer. Yale University Press. New Haven, 1945.

Trevelyan, George Macaulay. *English Social History*. Longmans, Green and Co., London, 1942.

Vernon, Raymond. *Metropolis, 1985*. Harvard University Press, Cambridge, Mass., 1965.

————. *The Myth and Reality of Our Urban Problems*. Harvard University Press, Cambridge, Mass., 1966.

———— and Hoover, Edgar M. *Anatomy of a Metropolis*. Harvard University Press, Cambridge, Mass., 1959.

Von Eckhardt, Wolf. *A Place to Live*. Delacorte Press, New York, 1967.

Whyte, William H., Jr. *The Last Landscape*. Doubleday & Co., New York, 1968.

Wingo, Lowdon, Jr. *Transportation and Land Use*. Resources for the Future, Washington, D. C., 1961.

Index

ibrar